For the
Love of
My Boys

A mother's story of parent alienation and abuse

Authored by

SHERRI-LEE JAMES

with SUSAN M. ROWE

ISBN: 1468198556
ISBN 13: 9781468198553

Library of Congress Control Number: 2012900742
CreateSpace, North Charleston, SC

Acknowledgments

Blake and Brett, I have written this book for you.

I have loved you since the day you were born, and I will always love you.

Motherhood is one of the greatest privileges some of us are given. With all gifts we receive, there are great responsibilities. I feel that I had to make the gravest decision a Mom could ever have to make. I felt that I had to put the welfare of both of you boys first, no matter the cost to myself. I recognized that there was only one choice for the safe welfare of our family. I knew the love that your dad and I had for both of you, and I believed that your dad would never harm you.

This book is the only way that I know how to tell you my side of the story, to let you know why I couldn't be in your lives even though I wanted to be more than anything. It is heartbreaking that we never got to experience the life that a mother and her sons should. I'm so sorry things didn't end up differently.

I love you and miss you. I missed you while you were growing up, and I miss you now. I do hope that someday you will understand.

Thank you, Susan, for taking on this challenge. I came to you with a compulsion, driven by emotion and commitment. I had a mission to share with my sons.I also had to satisfy my mind and heart. With the style and prose that you incorporated in my story, I could see my feelings and emotions come to life in the pages of this book. You were a sounding board for my story, and you used your talents to mold my information into a narrative that people will want to read. I thank you so much for the times you recognized the need to keep the book balanced while keeping my heartfelt emotions in check. You helped to keep me focused and reminded me of my objective for telling this story. Without you, I wouldn't be able to tell my story in such a thorough and complete way, and I can't thank you enough for helping me. You are an amazing writer. Don't give up on your dream.

Thank you Len for introducing me to Susan so that I could tell my story. You listened to me and you made the effort to assist me in my quest to reach a personal goal.

Andy, I have accomplished so many goals and have had so many experiences since you came into my life. You are an amazing person. You always encourage me to follow my dreams and to achieve my goals. You are so supportive and understanding, and you have accepted me just the way that I am. Andy, *you* are really my Knight in Shining Armor. Thank you. I will love you forever. LYF

Mom, thank you for always being my hope and strength, during some of the darkest times in my life. Each time that I thought I had hit bottom, you were always there to pull me out of that very deep and dark hole. You were there from the beginning, and you are still there for me today. Thank you for that. Everything you did was right, and you couldn't have done anything differently.

Dad, thank you for keeping your cool during these very stressful times. As my father, you are a great protector, and I appreciate that. During the writing of this book you have been my biggest fan. I really appreciated the feedback and support that you gave me. Thank you.

And finally, thank you to all of the wonderful people who were there for Blake and Brett growing up. Some of you knew I couldn't be there, and it helped me tremendously to know that they both had people that supported them and were willing to take an active role in their lives. You people know who you are, and I thank you. I will be forever grateful.

The late author and child psychiatrist Richard A. Gardner coined the term Parental Alienation Syndrome more than twenty years ago to characterize the breakdown of previously normal, healthy parent-child relationships during divorce and child custody cases. The definition of parental alienation is heartbreakingly simple—one parent deliberately damages and, in some cases, destroys, the previously healthy, loving relationship between the child and the child's other parent.[1]

Parental alienation is a social dynamic, generally occurring due to divorce or separation, when a child expresses unjustified hatred or unreasonably strong dislike of one parent, making access by the rejected parent difficult or impossible. These feelings may be influenced by negative comments by the other parent and by the characteristics, such as lack of empathy and warmth, of the rejected parent.[2]

---

1. www.afamilysheartbreak.com
2. www.en.wikipedia.org/wiki/Parental_alienation

A story of parental alienation and my continuing journey to rebuild a relationship with my sons that was almost beyond repair.

Table of Contents

Disclaimer

*Some of the names and dates have been altered
to protect the people involved.*

Only when we are no longer afraid,
do we begin to live...

—Dorothy Thompson

Preface

As a little girl, I looked forward to bedtime, when my parents would read me an exciting fairy tale. My favorites were when I found characters in the book that I could relate with, whose lives seemed possible to me. Everyone was happy. The characters would be adventurous and experience new places, meet new people. I always loved an adventure.

Are fairy tales a way that we can reinvent our innermost wishes and desires? Are fairy tales a way to give us courage when we are frightened or unsure of our feelings? In retrospect, I think that I believed fairy tales were real, that they represented real life.

In most of the stories there would be a handsome prince or a beautiful castle, or maybe just a horse to allow the hero to whisk the maiden away to live happily ever after. There always seemed to be a wonderful ending to each adventure. Many times the stories showed how courage and determination, as well as goodness and love would be rewarded if we just believed long and hard enough. I always expected that I would live a life very much like the fairy tales that my parents had read to me. I just had to believe hard enough and love long enough, and then everything would be as I had read it.

There were trials and tribulations in the stories, but there was always a reward for courage and determination. There was always someone who cared and someone who knew or hoped there was a way out. You just had to believe that everything would work out.

I dreamed of one day having my own Prince Charming as well as the little white house with the picket fence, with the children playing in the sandbox in the back garden. I always thought that if we loved hard enough and long enough that we would be able to live our own fairy tale. Unfortunately, life doesn't always turn out this way. It isn't always what we dreamed. Sometimes the fairy tale is not meant to be.

My story may not be a fairy tale, but as you read on and share in my experiences, perhaps you too will realize that with life, there is always hope. As in the fairy tales, I was definitely tested. I needed courage to overcome many obstacles, sometimes alone and sometimes with the aid of an unlikely hero. There were many times I wondered if I would ever really find my true Prince Charming. There were so many villains in the way.

Here is my story...

My father, a military man, had just accepted a new post back to Kingston, Ontario. Just like that, my family would be leaving me behind in Edmonton. I made the heart-wrenching decision not to follow them. After all, I was engaged to Eddie.

Because of this decision and the ensuing loss of my parental support, I was on my own (to some degree). Due to my parents not being able to fund a college education, I was now considered to be on my own and eligible for student loans. I had been about to give up on my college dreams, but with my parents' departure, it seemed they could now come true. I could be a college graduate!

Eddie was my safety net. At the time, he was probably my knight in shining armor too. He gave me hope for my future. With him, things were possible. He was a little bit older than I was and had a relatively good job in a warehouse. He was debt-free and even had goals in life. Looking back, I sometimes wonder if I only saw the surface. Did I really know Eddie, or was I just looking for someone to take care of me—a replacement for my loving father? Did I really love Eddie? How did I become engaged at such a young age? Eddie once told me that if he proposed and if I said no it would be the end of us.

How could I risk losing everything? I barely knew how to take care of myself. I had lived on military bases most of my life and wasn't sure I could depend on myself with just a high school diploma. Looking back now, I guess the only response to Eddie's proposal could have been yes.

But I am getting ahead of myself. First, I need to tell you about my own family history before I tell you about my time with Eddie.

The Early Years

I was raised by two wonderful parents, both of whom were raised in unbelievably strict environments. My father grew up in a rigid Pentecostal home in New Brunswick. For some, growing up Pentecostal was very stifling and restrictive. My father would tell me that women were not allowed to wear makeup or cut their hair, which were things I had taken for granted in my own youth. I couldn't imagine growing up like that.

He told me that television was completely prohibited. They went to church several times a week and even more on the weekend. The most extreme form of punishment growing up was being forbidden to attend church for a day. That was his routine. You learned to work within the rules.

At eighteen, however, my father chose to leave New Brunswick for reasons almost entirely separate from his upbringing. He wanted to see the world. He was an adventurer at heart, and military life could offer many new experiences for him.

There isn't much opportunity to see the world growing up on the East Coast. Jobs were scarce, so some boys often joined a branch of the military. My dad chose this life too, and joined the Army at eighteen. Army life can be very restrictive, as it runs on following orders and routines. As my father's childhood was also highly structured, the principles instilled in him as a young child helped him climb the ranks until he retired as Master Warrant Officer many years later.

My father had many career successes during his tenure in the Army. When he and my mother fell in love, there was a joining of two families. Those times could have been stressful, but they weren't. Perhaps there was camaraderie between him and my mother's father. My grandfather was also a military man and spent a large portion of his life following the rules of the Army. They had similar lives within a strict military family. As it was, the relationship between father-in-law and son-in-law was actually better than the relationship between father and daughter.

Kingston, Ontario was the home of the Royal Military College, the historical Fort Henry, and its own military base. For many, it was considered to be *the* military city in Canada. The majority of people in Kingston were connected to some aspect of the military. As my grandfather was also part of that life, my mother had had a very austere childhood. The regimented and authoritative life was forced upon my mother, and she felt unattached and emotionally crippled growing up.

It seemed fitting that my mother would meet and marry a military man. She met my father while he was on a posting to Kingston. She was a beautiful and popular woman with an incredible capacity for love. My father, a shy and reserved person by nurture and nature, was drawn to her. They both experienced childhoods that some only read about. They did not have open loving families. This mutual experience not only allowed them to commiserate, but it also helped them to heal the scars of the past. If you hadn't lived that kind of life, it would be difficult to understand and move past it, let alone to become such loving parents to your own children. They had such love inside them, just waiting to be shared with each other and their children. They had not learned this abundant love, but it had somehow been invested in them.

You might say that I didn't have a normal childhood since my entire childhood was spent on military bases throughout Canada. But it was just as normal for me as not living on a base was normal for you. Sure, it had restrictions and rules, but, then again, didn't everyone? The only real issue was that every few years we had to move to another base, but the structure was always the same. City life was only something I saw on TV until I was much older.

Life on the base is different than the city in some ways. There is no unemployment and there's only minimal crime. You live by the rules just like the city laws, but if you break the rules on base, you are not welcome anymore. Because of the bubble effect of base life, you can be completely unaware of the intricacies of life in the city. You don't know that your neighbor was laid off, or the amount of crime in your area. Base life is secluded. That can be good and bad all at the same time. You are protected from life outside your bubble but as a result you might grow up a little naive.

I was born in Barrie, Ontario when my Dad was stationed at Camp Borden, but since I was an army kid, we had moved five times before I even turned three. Sometimes Dad's posting caused the move, other times it was because of the house. For example, we lived in a house infested with snakes, or the landlord was selling the house. Finally, when I was three, Dad got posted to another base, but this time it was across the country in Penhold, Alberta. As Dad was an adventurer, he and my mother were very excited about moving to a new part of Canada and starting a new life there. When they heard about the posting, they told us about the majestic Rocky Mountains. Even to a three-year-old it sounded glorious. I couldn't wait to see them.

It isn't easy raising a family on a corporal's salary, and as a result my dad often worked a second job. Most of us think our dads can do anything. Well, my dad really could. To supplement his salary, Dad took a second job on a dairy farm. Because he had lived on a farm when he was young, he knew how farms worked. Everything was about timing, especially on a dairy farm. Every morning the cows had to be milked at precise times. If they weren't milked at the right time, well, let's just say the cows got ornery. As a result of the early morning milking, Dad thought it would be best if we lived on the farm. So we moved to a dairy farm with eighty cows and twenty-two chickens. What an experience! I couldn't have asked for a better education.

I loved spending time with my Dad, so every morning I would help by gathering eggs or by working as his "assistant" with the cows. He always made me feel special. One time, he was helping to birth some cows. Now, that might sound absolutely disgusting to many of you, but I thought it was exciting that I got to be part of the miracle of life. Not too many people get to experience the joys of life like that. It was hard work, but there were so many joys that outweighed it. I experienced that joy again while living on the farm; I was in the hayloft watching five beautiful little kittens being born. It was an incredible time in my life.

By the time I was six, I considered moving to be a normal part of my life. When I began first grade, my father was being transferred yet again. This time it was to an even smaller community than Penhold. We moved to Saskatchewan, to a place called Alsask. I bet most of you haven't even heard of the place. It is right on the border between Alberta and Saskatchewan and located about forty-five minutes from Kindersley, Saskatchewan and thirty-five minutes from Oyen, Alberta. Alsask is an isolated, barren, flat piece of land where the government had placed one hundred double-wide trailers for the military staff and their families. At least the trailers didn't have snakes!

Communities thrive in small areas because everyone looks out for everyone else. However there is also a downside, because everyone knows everyone else's business. There are few secrets hidden in small communities. Still, it was a nice community to grow up in, as we all could run about or stay home alone without anyone thinking any harm might come to us. If something went wrong, you could just run next door to the neighbor for help.

We lived in Alsask for three years—first through third grades. It was a pretty good life. I did well in school, and would continue to do so. Often I was the teacher's pet. Being the teacher's pet brought with it great opportunities but also jealousy from some classmates. Sometimes, that jealousy made it very difficult for me. But I will talk more about that later.

My sister and I were very involved in extracurricular activities. We both loved school, Brownies, gymnastics, and even Sunday school. As the community was small, my mother was both the Brownie leader and the Sunday school teacher; that always made me feel kind of special.

But once again, we had to move. We were excited about going back to Penhold, as we had many great memories of that time. That time the transfer lasted almost four years, until I was thirteen years old. My sister and I enrolled in many extracurricular activities, such as dance and guitar lessons, and we continued with Brownies and Girl Guides. I even volunteered at the local library. We were always doing something. Life was sometimes hectic but it was such a rewarding time.

I remember every Saturday the bus would bring us to Red Deer for shopping, and on Sunday the bus brought us back for swimming at the local pool. Traveling into town on the bus was a great adventure, and we looked forward to it every week. I never thought of us as different because we came from the base, but it was noticeable when people would stop and stare at us, or point to the big, green military bus.

I was a reasonably good kid growing up. I did well in school, usually earning honors, and was popular with my classmates. Living on the base was a safe and happy environment, and I enjoyed it tremendously.

However, when I became a tween, that preadolescent time when we all endure rites of passage, I had my first experience of being shunned. I had always been popular and hung around with the "in" kids, but when I was twelve there were some powerful struggles happening. At some point everyone was ostracized. As it was, I did not fare well at all when they decided to blacklist me.

One day when I showed up at school early to hang the Canadian flag, which was my job, I noticed something different about my so-called friends. Once others started gathering around, they purposefully excluded me. I was no longer welcomed to join the conversation. They were even whispering and staring at me. I was devastated and sick to my stomach. What had I done to be tossed out of the popular crowd? How could this have happened to me?

This lasted for a few weeks, and, as we all know, weeks to a tween or teen are a lifetime. No one spoke to me or included me in anything during school or after. In gym class I found out what it was like to be without a partner for badminton and to be the last person picked for the team. I learned how awful it was to be alone in the locker room while the other girls giggled and whispered. I'm sure they were whispering about me. It was very painful to lose my friends without knowing what I had done to deserve it. Of course, looking back now, there was no true reason for any of it. It was just part of that stupid time when kids did horrible things to each other.

But I didn't let it ruin my life. There was a school Valentine dance and I decided that I still wanted to go. I loved dances and wasn't going to miss it. Even though I didn't have a friend in the world (or so it seemed), I mustered up all the courage I had and went to the dance. I guess when you have nothing left to lose, you can have a fearlessness that allows you to stand up and just go for it.

After a couple of hours in solitude and posing as a wallflower, one of the popular girls came over and invited me to join her group. Perhaps she saw my courage in actually showing up to the dance, or perhaps she just missed my friendship. I'll never know why, but my exile was over. I breathed a huge sigh of relief and felt the weight of the world lifting off my shoulders. Despite being back with the "in" group, I knew things would never really be the same again. I had changed because of what they had done to me. Perhaps it made me wiser about how I treated people, or perhaps I never really let anyone in again, as I never wanted to be that vulnerable. My confidence had receded, and it was going to be some time before I felt valued again.

So, I was pretty happy when Dad announced one night at dinner that our time in Penhold was over. Our next move was a big one—we were moving to the big city of Edmonton. Well, not quite Edmonton, since the base, CFB Namayo, was located just outside in Lancaster Park. This was a huge move for my family, we had never lived on such a large base before, or so close to the city.

My sister Cathy and I were fifteen and thirteen, so we entered high school and junior high in Edmonton. My family experienced a lot of growing pains with this move, especially at our ages. Moving teenagers from the comfort of their small-town life and introducing them to the dangers and excitement of city life can be quite an adventure. And believe me, we tested our parents every chance we got. The crowd was tough, fast, and seemed older than the friends we had left behind. It was the beginning of my lost innocence.

Edmonton Daze

Moving has its good points and bad points. The good thing is that you can reinvent yourself with each move, getting rid of whatever it is that you don't like about yourself. However, most kids don't think they have anything to change about themselves when they are that young. Introspection doesn't usually start until you are older, and by then there are fewer opportunities for fresh starts.

One of the bad things about constantly moving is that you have to create a new social circle and new friends each time. Making friends at any age can be challenging, but the teen years can be absolutely brutal. The new kid on the block doesn't always get accepted, as most groups have been together since grade school. You either have to be strong and confident in yourself or you just survive somehow and try to fit in with whatever group accepts you. Belonging and feeling needed is important to everyone, but these feelings are overwhelming during the teen years and can overrule your values. Even though the base was just outside of Edmonton it still had the same fast paced energy that Edmonton had. It was in Lancaster Park (Edmonton) that my opportunity to change myself took a turn and changed my life. It was a big city and a big base for us. Especially compared to the smaller towns and bases where we had lived earlier. Alsask was a station with 100 homes and now I was living in a city with over half a million people. The pace of life, the size, the traffic, the opportunities, both good and bad, that come with city life were things I wasn't used to. I was like a tumbleweed caught in a tornado. Survival was paramount, and I did everything to fit in, but not with the best of people.

It was an exciting and terrifying time for my family. Even the simple task of driving into the city for work seemed formidable. I remember going in to the city that first week, and my mother was terrified to drive. It was her first time driving in such a big city. We were driving to her new office and suddenly the traffic light was flashing green. We were all used to red, yellow, and green, but what the heck was flashing green? Mom started to get nervous, horns blared, and my sister and I didn't help by stressing her out even more. Eventually we did make it to her office, and I think Mom gave only a small sigh of relief when we arrived, since she would have to do it all over again to get home.

At home in Lancaster Park, Cathy and I were doing our best to fit in. It just so happened that our new neighbor was one of the popular girls. She hung out at the teen center with the "in" group that we desperately wanted to join. It was those few people who would arrange parties for the group. This involved getting the booze and figuring out whose parents weren't going to be home that evening so there would be a location for the party. As far as we were concerned, our neighbor would help us meet all the "right" people on base.

I latched on to this group like a baby to its mother. At the time, I couldn't believe my luck in finding Marie as my neighbor. I thought I was going to be one of the popular girls. I couldn't imagine how my life would change because she was my neighbor. Or perhaps that's just an excuse and I would have changed anyway.

I started eighth grade at Guthrie Middle School. My school was located on base, so I could walk to school and go home for lunch every day. The class sizes were bigger than previous schools, with twenty students per class, but they were still small enough to allow for individual attention. As days went by, I found myself developing an attitude with a capital A. I was no longer polite, easy going, or the teacher's pet. I was a nasty, rude, and sullen teenager. I no longer even cared about being on the honor roll. It was like Mary Poppins met Marilyn Manson that year. I would write the vilest things on my binders, and when the teachers confronted me I gave them a deadly stare or, even worse, spewed the most hateful words from my mouth. I didn't even think twice about swearing at them. It was like I was possessed. Wanting to belong to the "in" group had somehow changed me.

It was October that year that one of the "in" girls invited me to a party at her house. We all gathered at her house because her parents were going to be out. It was a school night, so I was supposed to be home by nine o'clock. Being the new girl, I felt I had something to prove to the others, and my new friends wondered if I was up to the challenge. So I poured rye into three juice glasses and placed them in front of me. Then, one by one, I chugged them. Why wouldn't you down them? The liquor tasted awful and wasn't the idea to get drunk?

Soon after drinking that god-awful drink, I was hugging the big white phone, talking to God and making promises to Him to just let me live. The next phone call I made was to my mother. That phone call was brief and went something like this: "I'm in trouble. I need help. Please come and get me." Click. My mom was in a panic because I didn't leave any information about where I was. Luckily, I shared everything with my sister, and she was able to figure out where I was. The next thing I remembered was Mom scraping me off the bathroom floor and placing me in the car.

What a night! I barely remember going home and hearing my mom tell my dad that I would get all the punishment I needed in the morning with a blazing hangover. But my behavior that night wasn't enough shame to bring them. I lashed out at Dad and blamed him for my own failings. I screamed that it was all his fault for moving us every few years. It was too difficult to make friends every time, and I couldn't take it anymore.

After a moment of stunned silence, I realized I had actually managed to make my parents feel guilty that horrible night. However, my loving parents did not yell or scream or react to my outburst. I had acted terribly and although they knew my outburst was in part due to the alcohol, they also knew that something had changed within me. I was no longer their "good little girl." I had disgraced them. The truth was, I could see the sparkle diminish in their eyes, and it was my own fault.

The next morning didn't get any better. I woke up still drunk. Not only that, I really couldn't see. Of course, when you are young, you never think if you drink too much you'll go blind, but that's what happened. Now I know it was alcohol poisoning, but back then I was so frightened I would never see again. Unfortunately I had a science test that week, and I could barely see the test. The punishment for my stupidity (my lack of sight) dragged on for almost a week before I could see clearly again. However, it took almost a full year before I realized I was becoming someone I was not very proud of. You think something like that would change your actions, but, as you will see, the blindness didn't wake me up at all.

After that year, I realized I needed to make a change. I found a different group to be with and some great friends. They weren't the most popular kids, but they weren't nerds either. I had found that in-between group and settled in. Don't misunderstand: I was still a wild child, but I wasn't getting into as much trouble as before. We still had fun on the weekend and attended parties in town, but without getting into trouble. We didn't do any hard-core drugs or other illegal activities; we were just trying to survive our teenage years. The pace of life with this new group of friends slowed down just enough.

Cathy and I were enjoying the big city and finally convinced our parents to move from Lancaster Park into Edmonton itself. We all knew that hitchhiking was dangerous and constantly asking for a ride into town was very inconvenient. Since Cathy went to high school in the city and Mom also worked in the city, it just seemed best for everyone, except Dad, to live in Edmonton. Of course, he wasn't thrilled about moving mid-post, as he had the luxury of being able to walk to work every day. But his girls convinced him otherwise, and soon we moved to the base within city limits: CFB Griesbach would be the new base we would call home.

I changed schools in the middle of the ninth grade. My new school was Major General Griesbach. The people at school were nice, but since they had known each other for many years, it would have been hard for any new person to join in, let alone in the middle of the school year. They were polite, but I never really felt welcomed. I was still the outsider. I felt very alone that year, and, as a result, I ditched school more often than I attended. It was a major accomplishment if I made it to school all five days a week. Quite often I'd feign sickness and just go home at lunch and sleep all afternoon in my sister's warm waterbed, cocooned in her satin tiger-print comforter. One day, Mom came home from lunch and I thought I was caught, but I snuggled deep within the covers, and she didn't even know I was there. During all of this, my parents didn't really know what to do with me. I was uncontrollable.

My best friend Tina still lived on the other base at Lancaster Park, so on weekends we would alternate sleeping at my house or hers. She loved coming to the city. I always thought she liked to see me, but maybe she was just visiting to experience freedom in the city. It was certainly an adventure when she came to town because we did everything. Because she was a year older, she knew about some of the wildest parties in the city. When she came to the house on the weekend, it was like she was part of the family. My parents thought of her as their daughter too—she was there that much. We were very close, but when she wasn't around I was alone again. You would think that with all the opportunities I had to make new friends every few years I would have been good at it. However, I still struggled. If there's one thing they should teach in school, it's the art of making friends and accepting others. Perhaps then there would be less bullying, or maybe fewer teen suicides.

Finally I started high school. High school was overwhelming compared with junior high on the base. On the base, there were between forty and fifty students in each grade, in high school, there were five hundred students in tenth grade alone. I was lost in more ways than one, and having no accountability within the classroom didn't help. The teachers couldn't handle such large class sizes, so if you missed a class or two or three, they didn't say much. You were old enough, and supposedly responsible enough, to take care of yourself.

Due to the huge number of people, there was great diversity among the students. You had the preppies, whose families had money. Some had been taken care of their entire lives without ever having to work hard. Some were very spoiled, and a few were snobbish. Still, I wanted to be one of them. I wanted to wear nice clothes and have the perfect hairstyle. I wanted to be accepted and admired in school. But it wasn't meant to be because I was an army brat and everyone knew it. We had our own stigma to manage everywhere we went. The preppies were in a different class from us and were not going to let outsiders like me into their group.

Unfortunately, becoming a jock wasn't in the cards either. I was not an athlete. I had always felt clumsy and somewhat chubby, so I didn't get involved in sports. I had been a sickly child, and allergies and asthma had prevented me from joining in many athletic activities. I was even exempt from gym class. It wasn't until years later that I found out that my so-called asthma attacks had really been anxiety attacks.

So I gravitated toward the only group where I thought I would fit in: the headbangers. But that wasn't really where I wanted to be. Growing up, I loved listening to classical music and attending cultural activities, such as the ballet. I was 13 when my mother took me to my first ballet. It was really more of a modern dance production and I was hooked. I loved everything about it: the music, the dancers, the audience and the ambiance. So, why would I dress like a grunge with a lumber jacket and jeans, smoking and drinking? Acceptance. Acceptance is the one thing we all crave, even if we don't know it. It allows us to feel valued and validated. It lets us know that we are important, and we will crawl through the desert for that welcoming feeling.

Trying to be someone I wasn't was a difficult charade. Deep down, I wanted to be a girly girl with nice clothes and nice friends that I could be proud of. Maybe as a result of my misadventures over the last couple of years, I suffered through some difficult health problems. Just before Halloween, I developed mononucleosis. As you probably know, this is a highly contagious disease. As if my school attendance wasn't bad before, I was forced to stay home for several weeks. This put me so far behind the rest of my class that when I finally returned to school I was completely lost.

When I thought things couldn't get any worse that school year, they did. By that spring, I had a large tumor almost the size of an egg growing on my forehead. I felt that this was the last straw. Perhaps I really was doomed. Needless to say, I thought a lot about my own mortality. I kept thinking, *Why me? I'm only sixteen years old; I'm too young to die.* I've seen the TV commercials about how cancer affects every family, but why me? Of course, most times you can't tell if a tumor is cancerous until it is removed. My surgeon was very compassionate and understanding during all of this. However, when he said he didn't want to just excise the tumor but also shave a strip of hair on my head ear to ear and make an incision so they could pull the skin down to see more of the tumor, I almost had a nervous breakdown. But I went through with the surgery. Thankfully, the biopsy results came back and the tumor was benign.

I was thankful to be alive, but my self-confidence suffered a major blow. I had a shaved head and a scar with staples across my entire head. I was a female Frankenstein. My mother saw my insecurities, and, as the year was almost over, she decided I didn't have to return to school.

At the time, I thought that year was the worst of my life. I never really recovered emotionally. A large part of the year had passed, and I wasn't part of it. I didn't fit in at school and I wasn't sure if I belonged anywhere.

Changing high schools in eleventh grade rekindled that lost feeling once more. I felt that moving to a smaller school would help with my accountability issue. I moved to a respected Catholic school, but the cliques there were even worse. There was a strong Italian population, and they didn't think much of newcomers, and I didn't have the heart to try and win them over.

During high school, my only reprieve was working at a shoe store. I wasn't judged because I had a very strong work ethic. My supervisor praised me for my sales and gave me a financial incentive to do well. So, after some thought, I decided to quit school and go to work full-time. This was not a good time in my life, my only friend, Tina, had moved back to Ontario.

Now, I was alone.

Eddie's Family

E ddie's history is somewhat varied and very tumultuous. Ed Sr. was from The Pas, Manitoba. He grew up in The Pas, and when he was older he joined his brothers in Flin Flon, Manitoba, and worked in the local mine. I am not sure how Ed Sr. and Joan met because Joan grew up in Fairview, Alberta. However, Eddie's sisters, Kim and Gerry, were born in Flin Flon. After the two girls were born, the family returned to Alberta and started raising their family.

Soon after they moved back to Alberta, Joan and Ed started having difficulties in their marriage. Joan left Ed and moved back to Fairview. While separated, she met someone else. During the affair, Joan became pregnant with Eddie. Ed Sr. knew that the child was not his, but he convinced Joan to come back to him anyway, promising to raise the child as his own. It wasn't until much later in life that Eddie discovered that the man he knew as Dad was not his biological father and that his sisters were only half siblings.

So, Ed, Joan, Kim, Gerry, and Eddie moved to Edmonton. Life continued in its routine manner for the first five years of Eddie's life. Throughout this volatile time, Eddie's mom was faced with many challenges. The details are not well known except that she attempted to leave Ed on many occasions without success. Leaving Ed was not an easy thing to do. This was not because she didn't want to, but because he had such a strong hold on her, which was difficult to break. He loved her dearly and he wasn't going to let her go. One time she told me she dropped the kids out the bedroom window and then followed herself. She got away that evening, but it was short-lived. Ed tracked her down and brought her back home again. I'm sure it was a very stressful time for her and the kids—whether they wanted to leave or not. The tug of war between parents, even bad parents, changes a child. The first role models a child has are its parents. When children see and hear how their parents treat each other, they learn to incorporate this behavior in their own lives. Sometimes they act completely opposite their parents, and other times they replicate what they have seen. Eventually, life became unbearable and things got so nasty that Joan made the difficult decision to leave without the children. I think she knew that to escape the roller-coaster life with Ed, she had to leave Edmonton. Joan left Edmonton and headed to Calgary to start a new life. After a year or so, the oldest daughter, Gerry, joined her mother in Calgary while Eddie and Kim stayed in Edmonton with their father.

It's not easy to be raised by a single father, especially when your mom is not in the picture. For the most part, mothers are the nurturers and fathers are typically the disciplinarians. However, with only one parent, these roles are merged or abandoned. Life went on and the kids learned the new rules of their father's household, but there was no longer the buffer zone of their mother.

Ed worked as a trucking dispatcher his entire life. Many times he had to work the night shift, so when he came home, he slept all day long. There wasn't much in the way of parental supervision or guidance in those first years after Ed and Joan separated. It was even worse when he was drinking. And when he drank, it was to excess. They say that drinking changes people. Some say it liberates them—that when they drink, they become who they truly are inside, be it good or bad. And some days Ed was bad, even Eddie's friends were afraid of him.

George Bernard Shaw once wrote that, "Alcohol is the anesthesia by which we endure the operation of life." But you can't escape life. It may bypass you if you are not engaged, but life still happens.

By the time I met Ed almost fifteen years later, I thought he was like a big teddy bear. He had stopped drinking, but unfortunately he still chain-smoked. He was still hardworking and he loved spending time with his granddaughters. I couldn't see him as the hard man so many other people described. Sometimes the passage of time has a way of mellowing that inner storm, or maybe we lose the energy necessary to keep up the fight. For me, he was a hardworking, gentle man who lived a very simple life. His life was about going to work everyday and spending as much time with his grand-children as he could. When he wasn't with them, you could find him at the coffee shop with his buddies.

Eddie and Kim both had to grow up quickly and take on a great deal of responsibility. For Kim, the responsibility was overwhelming at times. As the female in the house, she was left to take charge of the house. Life was not easy with one physically absent parent and another mentally and emotionally not there. But Eddie did have it better than Kim in other ways as well. As a child, Eddie was involved in sports: hockey in the winter and baseball in the summer. In Ed's moments of clarity, Eddie was Ed's pride and joy. Kim didn't have the same connection and was older. She was a great hockey sister, attending games and cheering Eddie on, but otherwise she found her own diversions to keep her busy. They both looked forward to visiting Flin Flon every summer, until they became teenagers and friends became their priority.

Due to the volatility of their parents' separation, Eddie and Kim didn't see much of their mother until they were teenagers. Rebellion takes many forms in teenagers, and both Eddie and Kim did their share of rebelling. Kim got pregnant at a young age, and Eddie quit sports and school. From what I recall, Eddie told me this was the time when things really started going downhill.

Joan, Eddie's mother, moved back to Edmonton around that time. After she had left Eddie's father, Joan met George, and they married and had two daughters—Penni and Jolene. Although Joan had moved back to Edmonton, she only stayed a year or so. During that time, Eddie was able to spend more time with her, but it was never the same. Too much time had passed and the relationship had changed.

As luck would have it, George and Ed had similar professions. George drove a truck for a moving company. That summer, George asked Eddie to join him on the road to make a little bit of money. The money was good, but the habits weren't. George was a drinker and by the end of the summer, so was Eddie. Actually, the household was intoxicating, and not in a good way. Even after I met Eddie, it seemed like every time we visited them on the weekends, we were inebriated. But I was young and thought that drinking was fun. I guess I had forgotten about my blinding experience with alcohol in ninth grade.

After all the years apart, I think Eddie wanted to rebuild his relationship with his mom. When he was fifteen he decided to move in with her and her family to see if it might work. While working that summer, Eddie enjoyed the weekly paychecks and the lifestyle too much, so he decided not to return to school. Instead, he found jobs working for trucking and moving companies in their warehouses.

Living at his mom's house was completely different than his dad's. There was a more formal family structure with a mom, dad, and two sisters, but there was also a lot more freedom. If you haven't learned how to deal with freedom and responsibility, you may fall when you finally get the chance to spread your wings. It takes many attempts to find that balance between freedom and responsibility, some people never do. Eddie tried many times but could never quite get it right.

Not being a part of his mother's life for such a long time affected Eddie immensely. There were things he never talked about that were bottled up inside of him. He was frustrated that his mom hadn't been there for a good portion of his life. And now that they were together, he had to share her with two little girls, his half-sisters. This made Eddie very angry. He thought the girls had a much better life and upbringing than he ever had, and he resented them. Unfortunately, his anger got the better of him one night and he got into a physical fight with his mother's husband. Not long after that, George, Joan, and the girls moved back to Calgary while Eddie remained once again with his father.

Around this time, Kim gave birth to a baby girl named Lori and moved out of the family house to be on her own. So now it was just Eddie and his dad. With all the turmoil going on his life, he thought he could relax and settle down. Unfortunately, Eddie was about to receive another blow. During a heated argument, he found out that Ed was not his real father. This information destroyed Eddie. But instead of abandoning the man that gave up everything to raise him, he became more loyal to him than ever.

Learning that earth-shattering news had a tremendous effect on Eddie. Drinking became more than just a routine—it became an escape. Soon, he became an alcoholic. Jobs and cars came and went. He totaled a few cars as a result of drinking and driving. Soon after we met, he told me he already had his first impaired driving charge.

The drinking finally got the best of him. Even his father couldn't prevent the trucking company, where Ed had worked for so many years, from firing his son. Too many times, Eddie hadn't shown up to work, or he'd shown up unable to do his job, and the company couldn't take it anymore. It was very hard on Ed Sr. He felt ashamed and embarrassed.

This caused great distress between the two, and they would often have arguments about it. Now that Eddie had dropped out of school and had been fired from his job, Ed was frustrated. He'd always hoped for a better life for his son. Eddie continued to live at home with his dad, and, over time, Ed's sadness slowly dissipated. Eddie stayed with his father until a month before we got married. He was just twenty-three years old.

And Then Came Eddie

L ife in Edmonton held many changes for me. Looking back, I think my time in Penhold was a dream compared to Edmonton. When I left Penhold, I wanted to be a lawyer or a teacher. These were great aspirations, and with my good grades they were possible. However, within months of moving to Edmonton, those dreams evaporated as a new person emerged from my cocoon, and it wasn't a beautiful butterfly.

My rebellion was a quick progression from Mary Poppins to Marilyn Manson that year. During the mid-teenage years I tried to do and sometimes did, just about everything. The truth was I was a wild and rebellious child. I went from an honors student to a class-A bitch and was in desperate need of an attitude adjustment. Despite my terrible behavior my parents loved me just the same.

I was partying pretty hard and listening to the loudest, harshest music I could get my hands on, including Black Sabbath and Iron Maiden. Gone were the days of listening to *Hooked on Classics,* or Zamfir, or going to the ballet. My style was ominous and consisted of unflattering clothing combinations, such as a lumber jacket and black purse. I also learned how to get the darkest eye makeup. We would heat up the black eyeliner pencil with a match until it became almost liquid, and then we applied it to our eyelids.

I was a sight to behold at my ninth-grade graduation. I wore a satin cherry-red dress. The top was strapless and fitted. The skirt puffed out as a result of the crinoline underneath. The skirt had bows to pull up the fabric and make it look layered giving the dress that southern bell or Cinderella look. I wore a white hat and white gloves. I've always been a bit eccentric in the way I dress. I started at a very young age. In fact, I even bought a specific brand of cigarette to match my dress. I had a warped mind to even think of doing that. I was all dressed up but had a cigarette hanging from my mouth, just to be cool; of course, just not when my parents were near. After the ceremony with our parents, my friends and I went to a local restaurant for alcoholic drinks. Although we were only fifteen, we learned pretty quickly that it was much easier to get alcohol in a restaurant than anywhere else. Back then, no one checked IDs, and I think servers were uncomfortable asking people for their identification, so they didn't.

When we left the restaurant, my best friend Tina and I started walking down the street. We were still in our graduation dresses, so we must have looked unusual. Then a Corvette drove by with two young guys in it. They stopped the car and started talking to us. We felt on top of the world. A Corvette and two guys! Wow! The next thing we knew, all four of us were crammed into the two-seater, cruising around town. But we didn't mind being that close to the guys.

Summer started out great. We had a lot of fun hanging around and going to parties. Tina and I always hung around with an older crowd. It just made everything easier, and they usually had cars. Later that summer we met some guys who were closer to our age, but their older brothers also took an interest in us. We loved spending time with the older brothers, as they drove a Dodge Charger. That was one sporty car—you felt cool just sitting inside. It was nice to just drive around town in that car. Sometimes we would do crazy things. I remember driving on a deserted road where the driver got out of his window while the car was moving and crawled across the roof to the other side while the passenger slid over to drive the car. It was a stunt that could have gone horribly wrong, but thankfully it didn't. We had a few unique experiences driving with those guys, and that was just one.

Another night, a third guy, Tom, joined us. Tom was looking for sex and Tina and I just weren't prepared to provide that. Tina and I were planning on hanging onto our virginity until we met the "right one" and these guys just weren't the "right one". Tom quickly figured out he was going to have to get it another way. The guys decided Tom was going to get a prostitute. After cruising around the block where these girls hung out a couple of times he chose one he liked and invited her to get into the car. Tina and I were in the backseat and the prostitute got in the front seat. I really wasn't sure what to think at that time. I think I was stunned or just shocked that things like this really happened. The prostitute realized we were in the car and just assumed we were there for the same reason. She turned around and said to us, "Do you girls work?" I didn't know what she meant. As wild as I was, I was still pretty innocent. I was about to say that I was working at the Coliseum at one of the concession stands when Tina, knowing what I was thinking, quickly cut me off and blurted out "No." The girl thought we were prostitutes too. How embarrassing. All in one moment, I felt stupid. I felt enraged. I felt cheap.

Needless to say, I was experiencing life. The good girl image from my early years was being tarnished by some of my choices that year. One thing that didn't change was my love and respect for my parents. I made sure I was at home by curfew and always let them know roughly where I was going to be. I never stayed out all night and lied about it.

One night, when I was fifteen, my friends and I were invited to a party. We called our friend Rob. He always knew where the action was and how to get us there. We all met at the mall and waited for Rob and some of his friends. They knew the guy who was going to drive us that night was Eddie. Not only did he have a car, but he had a really hot car, a Mustang Cobra. There were six of us trying to squeeze into that sports car. Eddie agreed to drive us to the party on the condition that I sit in the front seat next to him. I felt quite flattered. I was definitely attracted to him. He was twenty years old, had a great car and he liked *me*. We had a nice time that night just hanging out and talking. But then he didn't call, nor did I see him for a few months.

The next thing I heard about Eddie wasn't good. Rob called me and told me he and Eddie had been in a car accident coming home from a party. They had been drinking all night long and decided to leave the party. Eddie was in no state to drive, but he did anyway. So he ended up hitting a road sign and crashing into a ditch. They were both okay, but the car was totaled. Unfortunately the brush with death didn't push Eddie to slow down at all. With the insurance money from the accident, Eddie bought a silver duel-tank Ford F150 truck. Because it had a sleeper behind the cab, we were able to squeeze quite a few people in the back on our trips. Once again, Eddie insisted I sit beside him in the front seat.

It had been a few months since I had heard from Eddie, which was reasonable, as he did have different interests from a fifteen-year-old girl. I'm sure it would have been awkward to have an underage girlfriend. But Eddie always came back, he never stayed away too long.

We spent a lot more time getting to know each other at the next party. As the evening progressed, things got a little hot and heavy and we snuck off into the bedroom to "talk" in a more private setting. I will never forget that when I asked him where he worked, he told me he worked on the docks. I asked how this was possible, as there was limited water in Alberta. Alberta is located in the middle of the prairies. It is the land of vast wheat fields and it is landlocked. The closest ocean is near Vancouver which is a fifteen hour drive from Edmonton. But he meant the warehouse docks.

By the end of that night, we decided we were going to be a couple. There may not really have been a decision to make. He was older, exciting, and I felt that he really liked me. He brought excitement and danger to my ordinary life, and I liked that. I felt special, and I didn't want it to end. He was a really nice person, had a job and a truck—what else could a fifteen-year-old want? I remember that night that I wanted to be home by curfew, and he respected that about me and drove me home. I liked that about him. He didn't make fun of me or criticize me for wanting to obey my parents.

I did call the party house the next day because Tina did not come home. To my surprise, she told me she had fallen asleep with Eddie. I felt betrayed. I told her Eddie was my boyfriend. I acted like the kid I was, but when your boyfriend is twenty, the reactions are intensified. Then Tina told me nothing had happened—they were just talking. I wondered why he was even interested in me after the way I had reacted.

And now you may be wondering about our age difference. Well, it was an issue, to me it didn't make any difference, but we knew it would matter to our parents. So I told my parents that Eddie was younger than he was, and he told his father and sister that I was older. It was our first secret of many. At times, the age difference came into play since he could go to bars and I couldn't. His friends were adults and mine were still teenagers. Eddie tried not to fall in love, but in the end his heart overruled his brain.

Believe it or not, Eddie was good for me in some ways. He grounded me. Up to that point, I was a rebellious, wild teenager. I was partying quite a bit. He hadn't done well in life so he encouraged me to go to school and to do well in school. Also because of Eddie's drinking problem I had to be more responsible so that I could take care of him. Or that's what I thought. Although being a caretaker for an alcoholic wasn't how I should have been spending my teenage years. Someone had to make sure he got home okay and be the mediator for the fights he was sure to be involved in. By that time, I was only drinking when I thought we were in a safe situation, like his mother's house.

I was a naïve young teenager with little self-confidence. I was thrilled that a guy with a hot truck wanted to be with me. He would pick me up at school, and I would do my best to make everyone see me leave with him. Sometimes I purposely stole a big kiss in front of friends I wanted to impress. I thought I was doing quite well for myself. Partying was a big part of my teenage years. As the majority of people we hung around with still lived at home, including Eddie, we often rented a hotel room for our gatherings.

On December 14, 1985, a bunch of friends got together and rented a hotel room so we could have a little Christmas party. Eddie rented the room, so he made the rules for the evening. He thought that he and I should have some time alone together, so he asked everyone to leave for a couple of hours. People left quite reluctantly. Eddie and I were talking and drinking, but he seemed agitated. He said that I was flirting with one of our friends, which of course I denied. It was Christmas and I was just being jovial. Before I knew it, we were in a screaming match and then it happened. He slapped me across the side of my head. He hit me so hard I saw the flash of light and I could hear ringing in my ears, I was in shock. I never imagined he would hit me. I left the room in tears. I thought the relationship was *over*. I was going to New Brunswick with my family for Christmas the next day, and there was no way I was going to see him ever again. That's what we girls are taught growing up, isn't it? If someone hits you, it's over!

The two weeks away at Christmas were quite enjoyable. I wasn't sorrowful that I no longer had a boyfriend—I simply enjoyed the time with my family. It was the first time we had gone away for Christmas. Mom always created wonderful holiday times at home. She took the time decorating the house and baking goodies for the season. It was exciting in some ways to spend it away, but in other ways I missed the festivities at home.

It was what we expected every year. Given what had just happened with Eddie, I was glad to be away for a while.

Needless to say, I was shocked to see Eddie at my door when we arrived back in Edmonton after Christmas. I asked him what he was doing there, and he said he had missed me. I just glared at him; I was so angry. Who did he think he was to treat me like that? Somehow he managed to talk his way out of that transgression. He said he didn't mean it and he'd been drinking, as if drinking was an excuse. He actually convinced me that it was all a misunderstanding and that I was overreacting. I bought his arguments and questioned myself yet again. It was the beginning of our very tumultuous relationship. The warning signs were there, but I wasn't willing to see them. I should have stood my ground, but I didn't. That is where the story really begins.

We dated for three years before we married. Yes, I was only eighteen when I got married, a child bride, and Eddie was only twenty-three, still a baby himself. We were two people getting married far too young. Looking back, I'm not sure why I even married him. Our three-year relationship wasn't exactly blissful. From the time I met Eddie, he had a drinking problem, and it grew worse. He seemed to be getting into more fights, with me, his father and with strangers. He was drinking and driving more, missing work; things never seemed to go right for him and it wasn't a coincidence. His drinking had a very negative effect on our relationship and his life.

During the three years we dated, Eddie had three vehicles. The Mustang was the first, but he drove it off the road, hitting a road sign and totaling the car. Then he rolled his truck over when he drove it into a ditch on the way back from Calgary, where he had been visiting his mother. He was still under the influence on the way home, but he didn't care. The last car was a Trans Am. I was with him when he wrecked that car.

We were on our way home and stopped at a red light. We were only a block away from my house. The light turned green and he started to turn left, but he didn't see there was car coming toward us. I started to panic and screamed just as the car drove into the back of the Trans Am. I remember the car spinning a few times and then finally came to a stop. As I jumped out to see if the other driver was okay, Eddie drove off without me. I was in shock and couldn't believe Eddie's behavior. I didn't care where he was going—I didn't want to be near him. After I confirmed the other driver was not hurt, I walked home. When I got home, Eddie was sitting in his car outside my house. When he saw me arrive, he left and went back to his house. He was still drunk.

What was I thinking? I should have seen the red flags. How many times did it have to happen before I woke up? Hindsight is twenty-twenty, but I guess I thought I could change him, and that time would be the last time he would do something so foolish and thoughtless. Love is blind, love is cruel, and love is forgiving. Looking back, I think I had too much hope that he'd change and too much forgiveness when he didn't. I didn't realize that by choosing to stay, I was accepting that I deserved it. My life with Eddie would always be filled with turmoil.

Because I was still underage, sometimes Eddie would go drinking with his buddies, disappearing for days at a time. By this time, I had very few friends. I had a hard time making friends in high school and my army friends had all moved away. I had a couple of friends at work, but Eddie made sure I didn't have time for them so they just moved on. I didn't know at the time that it was typical for controlling, abusive people to isolate you from family and friends. Getting rid of my friends was one thing, but my family was always there for me. When Eddie would leave, Mom would be there to comfort me or just be with me. We often spent our time playing Trivial Pursuit. By the way, if you don't know the answer to an Arts and Literature question, guess Hemingway.

Despite my rebelliousness, I still had a great deal of respect for my parents. There wasn't a whole lot they could say about my dating Eddie, but they did want to know where I was and that I was safe. I was still coming home almost every night, and I tried to be there by curfew. But when your boyfriend is in his twenties, getting home for curfew can be a bit awkward.

One evening, when I was trying to get Eddie home after a night of drinking, Eddie told me about the aliens that were coming for us. I didn't know what to do but to try to get him home. As we are walking home, he kept looking up to the sky and telling me they were getting closer. I wasn't really paying attention because I was holding him up and trying to navigate back to his apartment. I wasn't that familiar with the area and hoped we were going in the right direction. I was very relieved when we made it to the apartment without Eddie passing out on the street.

I propped him up as we climbed three long flights of stairs to the two-bedroom apartment he shared with his father. Inside, I managed to get him to the couch where he just passed out. I didn't really know where I was, but

I couldn't let my parents worry, so I called home. I explained I didn't know exactly where I was, but I was at Eddie's house and I was safe. I looked out the window and told mom I could see the big CN sign out the window. It was the only landmark I had and it wasn't much help. I suggested to my mom that I stay the night there and go home in the morning, when Eddie could drive. Unexpectedly, she agreed.

My parents weren't too happy that I was dating Eddie. They knew he drank too much and wasn't treating me well, but they also knew that if they had forbidden it, they might have lost me completely. Staying that first night with Eddie was the beginning of my withdrawal from my family, because after that I would spend the weekends with him. It wasn't long until I got to know the apartment and Eddie's father very well. The men and the apartment needed a woman's touch, and I loved being needed.

Often, I spent my weekends "babysitting" Eddie. Sometimes he would get so drunk that I thought he might just pass out anywhere, so I would sit with him until he could move again, or I would try to get him home. One weekend we were partying at a place in the countryside. In the morning he wanted to go home and was still too drunk to drive. I didn't know how to drive a standard, so I got a quick lesson that morning and I didn't do very well. Thankfully, it was an early Sunday morning and not many cars were on the road. At one intersection, the light had changed three times before I was able to get the car moving without stalling it.

Another weekend Eddie and I and another couple, Murray and Michelle, went to Grande Prairie. Murray had to pick up a truck he was going to restore, so we thought we'd make a road trip out of it. We checked into a hotel and the boys went to buy some beer. As I was underage, I waited back at the hotel. After twenty minutes, Eddie hadn't returned and I started to wonder where he was so I called Murray's girlfriend, Michelle. She was waiting in their hotel room for Murray to return. She hadn't heard from either Murray or Eddie. After an hour, I began to pace as my anxiety started to build. Had he really abandoned me in the hotel while he went out partying? I was just sixteen, I didn't know where I was, and I was stranded at the hotel. Many hours passed without any sign of Eddie, so then my anxiety turned to anger. I went to bed so angry that night just thinking about what he had done to me once again.

The next morning I woke up and realized Eddie still hadn't come back to the hotel. Then I started to panic. Where the heck was he? Did he get into a fight? Was he passed out somewhere? Was he laying dead somewhere? He was missing. I called Murray and Michelle's room and Murray answered. At least one of them had found their way home. I expressed my concern about Eddie not having come back to the hotel. Murray told me not to worry. He had been friends with Eddie since they were kids and he knew he'd show up eventually. He told me to meet them in the lobby and the three of us would go for breakfast. He was confident Eddie would show up before we were ready to drive back to Edmonton. He was right just as we got to the lobby Eddie came staggering in. He had spent the night in the drunk tank at the police station.

Eddie told me later that when he arrived at the bar the night before, he had to have a drink, and one drink led to another. It didn't take long for him to embark on a full-fledged binge. Unfortunately (or fortunately), the police saw him staggering across the parking lot and took him in. It was probably a good thing they did, given his state. He could have ended up in a lot more trouble or could have hurt someone else.

The stories go on and on. Because he was so controlling and obsessive, he really wanted me with him all the time. But there was also a double standard, as he wanted to be with his friends too. At times he was embarrassed about my age, so he would just leave me alone in the truck to wait for him while he spent time with his friends. Believe it or not, I waited for him. I don't know why I put up with it.

One time in the winter I recall waiting in the truck for hours. Eddie decided to stop at the trucking company where his friend Murray worked. Murray was done for the day and he was just hanging around drinking beer with his co-workers. It got very cold that evening, but I waited anyway. At some point, my common sense kicked in and I left the truck and went across the street to the hotel. I waited in the lobby where I could see the trucking building and was ready to run out if I saw Eddie leave. If he couldn't find me, there would have been hell to pay, so I had to be near.

I guess I was afraid more often than not because when Eddie got mad you didn't know what was going to happen. If we were driving and I said something or did something that he didn't like, he would start beating me right there in the truck. Once, this happened on the Yellowhead Trail outside Edmonton. We were arguing. About what I don't know; I'm sure it was something ridiculous. He had pulled the truck to the side of the road and just started screaming at me to get out of the truck. There was nowhere to go. It was a deserted area of highway. There were no cell phones back then, either. I felt totally lost both physically and emotionally. I begged and pleaded with him to stop. I was terrified I was going to be stranded there. Finally he calmed down. He was still angry and he wouldn't talk to me but at least he let me stay in the truck. We continued on our way.

You just didn't know what would set Eddie off or how he would react. One evening, we were getting ready to go out to a bar. I'm not sure what I said, but clearly it wasn't what he wanted to hear. One minute I was standing at the kitchen table talking to him, and the next thing I knew, my face was being rammed into the table legs. That was one of the worst times of my life. It was one of the few times Eddie left visible bruises, every other time the abuse was hidden. I was completely stunned. My face was swollen and bruised. But as quickly as it happened, it was over.

He told me to get myself together, as we were going to his sister's house. It was strange to me that I would go to someone else's house looking like that. But his sister showed no horror or shock when she saw me. I knew she knew what had happened, that Eddie had done a number on me because I was a complete mess. Gerry, his sister, matter-of-factly sat me down at the kitchen table and gave me a bag of ice to help with the swelling. Once it looked like you could touch my face again, she took her time and placed makeup to cover the bruised spots. Then we were off to the bar. Some bars were more lenient and did not check IDs when you were with an older person, so we tended to go to these more often.

I still couldn't understand why they didn't care that I had been beaten up. No one said a word; they just covered it up. Maybe they thought his behavior was normal and didn't make a fuss. It was something to cover up and move on. At the end of the weekend, Mom saw me and asked what happened. I didn't have the courage to tell her the truth, so I lied and told her I had been skating at West Edmonton Mall and wasn't able to stop, so I landed face first into the boards. That was my cover story—not very creative, I know, but Mom didn't question it. If only I'd had the courage that night to tell her the truth, my life might have turned out differently.

Life provides many paths, and sometimes we choose a path while other times it chooses us. Around this time, my dad had been at the Edmonton base for almost three years, so his post was almost at an end. One day when I came home from school, Mom told me that Dad was being posted to Wainwright, Alberta. This was another small town in the middle of nowhere, about three hours away from Edmonton. This time I actually didn't mind going and was somewhat excited. I think I was so accepting because I saw the move as an opportunity to escape the mess I was in. I wanted to return to simpler times. Although part of me loved the city life, deep down I was missing the real me.

However, Mom didn't feel that moving two teenage girls to a farm town was a great idea. So after she discussed the potential move with Dad, they decided that the girls would stay in Edmonton, and Dad would move to the new post and come home on weekends. Just like that, my chance to reinvent myself was gone. There was nothing to do but adapt and move on.

I don't want to mislead you, I wasn't a saint. I was young and trying to find my way in life. I was trying to find out what I wanted and who I wanted to be. One night I arrived at a party before Eddie, as he was going to meet me there later. I may have been getting a little friendly with one of Eddie's friends. Don't ask me why—to this day, I don't know. But when Eddie finally arrived, someone told him that I had been cozy with another guy. He was furious! He was so mad he actually forced my big toe in his mouth, and then he bit it so hard that I thought for sure he was going to bite it right off. I was screaming in pain, but nobody wanted to get involved. Once again, he attacked me, but no one came to my rescue. No one told him to stop. They continued on their merry drink fest and ignored what was happening. Finally Eddie stopped biting me. He must have thought that was enough punishment for a while, or maybe he wanted to join the party. I don't know how I survived. Whenever he was violent toward me, there was never an outcry or reaction from anyone, so I thought I was overreacting and became accustomed to the abuse.

When we had been dating about eight or nine months, my family went back to Alsask for a ten-year reunion. I was sixteen and I decided I wanted to go. It would be one of the few times I was away from him. I was looking forward to not only being away from him, but also to being with my old friends and being free. It took some courage to finally tell Eddie I was going away for the weekend without him. He made a couple of comments, but that was it.

As soon as I got there, I felt home again. Free—free from my old self, from Eddie, and the life I had been living. Staying in our old home brought me back to the person I had once been. It was good to see me again, even with a little bit of city attitude. It was an amazing weekend. We had a barbecue one day at one of the nearby farms. It was reminiscent of old times, the teenagers ran through the water sprinkler and the adults relaxed with some beer. It was great fun and very innocent. So, I decided I would stay an extra day and attend a wedding with some friends. I didn't call Eddie and didn't think about him too much, as I was having so much fun.

But I did have to return to Edmonton. So, the following day I did, and Eddie was waiting for me when I got home. He actually wasn't mad and took it in stride, perhaps because my parents were in front of him. But this calmness didn't last for long. When we were alone, he told me what would happen if I ever pulled a stunt like that again. It wasn't long before I resumed my role as caretaker for Eddie and his dad. I regularly cooked and cleaned for them. Part of me liked doing this because I liked being needed. I was a people pleaser and sometimes people took advantage of me.

You might think my life was all bad, but it actually wasn't. We did have some wonderful times together. When Eddie wasn't drinking, we would spend our weekends hanging out, just the two of us. In the summer, we would spend many lazy days enjoying the park. We would lie on the grass and watch the clouds drift by, or play Frisbee or take the dog for a walk. In the winter, we would often go on winter picnics. We would find a park that provided shelter from the trees and then walk for a bit, and then just sit down with our blanket on the snow and enjoy the warmth from the sun. It was very romantic. I loved those moments. He seemed to love me and treat me in all the right ways.

When he was good to me, I convinced myself that his rages of jealousy and possessiveness were just another form of his love. We loved to drive around to some of the nicer parts of town and dream about living there and owning those big homes. It was nice to have dreams that we both shared. If Celine Dion's song came on the radio, "I am Your Lady," Eddie would sing that he was my lady and I was his man. It was sweet—funny. He made me laugh.

Over the course of our relationship, I quit school. As I mentioned earlier, my health had been a big issue in high school, and I had started working in a shoe store. Eddie hated that I didn't finish school. He had quit school too, and he knew you needed an education to get ahead in life. It's because of his encouragement that I eventually returned to school and received my GED. Because of that motivation, I was able to attend college later and receive a diploma in accounting. I will always have Eddie to thank for that.

Love and Marriage

On many occasions, Eddie and I would just curl up on the sofa and watch a movie, eat ice cream, and drink Coke. It would make me laugh when all we hoped for was to get the two liters of soda on sale for $1.99. We walked back from the store to his apartment hand in hand, as if we didn't have a care in the world. Occasionally, Eddie would walk by the old school, and I would skip on the hopscotch tree, reliving my youth. Those were wonderful times.

One night while we were sitting on his dad's sofa, Eddie said, "If I ask you to marry me and you say no, it's over." I wasn't sure what to think. What was he really saying to me? I started to question what I really wanted in life. The little voice in my head was nagging at me. It was whispering to me that marriage probably wasn't what I wanted at eighteen. I still had my whole life in front of me. I had dreams and goals. While I did want to be married someday, was this the right time? I didn't want to break up with Eddie, but I really wasn't sure about marrying him either. I had experienced so many ups and downs that it was hard to catch my breath. But the little girl inside knew it would be absolutely thrilling to be engaged.

One beautiful fall day, when the azure sky seemed endless and the crisp air was fresh and invigorating, I decided to go on a bike ride after work. I was enjoying the peace, solitude, and, of course, the freedom of being alone on my bike. The wind was blowing through my hair and on my checks.

I felt alive. Eddie had worked the overnight shift, so I knew he would be asleep and would not wake up until later. We decided to meet around suppertime. So I was just enjoying my alone time, as I didn't think there was any urgent reason to see Eddie before dinner.

As I rode closer to his dad's apartment, I saw Eddie driving down the road in his truck. As soon as he saw me, he pulled over and jumped out. Before I could say hello, he was yelling at me. "Where the hell have you been? I've been looking all over town for you. I was going to f***ing propose today, and now you've ruined everything."

I was devastated. He said he had a wonderful setting planned for a proposal, and because it was going to be a surprise, I had ruined it. I felt my life was over and all the air had been sucked out of me. Then Eddie grabbed my bike and threw it in the back of his truck and shouted for me to get in. He continued yelling at me as he drove to the restaurant. I begged for forgiveness the entire way there. I apologized many times during that ride. I wonder now why I even bothered.

Throughout our relationship, Eddie wasn't exactly Prince Charming. So why was I begging him for forgiveness? I guess it goes back to wanting to be needed and valued. I really did love Eddie, just not what he did to me. In my mind I could compartmentalize the two without knowing it, and it would take years before those two parts talked to one another and let me in on the secret.

The rest of the evening proceeded as he planned. It was romantic. He had actually planned everything in detail, so I guessed that meant he really loved me. We went to our favorite restaurant, where I ordered my favorite dish, steak Neptune. The steak and crab were perfection and the white wine was delicious. When I went to the washroom, Eddie put the ring into my wine glass. As soon as I returned, I took a sip of wine and noticed the ring at the bottom of the glass. Even though I knew what was coming, I was still thrilled that he made such an effort to make it a wonderful surprise. When I put the glass back on the table, Eddie gazed into my eyes and asked me, quietly, to marry him.

When you're a little girl, you always dream about becoming engaged and getting married. You dream of the church, the white dress, and all the fuss that goes with planning a wedding. I was so thrilled and excited that of course I said yes. We didn't waste any time—we immediately started planning our wedding. When I told my parents about the engagement, they initially tried to get me to think about how this was a big commitment to make at my young age. I don't think they were happy at first, but they did relent as they knew that I wanted to marry Eddie so much. We were married about six months later, April 15, 1989.

The year we got married was also the year I started college. It was one of the worst years of our relationship. Of course, some of that had to do with being married and discovering our way through married life. We no longer lived with our parents and their rules. Now we had to set up our own house, and we set the rules. When we're young and have to follow someone else's rules, most of us rebel to some degree. Maybe we just test the water to see how much we can get away with, and other times we crush the rules and, with them our relationship with those around us. Eddie and I were so happy not to follow someone else's rules that we didn't realize that rules and structure were an important part of life and everyone needed them.

Although we still weren't living together, we had the apartment before we were married and I had keys to it. It was so exciting to go furniture shopping like an adult and get everything settled for our new home. There's something to say for buying things, other than clothes, and knowing they're yours, and part of your life.

The first weekend in our new apartment, Eddie's friends had a stag party for him. What a freaking disaster! I tried to get in touch with Eddie but couldn't reach him. Based on past history, I never knew what might happen, so I decided to go over to the apartment. I opened the door to an eviction warning. Bodies of drunken passed out men were laying all over the floor of my new home. My new home was defiled before I was even able to stay the first night. I was devastated. I just turned around and left without talking to anyone.

Several weeks later, Eddie had been out drinking with his friend Murray. I was with him but was fed up, so I decided to go to the apartment. Sometime in the middle of the night he staggered in, drunk beyond belief. He woke me up and told me it was over. He was leaving me, and he and Murray were on their way to Las Vegas that very night. I panicked. Not only was my fiancé leaving me, he was planning to drive while he was still drunk. I jumped out of bed and ran after him. In the parking lot I begged him not to go. I pleaded and cried and did anything I could just to make him stay. I stood there and watched him drive away that night not knowing what tomorrow was going to bring. Just like a lost dog, he returned the next day with his tail between his legs. And I took him back. Again. In a very dysfunctional way, we needed each other, and deep down I knew it would be a roller-coaster life with Eddie.

Eddie came to his senses later that weekend and, for a short time, changed his behavior. We didn't have any parties at our place and we did our best to live a relatively quiet life. We continued to plan the wedding. I had hoped my best friend Tina from school would be one of my bridesmaids along with my sister, of course, and Eddie's sister Kim. As the date got closer, Tina told me she was not going to be able to make it. I then asked a girl I worked with, but she refused, stating she didn't know me that well. I was somewhat deflated by both refusals, but the wedding went on, and I had Eddie's niece and his other sister Penni join as bridesmaids.

The night before the wedding was very hectic at my parents' house. I had moved most of my furniture out by then. Mom and Dad had a few out-of-town guests staying with them, so there was a lot of noise and confusion at the house. All I wanted was some peace. I found a place in what used to be my room and just lay on the floor. I recall laying there, staring off into space, and sporadically glancing at my dress. A typical wedding dress in the eighties was very full, with organza and lace, and it seemed like my dress took up most of the room. It was like a cloud whisping by. Staring at my dress brought me a kind of peace away from the hustle of everything. I was not nervous at all. I quickly fell to sleep.

The day of the wedding was a flurry of activity at the house. After hair, makeup, and getting dressed, it was time to leave. On the way to the base chapel, I discovered that my bouquet was still at the house. Dad then asked if I needed it, to which I replied, "of course." So we turned around and made the trip in record time, and I arrived a little more than fashionably late to the church. As Dad walked me down the aisle, he glanced over at me, squeezed my hand, and smiled. He didn't say a word, but the love in his eyes spoke volumes. Today his little girl was walking down the aisle as his child, and then she'd be leaving as someone's wife. My, how the years just flew by.

When I got to the end of the aisle, Eddie just stared at me. When we finally started to say our vows, Eddie was very emotional and started to sob. He cried so hard my mother didn't think he could finish them. But he mustered through it, and finally we were pronounced "husband and wife."

I think I heard Eddie exclaim a sigh of relief that the formal part was now over.

At the community hall, we posed for pictures and then, finally, the reception began. To my dismay, someone brought in a television to the back of the hall. After all, it was Stanley Cup season and the Edmonton Oilers were playing. Looking back at it, I think it made the night very unique. Only in Canada!

The night of our wedding, Eddie knew he had to be on his best behavior and he was. Eddie wasn't the kind of alcoholic that needed a drink every day; he was more of a binge drinker, if he started drinking, he couldn't stop until there was no more alcohol available. This caused me a great deal of stress, which only got worse when the provincial government decided that liquor stores could open on Sundays. But an alcoholic will find alcohol. Even before the stores were open on Sundays, he could find it if he wanted to. Open liquor stores seven days a week just made it easier for him.

That first year of marriage was difficult. We were learning more about ourselves and I started college. I was also very homesick. Eddie worked nights, so I was alone and didn't like it. I also had a part-time job for my own spending money. Being a new wife, a student and working part time was stressful. College was pretty tough. I had been out of the school atmosphere for some time, and I didn't realize the amount of homework and studying necessary in order to be successful. Part of my problem was, of course, Eddie. He really enjoyed his weekends, and I, unfortunately, was his babysitter. As soon as I got home from school on Fridays, we would get ready and go out to the bar. I wouldn't drink because I had to drive and maintain a clear head. I only had my learners permit but me driving without a full license was better than Eddie drinking and driving.

I also wanted to be the perfect wife. I tried to do everything I thought the perfect wife would do. I was married, and where I grew up, the wife took care of everyone else. And so I tried to take care of Eddie. At that time he was working the evening shift and didn't come until 4:30 in the morning. I would be up waiting for him, like a Stepford wife, with a warm breakfast after his long night at work. I did this for a long time, but as I was in school, it was to my own detriment. Because I wasn't getting enough sleep or just broken sleep, I sometimes fell asleep in class. My GPA wasn't that good, but through hard work and with the grace of God, I managed to graduate college. College graduates were not that plentiful in our family—in fact, I was in an elite group. I was so very proud of myself. I had come a long way from quitting high school, and now finally I was a college graduate. Could things get any better?

During some of the good times, Eddie and I took vacations. Because he was in a junior position at the trucking company, we usually took winter trips. Our vacation spot of choice was usually Jasper, Alberta. We loved to ski the slopes of Marmot Basin. They were refreshing and wonderful days, but the nights, well, the nights were an entirely different story. We endured more of Eddie's usual behavior, but somehow, being in a new location made it worse for me. I remember one night we were in a cab going back to the hotel when we saw an elk on the side of the road. As the cab stopped at the traffic light, Eddie got out of the cab and walked up to the animal. I waited in the car. The cab driver was very concerned and kept telling him to get back into the car. I had absolutely no control over Eddie so there wasn't anything I could do.

Thank goodness the elk wasn't in an aggressive mood or things could have gone horribly wrong. But the cab driver had enough. We were pretty close to the hotel, so he was kind enough to drop me off there. He wasn't waiting for Eddie to get back in the car. I left Eddie standing on the road staring at the elk like a lost soul waiting to be saved. I went back to the hotel room. I was exhausted. It took a lot of energy to do what I could to keep Eddie out of trouble. I crawled into bed. I had tried my best to keep him safe and that was all I could do. He was on his own now. I said a prayer for him and fell asleep.

I was in quite a deep sleep when I heard the banging at the door. I knew it was him so I got out of bed to let him in. I opened the door and to my utter amazement, he stood there with his pants around his ankles. I didn't ask one question. I was so mad that I just let him in the room. He walked to the bed and passed out within minutes. I never did find out about his pants. He didn't remember anything the next day.

A few months after our marriage, my parents moved back to Ontario. I remember it was a hot day in July when I stood at the end of the driveway of their home and waved as they departed. Life was moving on. I was happy for them, as they were returning to Kingston where Dad started his military career and Mom grew up. They were going home. My grandparents still lived there as well as my aunt, my mom's sister. I knew they would be okay without Cathy and me because they had family there. For me, it meant my family support would be far away. My sister still lived in Edmonton and we kept in touch daily, but she wasn't in any position to provide the support I would soon realize I needed.

It's hard for parents to watch their children grow up and move on, but it is normal. I'm not sure it's normal for children to see their parents moving on. I knew it was best for them but I felt so alone. Telephones are great, but it just isn't the same as being there. You can't see the pain or sorrow in someone's face without being there. You can't wrap your arms around a person and hug him or her. You can't be with someone in times of need, and you can't always visit when you want to. Yes, growing up and moving away has many perks, but it's hard to live without the love and warmth of our family's embrace.

Eddie and I didn't have a lot of money in those early years, but we would save up and treat ourselves to a special night out once a year. There was a fantastic restaurant in Edmonton called Sorrentino's. We loved to go there because the food and atmosphere were great. One night there, the waiter taught me how to eat shrimp scampi the proper way. What an experience! We always had a good time, and even Eddie wouldn't drink too much, maybe because it was so expensive. We could only afford an aperitif and one bottle of wine between us. I'm not sure why Eddie could maintain control in some situations and not others. Another evening, we really splurged and went to the Westin restaurant. It was truly fine dining. They even sent a sommelier over to help us make our wine selection for the evening. This was a wonderful and new experience.

When Christmas finally came that first year, we decided it would be wonderful to host it at our place. I think I needed to do something, plan something, so I wouldn't miss my family. So I tried to surround myself with everyone else to make our first Christmas special. Usually it was Eddie's sister who organized his family events, but with my family gone, we thought it would be nice for me to bring both sides of the family together to our place to celebrate. So my sister Cathy and her family came over to join the festivities as well.

On Christmas Eve, we went over to Eddie's sister's house. It was a pretty typical holiday with family sitting around, playing cards, and having a few drinks. Everything's typical unless there is an alcoholic in the family. For me, Christmas Eve is very special, so that night I dressed up in a beautiful dress and high heel shoes. Sometimes cold Alberta nights can drop down to minus twenty-five degrees Celsius and colder. Eddie's sister only lived a ten-minute drive away, so I wore my heels anyway. Little did I know that my planning was useless.

Eddie's drinking got pretty nasty that night, and I wanted to leave early to start preparing for the next day. We were planning to have ten people join us for lunch, and I had a million things to do, not to mention my Santa duties. As the night wore on, I was getting more tired and frustrated; finally, I reached my breaking point. I had enough and decided it was worth the effort to walk home, in my heels.

It was a bit of a walk to get to the main road, and by then I was freezing. Here I was on Christmas Eve walking home by myself. It wasn't the way I pictured Christmas Eve in my head. I felt alone. It was pure determination that kept me walking that night. I certainly wasn't going back. That would be admitting defeat. I was so grateful when a stranger pulled over and offered me a ride home. I wasn't far from home, but walking in the cold weather in my high heels I wasn't sure I would make it. The wonderful angel dropped me right at the apartment building.

Before long, I realized things were going from bad to worse. When I walked up to the building, I realized I didn't have my keys. I just buzzed every apartment in the building until someone let me in. It was too cold to remain outside, and at least I could stay warm. I had to sit in the hallway until Eddie decided to come home. Eddie sauntered in around two in the morning. I was too tired to fight him, and he was too drunk to communicate, so he passed out and I was finally able to do my Santa duties. I was relieved he made it home, but I knew he drove drunk, yet again.

The next day wasn't great either. The entire family was there, and I was doing my best to keep everyone fed and happy, but Eddie was so hung over he couldn't get out of bed. Kim helped me to cook my first turkey and thankfully dinner seemed fine. Eddie managed to get up from his comatose reverie to join us for supper, but his state ruined it for me. I was so angry with him that day that several times I pounded my way into the bedroom and told him exactly what I thought about him ruining everything. He did show some remorse, but he really wasn't capable of getting out of bed and joining the rest of us. It wasn't how I pictured our first Christmas together. It was a sign of things to come, that's for sure.

Children

They say one of the hardest periods in a marriage is the first few years, when you are trying to mold two lives into one. Ours was not a typical marriage, but somehow we did manage to survive the first two years. By the time I almost completed college, we thought we would take the next step and start having children. Since I had been on birth control for several years, we both thought it might take some time to get pregnant. Boy, were we wrong!

Our big plan after graduation was for me to get a job, work long enough to qualify for maternity benefits, and then get pregnant. But life had other plans. By the time I actually graduated, I was pregnant. I did manage to get a temporary job that ended in December, just in time for my January third due date.

Those months of pregnancy were wonderful. I felt special. And although most people talk about being sick throughout pregnancy, I really wasn't. Eddie and I were also getting along better, so things were pretty good all around. Eddie had been injured in a baseball game my third month of pregnancy, so he was immobile and therefore not drinking.

The day of the "life changing knee injury" we were enjoying a really nice day out in the country at Eddie's friend Murray's family farm. A bunch of people from surrounding farms gathered at a local baseball diamond for a casual game of ball. Eddie loved all sports and he was more than eager to play. Being pregnant I just sat and watched. The sun was shining, there wasn't a cloud in the sky I was just enjoying the day. Eddie's team was up to bat and Eddie was on second base. The batter hit the ball and Eddie started to run. Just as he came into contact with third base Eddie fell to the ground. He was clearly in pain rolling around on the ground holding his leg. I didn't think much of it. I thought that maybe he had twisted an ankle or something. Enough people had rushed over to see if he was alright so I just sat in the stands expecting that he would eventually hobble over and join me as a spectator. Unfortunately this wasn't the case. Eddie had seriously damaged his knee and there was no way he was getting up. An ambulance was called and we were off to the emergency room. I didn't have a license so Murray took me in Eddie's car to the hospital.

The night he blew out his knee was a nightmare. It was late by the time he was seen by a doctor. I was exhausted. Murray had tired of waiting and had gone home. Finally once Eddie did see the doctor we were told he would need to be admitted. He was going to need surgery to fix his ACL and MCL—parts of his knee. This also meant recuperation time; he would be off work for several months.

Not being able to drive proved to be very difficult for me during this time. I had a learner's permit and could drive with a licensed driver but not on my own. I had always depended on Eddie to take me anywhere I needed to go. I did take the bus but I wasn't dependent on it. That night, after we realized that Eddie wasn't coming home I called his sister Kim and she came to the hospital and drove me home. Over the next few days I needed to get to the hospital to see Eddie. The hospital he was admitted to was on the other side of town. Kim was wonderful and drove me whenever she could but there were many times I found myself sitting on a bus late at night making my way home. It was a very demanding time because of Eddie's convalescence, my inability to drive, and all the hormones surging through me due to my pregnancy.

We were still living in the apartment when Eddie came home from the hospital. He was really immobile, so we set up a bed in the living room where he stayed for the next few weeks. It was summertime then, and he was getting cabin fever, so I rented a wheelchair to get him out of the apartment. Eddie felt somewhat embarrassed being in the wheelchair, but he was so tired of lying in bed that he eventually began to enjoy the walks.

After a few months, Eddie's knee was good enough that he could return to work. His doctor did tell him that his career in the trucking/warehousing industry wouldn't be a career that would last his lifetime. Due to the stress of manual labor, his doctor thought it best to start thinking about a career change. I think Eddie wanted to exchange his blue collar job for a white collar job, and this was good timing.

During that year, we moved to a townhouse, as the apartment was small and we were expecting a baby. Life seemed to be progressing without any major catastrophes. We had been married for two years, I had graduated college, and now my dreams of being a mother were soon to become reality. I was so happy. One night before the baby was born; Eddie had a wonderful surprise waiting for me when I got home from work. When I walked into the house, Eddie had prepared a lovely meal for me. This was such a treat because I did most of the cooking. Eddie did a great job cooking, but that wasn't the only surprise that evening. At the time I loved to collect bells. Eddie had gone out and purchased a unique wooden bell with Chinese art on it. It was such a wonderful night for Eddie and me.

My son, Blake entered the world on a snowy December day. It was December 27, 1991, just two days after Christmas. I remember peering outside the window and holding my newborn while watching the light snowflakes slowly drift to the ground. I felt at peace and truly blessed. What a lovely Christmas gift to us. We were so thrilled to be parents. They say having children changes you, and it really does. Having Blake changed our focus. We now had a little man dependent on us for everything. It really was amazing to look down in the crib and see him sleeping away. I could just stand there and watch him breathe for minutes. Sometimes just my finger in his grasp would take my breath away. Blake was a really good baby. I was very thankful he didn't have colic and that he was so calm. It made being a mother so wonderful. I was able to stay at home with him for the first six months, for which I am grateful.

As anyone who has lived with an alcoholic knows, there are days when a normal life is just a dream. After Blake was born, it was very important to me to have him baptized. Even though we hadn't belonged to a formal church, I contacted the Padre that married us on the base. Growing up, I had attended church with my family, and I knew Padre Stenson from that time. He was happy to come to the house so Blake could be baptized at home. This was a very special day, so we set a date, ordered a cake and flowers, and Kim, Eddie's sister, made a beautiful white satin tuxedo for his baptismal outfit.

I was looking forward to that Sunday in May when Blake would be blessed and welcomed into the church. For Eddie, the baptism wasn't as important. The night before the baptism, he went out drinking with friends. And for an alcoholic there is never just one drink; the binging began once again. Throughout the night I kept thinking that he wouldn't do this just before his son's baptism, would he? He wouldn't ruin one of the sacred times in his son's life. But he did. He was too drunk for the ceremony to proceed.

I was embarrassed and devastated, but I needed to call Padre Stenson to reschedule. Most clergymen are very understanding and accommodating, and so was Padre Stenson. A few weeks later, Padre Stenson agreed to come back to our home. Eddie had taken away a little bit of the special magic that should have been there that day, but Blake was finally baptized at home in a beautiful, intimate family gathering.

Just before I returned to work after maternity leave, Eddie learned he was going to need another knee surgery. The timing was almost perfect. I was going back to work and Eddie could take care of Blake during the day. Because we loved being parents so much, we decided to try again for another child. Nineteen months later, on August 7, 1993, we welcomed our beautiful son Brett into our lives. Now we had a full family. We had been blessed with two healthy boys. I think deep down Eddie always wanted to have a "normal," family and I saw changes in him too, for a while. It was though he was try-ing to correct the wrongs of his own upbringing.

But calm and serenity doesn't last long when you live with someone who suffers from addiction. Many times they can only see themselves and become selfish. Those living

with them find ways to cope and make excuses, but eventually the house of cards begins to crumble. By the time Brett was born, Eddie had fallen off the wagon yet again. I was shocked and dumbfounded when a couple of days after I brought the baby home I had to take care of a newborn, a toddler, and everything else in the house. One Saturday afternoon Eddie went out to run an errand and hadn't returned. He didn't bother to tell me where he was going or call, nothing. I assumed he was out "celebrating" the birth of his son.

When he finally returned the next day, he did apologize, and I knew he felt bad about what happened. He suggested we all go away for family bonding time. The next thing I knew, we were driving to Red Deer, a couple of hours away. I really wasn't ready for this. I was tired. I had just given birth. My body really needed to rest. Once we got to Red Deer, Eddie decided we should go on a hike. He felt it would be a nice family thing to do. We walked for an hour or so from Rotary Park to Kin Kanyon. That was quite a trek considering I had just given birth a week before. Although I was happy to be with the family, I don't think that Eddie realized that perhaps I should not have done so much so soon. Again, he had a nice idea, but he didn't take anyone else into consideration.

When Brett was born, he was somewhat jaundiced. When we returned to the hotel from the walk, he was quite yellow. I was very concerned about him, so we decided to take him to Red Deer hospital. I was a bit panicked and felt somewhat guilty for not standing up to Eddie and refusing to go on the trip. It was just too much for us. Brett was less than two weeks old and didn't even have a provincial health care number yet. I was worried the hospital would refuse to care for him. Thankfully the medical staff was very kind and understanding and treated him anyway. They assured me that he would be just fine. They put him under the lights (that help to treat jaundice) for a couple of hours and then sent us home.

Life continued on and over time I became disheartened with Eddie's behavior. Maybe I thought he would change with a new baby. Maybe I hoped he would finally grow up and take responsibility. Maybe I was dreaming of things that could never be. A few months after Brett was born, Eddie came home drunk and insisted we drive to Calgary to visit his mom.

When I saw the condition he was in, I knew if I said no the confrontation would be worse than refusing to go. It seemed that I was afraid to say no too often. I packed the children up and off we went to Calgary. By the time we reached Red Deer, Brett was crying voraciously. He was hungry, so I begged Eddie to let me stop so I could feed him. He refused outright and I continued to drive with the baby crying in the backseat. When we arrived at his mom's house, Brett had all but cried himself out. I finally fed him while Eddie continued drinking with his family until he passed out.

As our family was growing, we decided we needed a bigger house and started looking for a new home. It was the fall of 1993, Brett was only two months old and Blake was almost two when we moved and I had a nice home where the boys would be able to play outside when they were a little older. Things were going relatively well except for the regular binges Eddie engaged in. When Blake was about two and a half and Brett was around nine months old, Eddie called me to pick him up. He was out drinking with friends and didn't want to drive that night, which was unusual. I was relieved that he didn't drink and drive.

Although it was one in the morning, I got out of bed, packed up the boys, and went out to pick him up. I pulled in front of the address he had given me, but there was no sign of Eddie. I didn't want to leave the boys alone in the car, so I took Brett out of the car seat and held onto Blake as we walked up to the house. As we approached, Eddie stormed out of the house with another guy. They were shouting at each other, and before I knew it, they started to fight. I scrambled to get out of there with the boys. Finally, after getting them safely into the car I went back and got between Eddie and his friend to break up the fight. I pulled Eddie away and managed to get him in the car and safely home. It was an incident that the boys really didn't need to see. Luckily they were too young to realize what was happening.

On another night, Eddie came home quite late from drinking. Because our front door was broken, we had to use the back door. Not long after he came home and crawled into bed, I heard noises near the back door. Eddie heard them too. Blake had been in bed with me and the commotion woke him up. Eddie said to call the police because some guy had followed him home and was trying to break into the house.

I heard the guy trying to remove the kitchen window. Blake and I were terrified. While I was on the phone with 911, the police arrived and caught the guy. The police showed me the guy's ID, but I had no idea who he was. However, he told the police that he and Eddie were out drinking and Eddie had invited him back to the house, but then Eddie wouldn't let him in. I told the police that given how drunk Eddie was, the guy was probably telling the truth. After that, I suggested they let him go without charging him. At times, living with Eddie was a nightmare for the boys and me. I wish I'd had the courage to do something about it back then. Somehow Eddie always explained everything away, and I swallowed every lie he gave me. My family really believes in the commitment of marriage. Marriage isn't something that you take lightly. Even if I had thought of leaving, where was I going to go? How was I going to care for my children and myself?

Life with the boys carried on like this for several years. Blake started playing hockey almost as soon as he could walk. His so-called hockey career was very important to Eddie. It was something they could share and dream about. Mothers want their little girls to be beauty queens; fathers want their boys to be sports stars. For many years to come, our lives involved Blake and Eddie's dream of Blake becoming an NHL player.

This privilege was bestowed upon Blake because he had been born first. Brett was still too young to play hockey, so we enjoyed our own time together. Brett and I really bonded during this time.

I really enjoyed being a hockey mom. The regularity of games and practices made our family life feel more normal. It was always hockey in the winter and T-ball in the summer. Eddie and I worked different social fundraisers, like bingo, to help pay for the sports, too. It was a real family affair.

Changes and Affairs

Our normal life didn't last long. We had been married for about four years when Eddie finally realized that he could no longer drive a truck for a living. His knee was in rough shape and his doctor convinced him it was time for a career change.

After some time and deliberation, he thought social work would be a good path. Maybe he commiserated with young people due to his own upbringing. Perhaps he thought his life experiences should have been an anchor and an inspiration for dealing with others who shared similar upbringings.

Since he hadn't finished high school, he first needed to upgrade some courses before he could apply for the program. When he was accepted to Concordia College, we were both so happy. Eddie always thought that education was a great way out, which is why he'd been so insistent that I get my college diploma. When we thought about him getting a college degree, it was like a wish was answered from heaven.

He had supported me through my two years of school, so now it was my time to do the same for him, and I was glad to do it. I thought that being in an educational institution would show him the error of his ways and would help him to incorporate better ways to live and deal with people.

I really supported him the first few months of school. When he had essays to write, he would give me the information and I would type it up. He would stand over me as I typed and would edit along the way. Although it was time consuming, I was glad he actually showed an interest in learning, and I was willing to help him any way I could. This wasn't easy, though, as I had a full-time job and two toddlers. Sometimes it caused some nasty arguments. Sometimes I didn't devote as much time to Eddie as he would have liked. It was a stressful time in our marriage, but I thought every marriage dealt with its own ups and downs. I thought we were in it for life, and I knew he loved me in his own way.

Eddie started making friends at college. At first I was happy that he had a different crowd of people to hang out with, but that soon changed. His classmates were young, and the majority didn't have any family commitments or responsibilities, so the party time atmosphere continued, but in different places. I often didn't see him between Friday afternoon and Sunday. That was one tough year, but we made it. Eddie graduated, and now he was ready to apply for the social work program. This was a great accomplishment, and Eddie was so proud he finally had a diploma. During that summer he worked for a trucking company. The extra income was a great addition and helped take off some financial pressure.

That fall he started the social work program at Grant MacEwan Community College. College life was very appealing to Eddie. Just like at Concordia, he found the party crowd early and continued his selfish ways. So the weekends were a blur to him, and I grew madder and madder.

After the first semester at Grant MacEwan, things were going downhill fast, and Eddie knew it. Our marriage was on a rocky slide, and Eddie continued to drink away his problems. It seemed that he was drinking now more than ever. He tried to straighten out and offered to go to a therapist. In fact, he saw a therapist regularly, but his behavior became very odd. Sometimes he would tell me things about his weekend jaunts, but they just didn't add up. He kept talking about a certain girl at school, Jodi. It seemed to me that there was definitely something between Eddie and this girl. He was more than just talking about his day.

I became very suspicious, so I called the therapist. I shared my concerns with him, and based on my interaction with him, I realized he thought I knew more about what was happening. He proceeded to tell me that Eddie wasn't having a physical affair, but he thought Eddie was having an emotional affair with a classmate.

Although his therapist confirmed my suspicions, I didn't feel better. I was devastated. Out of everything else that I had experienced with Eddie—the alcoholism and abuse—I really didn't think he would ever leave me for someone else. Family was very important to him. So, why would he abandon it? When Eddie came home that night, I confronted him. Of course, he denied it, but I didn't believe him. I knew deep down things didn't add up and that something was happening. I had been with him long enough to know that much about him. Unfortunately, that night we had a heated screaming match. Shortly thereafter, Eddie left the house. Infidelity was one vice I was not going to tolerate in our relationship.

You may wonder, considering everything I did accept, why this one offense was so upsetting. I really don't know. I grew up in a loving family and I never imagined I would be so subjected to deceit and unfaithfulness. Maybe it was the final straw; perhaps I only had so much forgiveness. I just don't know.

Going to sleep that night was almost impossible; I tossed all night long. My mind was racing. I felt that I had given so much for Eddie's love. As a result I had lost my friends, I had lost my youth by becoming his care-taker at such a young age and now I was losing Eddie. I was beginning to realize that our marriage might really be over. When I woke up, I felt sick to my stomach. I knew I was too distraught to care for the boys, so I called Eddie's sister Kim to take care of them for the day. Then I called a friend, Denise, at work who said she could meet me. We talked for a long time. Well, maybe I talked and she listened, but I needed an objective voice to give me some guidance on how to move forward.

Denise had experienced some of Eddie's behavior at one of our corporate functions; he'd had far too much to drink and behaved very badly. She encouraged me to move on and make a fresh start. She tried to persuade me that I didn't need that volatile atmosphere in my life. After all, I deserved better and I needed to grow as an individual. I probably wouldn't be the best version of myself if I stayed with Eddie because I was constantly afraid of what he might do next. Talking with her that day gave me courage to take some action.

The people where I worked knew a bit about what was going on. Even the partners of the accounting firm where I worked. Thankfully the part-ners were understanding and supportive and offered me assistance when-ever I needed it.

When I came home, I quickly gathered some of Eddie's things and put them by the door. I didn't want him in the house anymore. At that time Eddie was spending a lot of time at Jodi's house and I knew that's where I would find him. I called him to come over and get his things and move out. Due to his volatility, I took the boys out of the house and over to his sister's, where they'd be safe. I didn't want them in the middle of anything, and I didn't want them to see another one of Eddie's angry outbursts.

I sat nervously at Kim's not knowing how Eddie would react when he came home and saw his things packed up. It was the first time I had taken any action, and I was sure he wasn't going to like it. I thought he might come to Kim's because he knew I had so few places to go. Then I thought he might stay at the house and wait for me there to dole out his punishment. There were too many unknowns about Eddie. I tried to mentally prepare myself for any potential repercussions, but I had to take a stand. As long as I knew the kids were safe, I thought I could handle the situation.

When I finally got enough courage to go back to the house, after I thought he had been there and gone, I walked into a disaster! He must have been furious. He actually trashed the house. He kicked in the microwave stand and flipped the kitchen table, leaving everything strewn on the floor. When I saw what he had done, I quickly took the kids to their rooms and put them to bed so they wouldn't see what had happened. After they were settled away, I started to clean up the mess. I was exhausted, both physically and mentally, by the time I dragged myself to bed.

After a couple of days, we were both feeling a bit calmer and decided to sit down and talk about our marriage. We agreed that we both needed a break from each other and decided I would stay in the house with the boys. Eddie was going to stay with a friend. A few days later, I discovered that the friend was Jodi, the girl from school. He kept insisting they were simply friends and she was only offering him a place to stay while we were separated. I didn't buy it, but I accepted it because I wanted and needed time away from him. He said he had nowhere else to go.

The affair was really the beginning of the end. I had been through so much already that I wasn't sure I could take much more. The affair was the breaking point. Deep down inside my heart, I heard the whispers and the nagging that something wasn't right.

We continued with these living arrangements for a month or so. Eddie would come over to the house and take the boys out and spend some time with them. On occasion he would stay for a while and visit. One night I was out driving with the boys and decided perhaps I should give my marriage another chance. Perhaps I just needed to work on the relationship. I decided to start right then and drove to Jodi's apartment.

When I arrived at the parking lot, I called him from my cell phone and suggested we go for a coffee to talk. By now we were able to have a conversation without it turning into a shouting match; I thought things were getting better. And since he had always insisted there was no relationship with Jodi, I didn't think there would be a problem. Well, perhaps I did think there would be a problem since I thought he was lying about their platonic relationship and needed to confirm it.

He was not happy and let me know it. I asked him, "If she's just a roommate, what's the problem?" He was so furious that he came downstairs got into his Jeep and drove off. I guess I was infringing on his privacy.

I didn't let it end there. I was furious that he had no time for us. I don't know what came over me, but I followed him. It was like a high-speed chase you see on television. I followed him at high speeds throughout the city, weaving in and out of traffic. I had the boys in the car—what was I thinking? It was not one of my brighter moments, I wasn't thinking straight. We ended up at his sister's house. Right in the middle of the street, with the boys in the car, we started screaming at each other. This was not pleasant for us or for anyone who saw us. I was so emotionally drained, when we finished, he went back to Jodi.

Eddie came over the following day when he had cooled down. We talked—no, he talked and I listened to more stories about how he was just friends with Jodi and there was nothing going on between them. Once again, I believed him. Why was I falling into the cycle again? Why didn't I cut my losses when he moved out? Maybe I was thinking about the boys and that having a father in their lives would be better than not having one, and I could endure almost anything. Or maybe I just wasn't thinking.

During our separation I felt lost and alone. To fill some of the void I purchased a puppy, a Bichon Cocker. I needed something to make the boys feel happier, and I needed a little bit of happiness in my life. Eddie always wanted a cocker spaniel, a dog I didn't particularly like. But the Bichon was my dog. She was an angel when I needed a distraction. One day, when the boys were with Eddie, I picked her out at the kennel. I just had to wait a few weeks until she was old enough to leave her mother. She was an angel in so many ways that we named her Angel.

When Eddie would come over to get the boys and take them out for the day, they seemed to have a good time. But when they came back, the boys would tell me about how Jodi was with them. Then Eddie and I would argue about this. Still, really believing that they were sexually intimate was more than I could take.

A few days later, Eddie told me that Jodi was getting back together with her boyfriend and he wouldn't be able to stay there anymore. He wanted me to let him come back home. He told me that if there had been anything between him and Jodi, there wouldn't be anymore. When you are going through these situations, you don't always think logically or rationally. You do whatever you must, just to survive. Somehow my survival mode told me to take him back—I really don't know why.

So Eddie moved back into my (our) house, and for a while we tried to be civil to each other and get along, but the fighting soon returned. My trust in him was all but gone, and it's hard to have a solid relationship without trust. I questioned everything, all the time. He was still going to school and Jodi was still in his class. I couldn't see Eddie standing back when temptation was in his face. I know he did go back to Jodi at least once during that time.

So many things were happening that denial wasn't possible anymore. That November, Eddie went on a drinking binge again and went shopping. He was so pleased with himself when he came home with a gift of new, beautiful clothes. He spent a lot of money on these clothes. He really wanted to make his woman happy, and every woman likes her man to buy her things. Unfortunately that woman wasn't me anymore. Jodi was a plus-sized girl, and I was tall and slim. I was so angry and hurt; I told him he had bought for the wrong woman. I went back to return the clothes and was happy they refunded the money. Usually they have an exchange only policy, but I lied and explained that my husband didn't realize that the clothes in that store wouldn't fit me.

During my marriage meltdown, I was working at a public accounting firm. The tax season, January to April is extremely busy, and it is expected that you work ten hours a day, six days a week. As much as I appreciated work as my escape from the hellish reality I was living, some days were more than I could bear. Thankfully, I had a good relationship with Kim,

Eddie's sister, who was my savior on more than one occasion. She would often take the boys to her house for the day and play with them. It made the boys feel special, and it helped me too.

Sometimes I came home from work and all I could do was lie on the floor and cry. I cried so hard and so long, until the tears ran out. Crying is exhausting, physically and emotionally, but sometimes we all need a good cry. We need to think about our lives: where they're going and if we are living up to what we want for ourselves. For some, it doesn't take long to get to a light-bulb moment, but for others it takes years.

Eventually I gathered enough strength and courage to finally call my mother and talk with her about my situation. I was at the end of my rope, and I needed help—the stress was killing me. As always, she spoke to me calmly and reassuringly; she filled me with hope and encouragement and reminded me that I was caring, loving person who deserved to be happy. She reminded me that I had to pull my strength together and get some rest because I had two beautiful boys in my life and I needed to take care of them.

From January to April, life was a constant battle with Eddie. He moved in and out of our house a couple of times. He continued to reassure me that we were going through a rough patch and that he and Jodi were just friends. My life was like a yoyo of him moving in and out, and my trust went up and down. Finally, things came to a head. I received a phone call from Jodi's best friend, and she told me everything. She basically told me to pull my head out of the sand and to accept that my husband had a girlfriend. Then she told me they were having a sexual relationship. Although I had always had my suspicions and perhaps never really trusted him, hearing those words, which confirmed my husband's betrayal, defeated me.

I confronted Eddie with the new information, and he lost it. He started screaming again and left, although he didn't deny the accusation. He got very drunk that night and went over to Jodi's house and let her know how he felt about me finding out about their sexual relationship. He was in a rage for sure. He was so mad that he hit her across the face. Then, as he left her apartment, he ripped the door off the hinges. I guess she hadn't seen this side of Eddie before because she called the police and Eddie was arrested.

I was the one Eddie called from jail. I was the one who called a lawyer to get him bailed out. And I was the one who took him back, again. He was the father of my children and I believed strongly in the union of marriage. I wanted to do everything I could to make it work. Obviously, Eddie couldn't return to Jodi's place after the incident, so he moved back in with us.

Attacking a fellow student while you are studying to become a social worker does not bode well for your status as a student. Word about what happened to Jodi got around quickly and it travelled right up to the instructors. One of the instructors felt quite strongly that Eddie shouldn't be allowed to continue in the program. He went so far as to obtain the transcripts from Eddie's trial. Eddie had gone to court over the altercation with Jodi. However, both Jodi and I wrote letters on his behalf, stating that it was a one-time incident and Eddie was a really good person. Eddie had convinced us to write these letters. How could I not? He was getting an education. He was trying to improve his life. This was all he ever wanted and this was what I wanted for him.

The judge was quite lenient and gave him a conditional discharge. This meant that the incident would not appear on his criminal record as long as he completed his assigned community service. Eddie still had the issue of his standing at the college. With the transcripts in hand, the instructor went to the administration and requested that Eddie be removed from the program. This was a lengthy process. In the end, Eddie was able to finish the semester, but he wasn't able to return to the program the following year. However, because he wasn't expelled from the college just the program itself he was able to register for the university transfer program, which he hoped to complete and eventually get his master's degree.

After the trial and the expulsion from the social work program, I thought Eddie's relationship with Jodi was over. Unfortunately I was wrong. In May, I found out that he took Jodi to Grande Prairie, to meet his biological father. Meeting his biological father was a huge event in Eddie's life, and I felt that he should have done this with his wife and family, not his mistress. Devastated doesn't even begin to describe how I felt. At the time, I asked him to leave. I begged him to leave. He wouldn't. He had the best of all worlds: a family and a mistress. He knew he was screwing it up by continuing to see Jodi, but it was like he couldn't help himself.

Living together after that was almost unbearable. Frequently, in front of the boys, I would scream at him to get out of my house. I told him how much I hated him and couldn't stand to have him in my sight. I was overcome with emotion and wasn't thinking about anything but the pain that I felt. I told him I hated him many times. It was a terrible living situation, and I tried to work as much as I could just to avoid him. When we weren't fighting, we were trying to make it work. It was a roller-coaster ride that wasn't healthy for anyone: not for me, not for the boys, and not for Eddie. It was a nightmare. I realized very quickly that it had been wrong to allow him to come home. It was another regret to add to my growing list. I couldn't even sleep in the same bed as him.

By now I had lost any desire to make our marriage work. I knew there was no possibility of spending the rest of my life with Eddie. I needed to get out of the marriage, but I didn't know how. My resources were limited and my family lived so far away. I was beginning to understand the situations I had seen in movies about abusive, possessive people, and how they trapped and manipulated those closest to them. But I never thought it would happen to me.

One time, I actually did try to leave Eddie. It reminded me of the movie *Misery*. Love, if you want to call it that, wrapped tightly in a blanket of hate. I had been doing a lot of reflecting, and I realized I couldn't continue to live with Eddie. I had been treated so poorly for so long that I was finally ready to move on. It wasn't working for any of us, Eddie, the boys and certainly not me.

I told him I was leaving him and I was on my way out the door when he grabbed me and pulled me back. He took my car keys and dragged me into the boys' bedroom and threw me on the bed. I was terrified. It remains the most terrifying night of my life. I didn't know if he was going to kill me that night or if he was ever going to let me leave the house again.

He yelled and screamed at me. He berated me. He called me a whore and a slut in front of my children. I was shocked, desperate, and full of fear. He had been bad to me before, but this time he was so incensed and vicious that he reminded me of Jekyll and Hyde. While the boys and I were huddled on the bedroom floor, he stopped screaming for a moment and went to the kitchen. When he returned, he had a large kitchen knife in his hand. My heart was in my throat when I saw the knife. My first thought was, *this is it, he is going to kill me this time.*

What seemed like forever lasted only a second or two. He did threaten me, but he didn't physically attack me with the knife. Instead, he walked to the closet and then proceeded to take my clothes and cut them up. He sliced and ripped them to shreds in front of the boys and me, all while berating me. All abuse is unwarranted, but there is a difference between the aftermath of physical and mental abuse. Physical abuse eventually fades away with the sting of the bruises, but mental abuse dwells in your psyche and lives for a very long time. It affects how you deal with others and how you see yourself. I have always thought mental abuse was so much worse.

The boys and I were huddled in the corner of the room in fear of what he might do next. It was like he was possessed. I couldn't remember another time when he was so angry with me. He knew this was hurting me. We didn't have a lot of money, and I needed those clothes for work. He knew that by taking my clothes away from me, he would be taking part of my confidence. It would take me a long time to be able to buy those clothes again and being professional was very important to me.

Eventually he stopped cutting my clothes out of boredom or frustration. The boys were very quiet during all this. They didn't talk, they didn't cry. Maybe they were also in shock and terrified of what might happen next. We were all exhausted and then a moment later, Eddie took Blake by the hand and they both left the room. Blake glanced at me for a moment, but he turned around and walked out with Eddie. Brett and I remained in the room and huddled together for comfort. Eventually, we fell asleep wrapped in each other's arms.

The next morning, life wasn't any better. I woke up exhausted; my mind couldn't rest. There were memories I couldn't suppress long enough to have a restful sleep. And part of me thought I would never really feel safe again. I was so dehydrated that morning from all the crying the night before. And yes, I was still terrified. What was the morning going to bring? Had Eddie calmed down, or would the abuse and torture continue?

I got up, got dressed, and went into the kitchen to make breakfast. I tried to pretend that everything was normal. Because of everything that was happening in my life I was taking anti depressants. I was in the kitchen, I had just taken my medication and was putting the bottle back on the counter when Eddie came in and started the verbal onslaught once again. He was making fun of the fact that I was on anti-depressants. He said: "Ya you better keep taking those. You are f***ing nuts!" We started arguing again. He was telling me that I was worthless and I didn't deserve him or my children. I tried to just tune him out. I was desperate for him to stop. I knew if I said anything it would just be fuel for the fire. I silently carried on with breakfast. I went to the fridge to get some jam and that is when he couldn't stand my lack of response anymore and he really got angry.

He pushed me to the floor so hard I hit my head. Flashes of white light lingered in my vision for a few minutes. As I fell, some of the eggs also fell to the floor, leaving quite a mess. When I tried to get up, he held me there and told me to clean it up. Then he walked over to the toaster and took the cold toast and jammed the toast on my head, rubbing it in my hair. The boys witnessed everything. They just stood in silence and watched how their daddy threw me to the floor and mistreated me yet again. Finally, he left me to clean up the mess and then myself too.

We were expecting Eddie's sister, Penni, from Calgary later that day, and he knew we needed to get it together and look like a normal, happy family. When I emerged from the shower, he told me we were going shopping. This was the honeymoon part of the abusive cycle. He usually tried to make up for his behavior by taking me places or buying me things. I just wanted the nightmare to end, and I didn't want to entertain anyone. We spent the rest of the day buying me clothes and having lunch with his sister. My attempt to leave had failed. In an abusive relationship, it is always important to have a full tank of gas and keys outside the house. Eddie took my car keys from me that day, so I couldn't go anywhere. I felt like a prisoner. Never forget to have a plan and then another plan, just in case.

We did have a small honeymoon period after that. A honeymoon period in that Eddie was very sweet to me. He tried to help out around the house; he'd help out with meals and the boys more than he normally would. I was grateful that there was a bit of peace but I was still desperate to leave.

The peace in the house lasted for about four months before the arguments started again. During one of our arguments Eddie's actions crossed the line once again. This time we were in the middle of a very heated argument and Eddie grabbed a kitchen knife and held it to my throat. The frequency of these incidents didn't make them any less frightening. You never knew what he was going to do. Was this the time he would lose control and kill me? While he was holding the knife to me throat he said: "First I'm going to kill your mother and then I'm going to kill you." I was terrified. My adrenalin was rushing through my body giving me a bit of strength and courage. I managed to push myself away from him and when I did he seemed to realize what he was doing. It was as if his anger caused him to zone out. My mother was thousands of miles away in Ontario so I wasn't worried about her but I knew I should be very worried for me.

After he said that, I knew I had to get away from him, and so did he. But I needed to recover from all this fighting first so I could plan better. I went to Kananaskis for the weekend. Kananaskis is a small resort style village in the Rocky Mountains just outside of Calgary. I had never been away by myself before and I really loved it. The first evening I sat in the piano bar listening to Jacqueline Dolan play the piano. I enjoyed it so much that I bought her CD. There was a true sense of peace and solitude when you gazed out at the majestic mountains and saw the sun setting above the ridge. The fresh mountain air and the utter stillness of the area brought peace to my soul.

During the weekend, I called Eddie a couple of times to see how the boys were and gauge his reaction to our latest incident. He was feeling very insecure because I was away and he knew I needed the time away. I think I felt that because Eddie had *let* me go away, he had given me a gift and therefore had redeemed himself. It's strange to think that way, I know. That is the thought process of an abused woman. He did his best to be caring and kind, and he was sweet on the phone: another honeymoon cycle. The cycle of abuse was now spinning faster. I got sucked in and agreed to come home and make a fresh start. That was July, 1996.

My weekend away did help. The commitment of marriage had been so ingrained in me growing up that I still wasn't ready to walk away from that commitment. We tried to make a new beginning, and that summer was rather pleasant. We did a lot of family activities like taking picnics and taking walks in the park. One of my favorite moments was our trip to the Legislature grounds in Edmonton. They had these wonderful wading pools located between two buildings. On hot summer days, we would take the boys there and play all day. The boys would splash around, and then we'd have ice cream treats when the ice cream cart came by. They had so much fun, and so did we. It was a beautiful memory.

For a few months, we were a happy little family. Once summer was over and Blake started hockey again and Eddie went back to school, the old Eddie resurfaced. Constant arguments, screaming, and yelling were now the norm. We drove to the kids' events in separate cars and we slept in separate beds.

We both knew that this wasn't a good life, but how good was the alternative? What was the alternative?

The Other Affair

I began to regret my decision to give my marriage yet another try. After countless cycles of abuse and remorse, I knew in my heart it was over. I had asked Eddie to leave, but he wouldn't. In fact, he became even more adamant about staying. He had been desperate for a family his entire life, and that meant father, mother, and children together. I knew his childhood wasn't the greatest, and I knew deep down he had missed the loving memories that I had experienced, but that was no reason to treat me so terribly. I had suffered for too much and for far too long to continue. But I didn't have the courage or the resources to take the final step to leave Eddie.

I had the perfect job at the time. The company was really flexible with our working hours, and, for the most part, we worked the times we needed to. We were paid by the hour, so if you didn't work, you didn't get paid, and, conversely, the more you worked, the more you were able to bank the extra time and take days off when needed. I really loved this flexibility.

Because of this flexibility, I was able to create some amazing memories with the boys. One day in December 1995, Blake was four and Brett was three, such an adorable age for children. They are still discovering new things and they are filled with innocence and curiosity. At that age joy is found in the simplest things. We woke up that morning and we looked out the window to see freshly fallen snow. The snow was beautiful as it glistened in the early morning sun. It was like a dream sequence from a movie. As the boys were very young, snow was a still a novelty. So instead of going into the office that morning, I took some time off to be with them and play in the snow.

I got them all bundled up in snowsuits and mittens, and off we went to be adventurers. We made a couple of snowmen and started to make a fort too. Then we all lay down in the snow and made snow angels. We had such a wonderful day. My boys were my angels through all the turmoil with Eddie. I loved spending every minute with them, and those memories helped me survive some of the terrible times I had with Eddie. Through all of this, I still had Eddie to thank for my boys.

It was really no problem for me to work extra hours during this time because there was always work to be done, since it was tax time. I really took advantage of this opportunity whenever I could. Sometimes I would go to work a little later, after Eddie had left for his job, and stay later, but I was always home in time to put the boys in bed and read them a story. Eddie wasn't happy about the hours I worked, and I wasn't happy being at home with him. It was a stalemate.

When I began working at the accounting firm, I tried to include Eddie in some of the social functions there. Unfortunately, I invited him to one of the Christmas parties, and, not surprisingly, he had too much to drink. During his stupor, he thought he would impress my colleagues by telling them he had a gun. It was a strange sort of conversation because, to Eddie, it was just a matter-of-fact statement that showed he was one tough guy. This proved to be a big mistake, and I was told to never bring him to another social function again. He was no longer welcome, and I understood why. My colleagues only saw Eddie occasionally, but I had lived with this my entire adult life. I never knew what he might do next.

Eddie's behavior at my Christmas party proved to be another nail in the coffin of our marriage. Eddie had supported my decision to get a college education. He took care of the household bills, so he helped financially and, in his own way, emotionally. He loved that I was becoming a professional in the industry, and I think he was proud of what I had accomplished. Now he was feeling insecure about my new life and that I might be outgrowing him. He didn't come out and say anything, but it was in the little things and the snide comments he would make about my job, or things I was able to do because of it. I knew I had changed, too. I had to change both professionally and emotionally. I had listened to how other people led their lives and how they dealt with their life situations. None of my colleagues had ever experienced what I had. Maybe I was becoming stronger just by surrounding myself with professional people and interacting with them.

The accounting firm did a lot of great things to support teamwork among its employees. Every year we had a pub-crawl; the company hired a bus to take us to some bars in Edmonton. Because I met Eddie when I was fifteen and got married at eighteen, I had never experienced the nightlife in the same way that other young people had. I had always been busy keeping Eddie out of trouble or bringing him home inebriated. There was never time for me. I got lost in the relationship.

To complicate things even more, I was also on antidepressants to help deal with the mayhem in my life. Alcohol and antidepressants do not mix well at all. That first pub-crawl was so much fun for me. I loved living my youth (for me it wasn't reliving, as I never had the chance to do it when I was young). So, of course I drank far too much and was so relaxed that I thoroughly enjoyed being out. I did come home at a reasonable hour and crawled into Blake's bed. I hadn't been sharing Eddie's bed for some time now.

The next morning wasn't very good. I wasn't familiar with dealing with hangovers because I'd only had to deal with Eddie's. That was easier. But I had two boys to take care of and we had made plans that day to get their hair cut. I wasn't going to let my hangover interfere with my commitments to the boys. So, I got up and got dressed and tried to make myself presentable (not an easy task that morning). Then, I got the boys ready, and off we went to the mall for the haircuts.

We went to Sears because I had one of their charge cards, and it was easier to pay that way. However in the middle of the cut, I wasn't feeling very well. My stomach was queasy and my head started to spin. I had to excuse myself for a few minutes because I knew I was going to be sick. My feet didn't carry me quickly enough, and I realized I wasn't going to make it to the washroom in time.

I had to find a place now, or I was going to make a mess right in the aisle. I looked around and noticed an open garbage can beside a freezer. The bottom of my stomach heaved and regurgitated its contents into the can while onlookers just stared at me. At that moment, I no longer cared; I was just relieved I made it to the garbage can and not the freezer. The relief was palpable. I took a deep breath and finally found the washroom to freshen up before I went back to the salon for the boys.

I returned to the boys just as they were finishing their cuts. Eddie was pretty good about the whole incident. After all, what could he say after putting me through similar events every time he drank too much? He didn't really like that he wasn't welcome on the pub-crawl with my coworkers, but he grudgingly accepted it. I actually thought he would rub it in about me getting sick in public that day, but he didn't say a word.

While I was working those long hours, I started to get friendly with one of my coworkers. I worked the accounting side and he was involved on the computer side (IT). Because I was willing to work the extra hours, the partners had been very good and allowed me to do some business development work. Doing this type of work required me to create and demonstrate presentations that took place in the evening and sometimes out of town. My coworker Charles often helped me with the software and the computer aspects of my presentations because I was technologically challenged.

I loved my new responsibilities as a business development consultant. I loved planning and organizing receptions for potential clients, even if it did mean I had to stay late. I felt valued and knew I was providing the company with a valuable service. There were three of us usually involved in these events: Charles, the receptionist, Lori, and me. We started to develop a really great friendship spending all that time together planning the events. Lori would talk about her boyfriend, Charles his girlfriend, and I often chatted about my family (although very few people knew exactly what was happening at home).

During one of our discussions, we talked about the Corporate Challenge taking place in Edmonton. That was like a mini corporate Olympics for business people. Corporations were encouraged to form teams and participate in various sporting events over a two-week period. This was another great reason to be away from Eddie.

The Corporate Challenge took place in late April and early May, and I registered for mountain biking and running.

Training started a few weeks earlier and took me away from home for several hours a week, a godsend at times. I missed the boys terribly, though, and I did make sure we had our time together. It was just so hard to be home with all the tension and anger in the house. At this point, quality time was much better than quantity. Training occurred during tax season, so some weekends I would have to work at the office in the morning and then spend the afternoon mountain biking for training. It just so happened that Charles was also an avid mountain biker, and he was able to provide me with the equipment and the training that I needed to compete in the race.

I looked forward to those training sessions every week. It felt so amazing to travel through back roads through the mud and slush of springtime with the wind in your face. It was refreshing and invigorating. And free from reality. I had so much fun spending time with Charles. He was always encouraging and very kind to me. He thought of me as an equal, and he treated me with respect. This was something I was not used to.

All this time away wasn't helping my marriage, such as it was. Nor was it helping Charles' relationship with his girlfriend. One evening after about twelve hours at work, one of the partners suggested that Charles and I join him and one of his clients for dinner. We had a great evening of feasting on crab and relaxing. It was a lovely, peaceful evening spent in good conversation.

A week later, the same partner had access to a stadium box at the baseball game. He invited a few clients, and some people from work, including Charles and his girlfriend, and me. I had so much stress in my life at home and with the long hours at work that it was nice to spend some time relaxing. I really enjoyed myself that night, though it was quite possible that I flirted with Charles more than I should have, but things between us remained innocent. We were only good friends.

Every year the accounting firm had a big tax party at year-end, April 30. Tax season was always a grueling time for everyone, and our office tradition was to let loose once the last tax return was filed. Spouses were always excluded from tax parties—not that Eddie would have been invited anyway due to his past history. Every year, the celebration would go on until the wee hours of the morning. This year was going to be no different.

Eddie seemed aware that there was something else going on in my life other than work, and at times he seemed desperate: desperate in his relations with me, in the way he dealt with the boys, and in his general demeanor. In prior years even though our marriage was suffering, I still tried to remain respectful of him and the vows I had taken. Perhaps it was out of fear of what could happen—I don't know. It was pretty clear to Eddie that our marriage was in name only. But he continued to hang on to any thread of hope that materialized, whether it was real or not. He knew forbidding me to go to the tax party wasn't going to work but he was not happy about me going. For me the year-end celebration continued, although I did intend to be home around midnight. I didn't want to aggravate the situation any further.

The feelings that Charles and I had for each other had been building steadily for a few months. Those feelings came to a head on April 30, 2007. Charles and I both attended the end-of-tax-season party and had a few drinks. De-stressing with several drinks helped us both become very relaxed and social. Our pent-up feelings, the relaxed mood, and a couple of drinks formed a volcano ready to erupt. We could no longer deny we were both attracted to each other. At the end of the party, Charles and I exchanged glances and a few unspoken words. I took that leap into the forbidden and went home with Charles that evening.

Here I was, a married woman of eight years with two beautiful children, doing the unthinkable and getting involved with another man. Not to mention a man who was in a relationship with someone else. Infidelity was something I had always abhorred—both with Eddie and in general. Why was I committing the same sin? Who was I to condemn him for cheating on me when I was living a lie? In some respects, the fact that I had breached my vows finally confirmed my marriage was truly over. Eddie and I had been sleeping in separate beds and were living separate lives. This was the event that told me I had to move on with my life and move out.

I arrived home later than usual that night, around two in the morning. Eddie was up pacing the floor. When I opened the door he started with his verbal onslaught. He had his suspicions; my late arrival seemed to confirm them. Although he was furious, I told him I had gone to a coworker's house for an after party and was too tired to deal with him that night. I didn't have the energy or the desire to start a screaming match nor allow him the opportunity to be abusive.

I peeked in on the boys, and I was relieved to find them both settled in their beds. I discovered much later that Eddie had shared his concerns about me and our marriage with Blake and had told him some very nasty things that night. Little did I know how much that night would change my life.

It seemed that Eddie and Charles's girlfriend were both aware that something had happened that night. It was a good thing I did go home because Charles's girlfriend arrived at his house pretty early the next morning, while he was still sleeping. She stormed into his bedroom and told him that she'd had a dream he had slept with that girl from the baseball game. Charles was shocked.

Groggy and still half-asleep, he did a quick scan of his bedroom to make sure I had left no evidence behind. Technically May 1 is a holiday at the accounting firm, so neither of us was required to go into the office. We both did, and I was surprised when he relayed the morning incident with his girlfriend. After that night, we did slow things down quite a bit, but we still continued to socialize in work settings. Charles had treated me so well that I couldn't allow myself to settle anymore. Being with Charles gave me the strength and the push I needed to leave my marriage. I knew I had crossed the line, and it wasn't right to live with Eddie anymore.

Luckily, my mother came to visit the very next day. She could feel the tension between Eddie and me. She even witnessed some of the violent arguments that took place over the next couple of days. One day, when Mom was in the house, Charles called about our home computer and a problem I was having with it. I took the call and then went into the bedroom and closed the door. I realized now I could have handled that situation better, but that's the way it happened.

Eddie was quick to realize who I was talking to and became very enraged and flipped over a kitchen chair. This was mild compared to other incidents with Eddie, but it wasn't something Mom had ever experienced, so it was a very big deal to her. She took me aside and talked to me about what had happened. Needless to say she didn't know all our past history, but she knew this was a dangerous situation. She insisted I leave Eddie, and soon.

The following day, Mom and I looked for a place for the boys and me to live. We found a house about twenty blocks away. We thought it would be close enough for the boys to go between their father's house and mine, yet far enough so that we wouldn't bump into each other at every turn. But the catch was the house wasn't available until May 15. Mom wasn't comfortable with me staying in our house, so I moved in with a friend, Darla, until the new house was ready.

Eddie was devastated when I told him I was actually moving out. He knew it was coming, but it wasn't something he wanted. I will never forget his words the day. We were both in tears and he said to me, "All I ever wanted was a normal family." It broke my heart that I couldn't give him that.

Post-Separation

Moving day had the full gamut of emotions for me. As I looked around the house and all the memories there, I thought my heart would break. I glanced at the pictures on the wall, the toys scattered about, and the boys' clothes on the floor, and I started to get very emotional. I had so many dreams when I was first married, and then later when the boys came. This ending wasn't part of those dreams. But I knew leaving Eddie was the right thing to do. I had no choice in the matter; Eddie wasn't going to leave me with the boys. So I had to leave the house. We had agreed that the boys would spend half their time with Eddie and half with me. It was heartbreaking for everyone that the boys wouldn't have two parents in one house, but there was no other option. The marriage was over.

At this time, I really thought I hated Eddie. I was venting to a person at work, and she told me that love and hate were very close emotions. She told me that until I no longer had feelings for him, I hadn't really stopped loving him. She was right. I think as angry and hurt as I was, I still loved Eddie. I still believed in him. He had done some very horrific things to me, but in my heart I felt that wasn't who he really was. I felt that he was just expressing his anger toward me. He didn't want our marriage to end, neither one of us did, but there was no way it could go on.

I also still believed in him as a father. I saw him interact with the boys when he was in a good place, and I never doubted his love for them. Blake and Brett were everything to him. I could also see how happy they were when they were with him. I knew how much I was hurting Eddie by leaving, I couldn't hurt him more by keeping him from his children. I didn't think it was fair to the boys to keep them from their father. They loved him very much. I realized that he had done some stupid things and he had used the boys to hurt me. I knew the boys had seen and heard things that no children should ever experience, but I felt that things would improve once I removed myself from the house. I felt that if I left, Eddie wouldn't be so angry, and he would go back to being the good person I believed him to be. I felt that the boys would enjoy both parents in a much healthier environment. It was all that kept me sane at the time.

I knew that by leaving, I was probably saving my life and the boys' lives as well. I also knew that as bad as Eddie treated me, he loved the boys dearly. I had never lived on my own, and it was an adventure I was about to commence. A mixture of emotions swirled inside, and at times I didn't know if I could even make it on my own. It was going to be the three of us: Blake, Brett, and me. It would be a fresh start and, I hoped, a life with a lot more peace.

Just like when I was young, moving from base to base, I had begun to find my own friends and my own social group. They were all there for me that day to help me set up the newly purchased furniture (acquired by a store credit card). In order to leave my marriage, I had to leave with nothing. It was dangerous enough to take my personal belongings out when Eddie wasn't there; trying to take the furniture might have been deadly. It just wasn't worth the risk. I justified this by telling myself it would be better for the boys if everything looked the same in their house.

My parents were very aware of the situation, and they helped by contacting some of their friends who took me back to the house one night when Eddie and the boys were away. I took a chair that I had purchased for the boys. There was a time when both of them liked to sit with me, and I told them I'd have to get a chair big enough for three of us. This was the chair that meant the most to me because I associated so many nice memories of me and the boys with it. I took a few other items, like school books and my wedding dress. Don't ask me why I took the dress: I just took it. I guess it was because marrying Eddie was a huge event in my life. No matter how it turned out, we were together a very long time and I wanted something to hang onto.

The thought that I would be free, living a life of peace and happiness with my boys and the joy of moving into my new house, was short-lived. Once I moved into my new home, we made our joint custody agreement formal in a court of law. If this was a normal situation, this would have been a great agreement.

The intention was for the boys to see us equally, and we lived close enough that school or sports wouldn't be an issue. However, life with Eddie, whether we lived together or apart, was always going to be an issue. Physically leaving him stirred the pot even more. He twisted everything I said and did and turned every little thing into a major issue. Pretty soon, things got very tense between us.

My dream of a calm and somewhat normal life died rather quickly. The boys didn't like going back and forth, and Blake would often cry that he wanted to be with his dad. Since Blake was born, he and Eddie had a unique relationship and they had bonded so tightly that there was never enough room for me. I think he was more comfortable with Eddie, and even when he was with me, he would call his dad and ask to be with him. Blake had always been devoted to Eddie, and this became even more pronounced after we separated. Blake was so loyal to Eddie that he stole my address book out of my purse and gave it to him. Eddie then used the address book to contact all my friends and tell them horrific stories about me.

I would receive trash calls daily from Eddie. We usually screamed and yelled at each other on the phone while the boys stood by and listened. This is probably what Eddie experienced with his own volatile family growing up. Like father, like son. Now I was seeing my kids continue the cycle.

Life during those first few months after moving out were just as bad as life with him. Maybe it was worse. He was continuously driving around my house when I didn't have the boys to see what I was doing or who I might be with. The kids were in the car with him, and I'm sure they were hearing all kinds of slurs and slander from their father about me. Eddie would eventually turn the boys away from me by constantly telling them lies about me.

One morning I was bringing the boys back to Eddie before I went to my company's annual golf tournament. When we pulled up to the house, I let the boys out and then started to walk up to the door, but the boys quickly ran inside. Somehow Eddie got hold of me and pulled me inside the door. He pushed me against the wall and held me there with his body weight. I saw the pure black hatred in his eyes. I knew something bad was going to happen.

Then his hands grabbed my throat and he started choking me. I thought for sure, this time Eddie was going to kill me. Between gasps of air, I tried to tell the boys to call 911. I thought that by living in a duplex the neighbors would have heard what was happening and call for help. This wasn't the first time I wondered that. During the many incidents of violence, our neighbors never once came to my aid or even asked me later if I was okay. I guess they didn't want to be involved.

Blake just sat there on the floor and watched. Brett was still quite young and didn't really know what to do. He did eventually run to the phone, but by then Eddie had let me go. I just ran out of the house and sped away in my car. I drove to the golf course to the company function. While I was there, my colleagues heard my name being paged on the loudspeaker. It was Eddie. He had been repeatedly calling the golf course, and he knew this would cause me embarrassment and grief at work. He wanted to do anything and everything to make me unhappy.

My first thought was that something had happened to the boys, so I did call him back. But no: this was just another part of the cycle of humiliation. Yeah, I know, why didn't I go to the police? The situation escalated and I didn't do anything to stop it. I just don't know why. I couldn't be the reason my children's father went to jail. I know I said it a few times, but when you are in these situations for as long as I had been, you don't think straight. A life of "should haves" or "ifs" seemed to swallow me whole.

After I moved out, Charles was still part of my life. He made the transition much easier, and he was a great support to me when I questioned myself or felt down. Being with him was fun and light, and he made me feel good about myself. When I didn't have the boys with me, we would meet friends and enjoy a peaceful adult evening. Sometimes it was food and drinks at a local restaurant, Earl's. Sometimes, just feeling "normal" for an evening was enough for me.

One night Charles drove me home from Earl's restaurant. It was around ten o'clock and dark outside. I invited Charles back to my place. When I arrived home, I didn't realize Eddie was in the neighborhood. It wasn't long before Eddie did a drive-by, and he realized I wasn't alone. In his usual fashion, Eddie had been driving his Jeep circling the house with the boys in the car. They should have been in bed by then, but when Eddie discovered I was out with friends he decided to track me down.

He parked in front of the house, left the boys sitting in the car, and banged on my front door. Charles and I realized very quickly how dangerous this situation could be, so we escaped out the back door. We ran to the neighbor's, but Charles wasn't fast enough. Eddie had caught up with him and started pounding him with clenched fists. Luckily, my neighbor saw what was happening and came out and started yelling at Eddie, and then Eddie drove off.

Regrettably, Charles left my house with a black eye, a few sore muscles, and the realization of what I had been dealing with for so many years. Someone had called the police and they came to take everyone's statement, including my neighbor's and Charles'. The police really wanted Charles to press criminal charges; at that time, it was the victim's choice whether or not to lay charges. Charles didn't want to get involved any further. It seemed like every time the police were involved, even momentarily, nothing ever became of charges against Eddie. It wasn't a good situation for anyone. Perhaps if the charges had been laid, Eddie would have learned that he couldn't get away with treating me or anyone else so badly. But that didn't happen. Only a few days later, Charles decided it was in his best interest not to see me anymore. He'd had enough of the drama and he had his personal safety to think about.

After I moved out, Eddie was still making a huge effort to save our marriage, not that I gave him encouragement. He would try to force me to join him and the boys during family activities. This was a recurring ploy. He would use the boys to guilt me into spending time with him. I wasn't very strong during this time, and one evening he convinced me to go to the movie *Faceoff* with him, without the kids. It was a good movie, but I didn't get to enjoy very much of it. Throughout the entire movie, Eddie taunted and berated me about Charles. He didn't realize that he had beaten Charles right out of my life.

Eventually I had enough, and just before the movie ended, I got up and left the theater. This was a very big step for me: I had stood up to his insults and taunts and indirectly told him I wasn't going to take it anymore. This would never have happened in the early days. I never had the courage. Maybe being in the dark, crowded theater helped give me courage: I couldn't see his face or the anger in his eyes. It was a small step along my journey to self-worth.

Eddie's birthday was in June, and that month U2 came to Edmonton for a concert. They were playing at the stadium close to my house. I felt sorry for Eddie and decided to go to the concert with him; it was also one of my favorite bands, so I was excited to see them too. I know what you're thinking: why in the world would I choose to spend time with Eddie after everything he did to me? But like I said before, it is the cycle of violence: he drew me close, manipulated me through our children, and I think that part of me loved him. So, I went to the concert with him.

When I got to the concert I decided to have a couple of drinks. It wasn't my job to be responsible for Eddie anymore and I thought a couple of drinks might help me to get through the night. Unfortunately two drinks turned into too many drinks and I wasn't in a good state when the concert ended. I should have known better, but I didn't. Eddie had to bring me home, and he put me to bed. After I was safely in bed, he went through my house. He took some of my lingerie and my wedding rings and God knows what else. I knew I had screwed up by going with him in the first place, but drinking too much and letting him into my house were big mistakes. I had to be stronger. I could never allow that to happen again. My home was supposed to be my safe place, but it felt violated.

It was only a week later that I received a phone call from Eddie. He told me some sad news: his mother didn't have long to live. She was dying from breast cancer, and it wasn't going to be much longer. She was on her deathbed and she wanted to see the family. Eddie asked me to go with him and the boys to Calgary to see his mother. I had known Eddie's mom for many years, and I thought I owed that to her and the boys. I knew it was something that I had to do, however reluctantly, with Eddie.

After I finished work that Friday, we all piled into Eddie's Jeep and headed to Calgary. Eddie's mom was in the hospital, so we decided to stay in a hotel. I started calling hotels from my cell phone during the three-hour drive to Calgary. But this was early July in Calgary: we had completely forgotten it was Stampede week. The Calgary Stampede is known as the biggest outdoor show on earth. It is the world's largest outdoor rodeo that lasts for 10 days in July. There are concerts, stage shows, a carnival, chuck wagon races and more. The prize money from the rodeo is quite significant and it draws tourists from around the world. The entire city gets into the spirit of the rodeo decorating storefronts, restaurants and offices in western décor and everyone dresses in western attire for the whole 10 days. It is a huge event and getting a hotel room during this time is almost impossible. I don't know how many hotels I called, but eventually I found a reservation at one of the more exclusive hotels, the Westin. Normally this would have been a treat for us, but under the circumstances it only made the trip almost bearable.

I booked a room with two queen beds. There was no chance that I was going to share a bed with him. Eddie was upset once again. I guess he thought that sharing a room while his mother was dying might bring about reconciliation. For me, the marriage was completely over. I had only agreed to the trip for his mother, the boys, and for myself. I wanted to say good-bye. We barely survived the weekend and the drive home.

Eddie's mother died the following week on July 17, 1997. I had the boys that night. It was late, and we were all in bed when we heard the banging on the door. At that instant, the anxiety flooded me. I physically felt sick to my stomach. This wasn't going to be good. I opened the door to find Eddie there, drunk as could be. Then he told me his mother had died and he needed me to take the boys for a few more days. Of course I had no problem with this, but somehow another argument broke out between us. I was still half-asleep and groggy when I opened the door. That quickly changed when he grabbed me by the throat, pulled me out of the house, pushed me against the brick, and dragged me across the wall until my head went through the glass portion of the screen door. I was terrified. I wasn't sure what would happen next, and I wondered if he was finally going to kill me. He was so angry and hurt that I knew he wasn't thinking clearly. I felt like he held me there for a very long time, but I'm sure it was only seconds. Glass shattered everywhere. There was a large lump in the back of my head, and there was glass all through my hair, and my back had some pretty serious scratches from being dragged across the brick. I was stunned more than injured. Eddie let me go and just stood there like he wasn't even aware of what had happened.

The boys had been awakened by all of the commotion; they just stood and watched the whole incident. My neighbors, who happened to be my landlord, were getting fed-up with all the commotion. It only took a few minutes before they called the police. We lived in a residential neighborhood and they had three small children. The last thing they wanted was to have a crazed person threatening their neighbor for fear that the violence might spill over into their house.

They rushed over to see if they could do anything. Eddie, in his drunken, emotional state, started fighting with my neighbor. The police arrived just before things got ugly. Again, the boys watched their father melt down and pummel an innocent bystander and their mother. The police talked to Eddie, but because his mother had just died, they were quite compassionate and they let him go with a stern lecture.

By the time Eddie was removed from the premises, I was a wreck. I was shaking uncontrollably and sobbing. I was so relieved that my life was spared that I basically had a breakdown. I was getting so tired of these situations. The police stayed a while with me until I felt safe. I wasn't sure what I was going to do because Eddie just wasn't letting up.

The day before his mother died, I decided to place an ad in the newspaper to give away my dog, Angel. The dog was now living at Eddie's house because I wasn't allowed to have pets at my new house. I saw that the Angel was being taken care of poorly and decided I couldn't let it go on. She was always left outside, and I wasn't sure if she was being fed regularly. Eddie had so much going on his life I think the last thing on his mind was taking care of the dog.

The next morning the phone was ringing off the hook with potential new owners. One man wanted to come over right away. Still groggy and recovering from the incident the night before, I put the boys in the car and drove to Eddie's house. He wasn't home, so I took Angel from the back yard.

The man loved her instantly, and I knew it would be a good match for the dog. However, I just gave the boys' dog away without explaining to them what was happening. I really wasn't thinking straight. After what had happened the night before, I was only thinking about survival: mine, the boys' and Angel's. They asked me what was happening and all I said was that Angel was going away for a while. I told them she needed better care. My focus was not on the dog but what I was going to do to escape this horrific reality for a couple of days. I needed some time to regroup and collect my thoughts. I really regret the way I handled things, and if I could do it over again, I definitely would.

We all had so much turmoil in our lives that I didn't think it was fair for Angel to be mistreated as well. I thought that I could at least save her from this misery. My life was spiraling downward, and I didn't want to take everything in its path with it. The boys never forgot how I gave away their dog and are still angry with me to this day. I've apologized countless times, but it's unforgivable for a mother to take away her children's pet.

Because of Eddie's mother's death and our separation, Eddie's behavior became even more erratic and dangerous. I knew the boys and I needed to get away for a few days, to hide out and escape the drama and stress of what was happening around us. I phoned a camping store and rented a bunch of equipment, and the boys and I packed some things and went on our own camping adventure for a few days.

It was quite an event. I had camped all my life, but I had never been in charge of setting up the tent, chopping wood, or getting the water. It was refreshing and wonderful. It gave me a sense of confidence that I could do these things without anyone else. Both Brett and Blake loved our camping adventure. They helped me gather the wood and set up the tent. They felt good helping me out. The next few days were wonderful and peaceful, and I loved sharing that time with both of them.

It was July, the weather was beautiful, the beach extraordinary. We swam, played on the beach, went on excursions around the park, and ate ice cream. The boys' favorite flavor back then was mint chocolate chip ice cream. One afternoon I bought each of them a cone, but in less than a minute Brett's had fallen to the ground. He was so upset. Of course, he didn't have to be because it really didn't matter at all to me. It was so wonderful that I could just go and buy another one for him without anyone getting angry. There was no

yelling or screaming or violence. Once I bought him another, he was one happy boy.

On the fourth day, we packed everything up and went back home to Edmonton. The timing of our return was perfect. I was starting to get

nervous that Eddie was going to figure out where we were and would
come looking for us. I really didn't
need him interrupting my camping
adventure with the boys. When I got
home, I brought the kids back to his
house and luckily it all went well. He
didn't suspect that we had been away.
As long as he knew where I was and
felt that he was in control of the situation, things went relatively well.

We continued with our liberal
visitation schedule for the boys.
However, it was a double-edged
sword. When I didn't have the kids,
Eddie was frustrated because then I
was free to do what I wanted. I think
he thought that it wasn't fair, that I
should not be able to have fun or even think about myself when I didn't
have the boys. He continued to try and control me when I wasn't with the
boys, and he made sure I didn't have a good time with anything or anyone.

One night when the boys were with Eddie, I went out with a group of
friends and we decided to go dancing. Eddie figured out where I was and
dragged the boys to the club. I was sitting at a table with my friends, and
I saw him come in the front door. Instantly I felt a cold shiver run down
my spine and I began to shake with terror. I told the bouncer that I needed
protection and he escorted Eddie out of the club. This infuriated him even
more.

But he made sure I left the club in his own twisted way. He left Brett
standing in the parking lot alone and then told the bouncer to tell me that
my son was there. It was so awful that he was using our son in that way,
but I never knew what he would do next. Of course, I left immediately and
took Brett home.

It didn't matter what the situation or event was with Eddie. Whether
he had the boys or I did or we were meeting to pass the kids to the other,
there was bound to be some argument or worse, trouble with a capital T.
Eddie was working evenings and I worked days, so we had it worked out

that the boys would spend the evenings with me and I would drop them off in the mornings at his house. This minimized their time with a babysitter.

Eddie regularly caused trouble for me that summer. I was a nervous wreck because I didn't know when or what the next situation would be. I had to be alert all the time. It's very tiring and difficult to always be on alert because you never get to relax. Eventually, it catches up with you, or you may slip up and the worst happens.

I knew it couldn't continue much longer, I just couldn't take it anymore. There were nightly screaming matches on the phone, and then there was the stalking. Whenever we exchanged the boys, I encountered abuse and violence. It got to the point that I would only meet him in a public place to do the exchange; we chose the McDonald's parking lot. Unfortunately, this was years before women's shelters began assisting with exchanges between parents, so I didn't have the opportunities separated parents have today.

He was always trying to intimidate me during these exchanges. He would tell me that in order for me to have the boys, I would have to go to his Jeep and get the boys myself. Of course, this meant I had to be pretty close to him physically, which also meant the chance of something bad happening to me increased. Danger had been part of my life for so long that I was almost accustomed to it on a daily basis. But you do what you have to do.

I lost at least two cell phones as a result of having to meet Eddie to exchange the boys. I thought I would be safer if I was on the phone with someone during our meetings, in case things went horribly wrong. The first time he saw me on the phone; he pulled it out of my hands and smashed it to the ground. I lost the second phone when I did go to his Jeep to get the boys. While I was doing that, he went to my car, took my phone, and threw it in the garbage dumpster. It went far too deep for me to retrieve it. The cell phone wasn't worth the degrading experience of climbing into a dumpster in front of Eddie, so I left the phone and Eddie in the parking lot.

He was relentless. He would show up everywhere, even church. I started going to church on Sundays with the boys and their cousin Courtney. This was really nice for me and the boys. I had support at church and it felt healthy and normal. It also gave me peace, even if it was only an hour at a time. I prayed a lot during those times for the strength and courage to make it through.

One day, as we were leaving church, Eddie showed up. He followed us as we walked to the car. He was taunting me and calling me nasty and vile names. He accused me of going to church to find someone to sleep with. It was so demeaning. He said these things right at the church—in front of the boys and my fellow parishioners. We did get safely home, but it was just another day of harassment and stalking. All I wanted was a nice, peaceful Sunday at church, but it wasn't to be.

One summer day that I had the boys, one of the parents from Blake's hockey team called and asked if the boys and I would like to go to the lake with them. They had a cabin and boat, and their kids were the same ages as Blake and Brett. I was really excited. It was going to be a great day. We had never been invited to this type of outing, and I thought it would be good for the boys to be in a calm social setting with their peers. They could see how a normal family interacted.

I should have known better, but when Eddie called to see how the boys were doing I told him what our plans were for the day. He was furious. How dare we have fun, and especially family fun, without him. He actually phoned the family and told them what he really thought about me going to the lake with them in very ugly terms. They called me shortly after and said it was best that we didn't join them. They said Eddie was too angry and they didn't know might happen. It was too much drama for their peaceful day. One more win for Eddie.

I'm sure you are wondering why I didn't go back to court and have the custody agreement amended so that I would have full custody of my children. There are a few reasons. I really believed that I was the cause of Eddie's behavior. I always felt I was the one who caused him to be so angry.

I believed that if I weren't trying to leave him, he would have been less angry. I believed he would have stopped acting out and would have settled into a great social worker and good father to his boys.

I was also very afraid of him. I knew that I had pushed him very close to his breaking point. What would have happened if I pushed him that little bit more by getting sole custody of the boys? What would happen if he really reached his breaking point? I feared for my life and the lives of my children. I felt that appeasing him was making the best out of a very dangerous situation, that it was the key to our survival.

In August of that year, I met a wonderful man named Bryan. Darla, the friend I had stayed with in May, invited me to a baseball party. I really clicked with a friend and teammate of hers, Bryan. It was refreshing to find someone who actually cared about me and treated me well. He loved to make me happy. It was really wonderful. During all my years with Eddie, I had never felt valued for being myself. There were times when I thought I didn't deserve to be happy and thought the abuse I received from Eddie was going to be my life forever. My self-confidence and self-esteem were so low I wasn't sure I could even crawl to the basement of life.

But with Bryan everything was different. He was a gentleman in every sense of the word. It didn't take long for Bryan to have a full understanding of the complications in my life. I had so much baggage that it would have been difficult for anyone to really understand it. He was tremendous in his understanding and he allowed me time for everything. He did his best to keep me safe and supported me during my visits with the boys.

He knew during these times that I might be at risk, but he knew that spending time with the boys was both necessary and important to me. Because of the situation with Eddie and his behavior toward me, when I didn't have the boys I started to spend more time away from my own house and more at Bryan's house. He lived on the other side of town, so it was safer and I could even relax there. I felt I could easily go for a walk or a bike ride and not worry about running into Eddie. Then when it was time for my boys, I stayed at my own house and everything was fine. In the beginning, life with the boys was separate from my life with Bryan. This was partly because of what Eddie might do and also because I needed to understand and feel comfortable in my relationship with him before I introduced him to the boys.

By September, the boys were back in school. Brett started kindergarten and Blake was in second grade. Eddie was also back in school, so the boys had to go to a babysitter after school. Depending on the schedule, either Eddie or I would pick them up from the babysitter's house. Things with Eddie still weren't any better, and having the boys back in school made things even more complicated. He didn't like the joint decision-making regarding school issues, nor did he like having to see me at the school for school functions.

Eddie started to realize that I was seeing someone and was spending less time at my own house. This really made him angry. Our confrontations escalated. He convinced Blake that I wasn't a good mother, and soon Blake stopped visiting me altogether. Brett was still coming to me, but Blake refused.

By this time I'd had enough! I did go back to court to let the judge know that Eddie was not following the court order. Eddie didn't show up for that hearing, but his lawyer was there. Sitting and listening to lawyers going back and forth made me feel helpless yet again. We had been to court many times, and Eddie just ignored all the court orders. All Eddie's prior experience with law enforcement led him to believe he could do what he wanted, that there were no repercussions.

Eddie "let" me see the boys only when he wanted to. Finally, I couldn't take it anymore, so when the judge said I could have my say, I did. I explained we had been to court many times and Eddie had ignored the court orders. The judge told his lawyer that if Eddie didn't abide by the orders, there would be consequences. I also told Eddie this, but it still didn't matter. There was no follow-through, so once again he decided when I did and when I did not have access to my children.

My lawyer was reasonable regarding his fees, but he still cost one hundred dollars an hour. I was a single mother struggling to pay the bills; sometimes I didn't have enough money to buy simple things like milk. I was earning about $24,000 a year: not enough to support the kids and me, but too much to qualify for legal aid. Eddie and I did try mediation because the Court required it, but it wasn't successful. The mediator was very worried about my safety and she felt that it was necessary for Eddie and me to be in separate rooms. How can you mediate when you aren't able to be in the same room together? It was so serious that at the end of my session, she kept Eddie a little longer to ensure I was safely in my vehicle before he left.

Continuing a long legal battle that had no real impact on my life didn't seem realistic for me. Moving out of Eddie's house had resulted in a great deal of debt, and I was using credit to make ends meet. Credit would only last so long before I got into more trouble. I had to make some difficult decisions.

After the court date, I took a step back. I stopped trying to force Blake to see me, and I accepted that I was causing turmoil in his life. The last thing I wanted to do was cause more hurt. In his mind, visiting me would be completely disloyal to his father, and he couldn't disappoint his dad. I tried to see Brett whenever I could.

One day, I drove to Eddie's house to get Brett, and it turned nasty. Eddie came up to the car and started banging on the window, yelling and screaming telling me what an awful person I was. He called me whore, bitch, slut, and other derogatory names you couldn't imagine. He said I was a terrible mother and no one would ever love me. Then he said he was going to kill me. I broke down. He had broken through the last shred of confidence I had. I left without Brett and drove back to Bryan's house. Bryan held me and comforted me while my heart broke in two.

The last straw for me came when I was at work and drove home at lunch to check the mail because I had been staying at Bryan's almost all the time now. Thinking that Eddie would be at school, I assumed it would be a safe time to check on the house. After I picked up my mail and started driving back to work, I looked in the rearview mirror and saw, to my horror, that Eddie was tailing the car. He was so close it looked like I was towing his Jeep. It was terrifying. Was he going to run me off the road? Would this be the end?

I didn't know how to get away from him. My heart was pounding. Then he pulled up in front of me and forced me to pull over. Once we were pulled over, he came over to the car and started pounding on the driver's window. He pounded so hard he broke the window; the glass shattered around me. I sat there covering my head while the glass showered over me. I was shaking. I'm sure I was in shock. I was just praying that there wasn't more to come and that it would finally end. I knew he was not only mad, but that he was deranged. He could do anything. I was grateful that the sound of the glass shattering must have shaken him out of his trance, so he went back to his Jeep. He just sat in his Jeep and waited. He knew he had done wrong and there was no sense trying to avoid the police.

Somebody notified the police and they arrived fairly quickly and were ready to charge him. I just couldn't do it. I wasn't strong enough. If I did it, what would Eddie do to me then? Up to now, nothing was ever formalized with the law so would he finish me because of my involvement with the police. I couldn't chance it. I think I was frozen by fear.

I talked the police out of charging him. He was the father of my children and I couldn't take him away from them. I had a precarious relationship with the boys now, once again, I could not be the reason he was sent to jail. So Eddie left, and the police did too. I called Bryan to come get me. He helped me calm down, and I returned to work later that afternoon.

The police were aware that this was a domestic violence situation. They accepted that I didn't want to press charges, but they did encourage me to go to the main police station and speak with someone about what was going on. I did this and the police officer convinced me to tell her about all the incidents in order to put them in an information file, which would be maintained at the station. She thought it would be good to have the history in case something did go horribly wrong.

As the weeks went by and Eddie realized that I was moving on with my life, he found every opportunity to make it more difficult for me to see the boys. I wasn't seeing Blake at all now and Brett only occasionally. Eddie actually said to me, "I've got Blake turned against you and now I'm working on Brett." In that moment, I saw the future and I knew. I knew I would not have a close, loving, friendly relationship with the boys. Eddie was going to guarantee it.

My relationship with Bryan only strengthened over the next weeks, so I began to introduce him to Brett. Brett enjoyed spending time with Bryan and me. We did all sorts of things together and it was a peaceful, fun time. As Bryan's family lived in Grand Prairie, a town about five hours north of Edmonton, we decided to take Brett for a visit on Thanksgiving. He had a great time and was able to experience what a calm family gathering was all about. He went for a ride on a quad and couldn't stop talking about it. It was also a special weekend for us. Being thankful for my boys and Bryan meant the world to me in a year filled with turmoil.

I remember Brett was with us at Bryan's house for Halloween in 1997. It was such a great night, taking him door to door to trick or treat in his pumpkin costume. He was still very young and he got scared at one house, so I had to bring him home early. It's funny how the little things that others take for granted are the memories that remain in our hearts. It was a beautiful night.

I tried hard to see the boys whenever I could. Eddie was very dangerous and always threatening. Despite the court order, he had complete control over when I could and couldn't see my children. He would phone me daily at work and threaten me. One time I picked up the phone and all I heard was, "Whore, slut, c**t, f***ing bitch. You're dead! You f***ing bitch! I'm going to kill you! You're dead, bitch!"

I did get a restraining order, but he used this to hamper the exchange of the boys. He would tell me that I couldn't pick them up and he couldn't bring them to me because of the restraining order. He did everything he could to keep them from me. No matter what I did or how hard I tried, I just couldn't seem to gain any ground.

Not a moment went by that I didn't think about the boys. It is very strange, I know, but I still felt that they were safe with him. He loved them, and they weren't trying to leave him, so I didn't believe they were in any danger. The danger occurred when they had to see their father and me in the same place. That was never safe and you never knew what was going to happen. I would check in with the teachers at school, and they never expressed any concerns. The babysitter never expressed concern. My mother and my lawyer kept reassuring me of the fact that the boys were going to be fine. It was my safety that was in jeopardy. By this time I was one hundred percent in survival mode. I was doing whatever it took to see my boys as much as I could while still ensuring my survival.

I know you are asking yourself why I didn't take the kids and run far away. Why did I let this continue? How could I leave the boys with this man? Brainwashing is a tactic used by manipulators and people with deviant minds. They probably don't even know they are doing it. Eddie had instilled so much fear in me that I believed I needed to do whatever pleased him.

Recently in Calgary there was a trial where the Crown alleged that a Regina man allegedly tortured by his roommate reacted like an abused animal. The article written by Bill Graveland of the *Canadian Press* (Graveland 2011) states that: "the Crown says a man who was allegedly tortured by his former roommate reacted to the almost daily beatings like an abused pet or battered spouse and couldn't flee the relationship."[3]

---

3   www.globalnews.ca; Canadian Press, 2011

"His personality combined with the abuse conditioned him to try and make the accused happy, not to make any mistakes, and not to get beat again," Crown lawyer Jayme Williams told Queen's Bench Justice Sheilah Martin.[3]

Dr. Kris Mohandie is an American forensic psychologist and an expert on the assessment and management of violent behavior, as well as on cases of people being taken captive. He wrote in the *Journal of Threat Assessment* in 2002 that, "A person may be held captive in several ways. While some captivity is maintained through physical control mechanisms, such as restraint or overt force, most is facilitated by psychological coercion-induced helplessness." Mohandie said that control mechanisms can include isolation, verbal abuse, humiliation, threats, and torture.[3]

I had been with Eddie since I was fifteen years old. The teen years are very formative years. He'd had many of years to mold me, form me, and to control me. I was definitely his captive. I didn't have any family close by, and my financial resources were limited. I was only twenty-seven years old. I didn't have enough life experience to know what to do. To take any steps to end my relationship with him was quite incredible. It said a lot about my commitment to Eddie.

The Long, Hard Decision

One day close to the Christmas holidays, I stopped by the babysitter on my lunch hour to see the boys. It was very impromptu, but I needed to see them. My heart was aching for the boys, especially at Christmas. They had made Christmas decorations out of Play-Doh. They had them ready for me in a box they had wrapped in Christmas paper. There was a candy cane, a wreath, and a bell. A tear fell from my eye as they gave them to me. My heart was breaking and the boys didn't even know it. I still have these ornaments and cherish them to this day. They still decorate my tree to remind me of the boys.

We were having a really nice visit together, playing and talking about Christmas, when Eddie showed up. I don't know how he was always able to figure out where I was; maybe he always knew because he was stalking me. He was furious that I was there with the boys. I knew I had to get out of there or there was going to be trouble. I ran out of the house and got in my car. I drove as fast as I could to get away from him. Unfortunately I ended up blowing something in the engine. I had to pull over and smoke was billowing out the exhaust. I was terrified when Eddie drove by. When he saw the smoke from the car, he just drove on. I guess he realized he had scared me enough; he didn't need to do anything else.

That was my first Christmas without the boys. It was very hard. Bryan and I went to Grande Prairie, so at least one of us could be with family. It was painful not being with the boys. I called them, but the conversation didn't go well. I know it wasn't easy for them, as their dad was close by, listening to every word. They were loyal to their dad in every sense of the word, and I was confusing them. That week my heart broke. A piece of me was swallowed up and spit out. My boys and I would never be the same.

Shortly after Christmas, I realized that something had to change. I was a nervous wreck and I knew that I couldn't go on that way anymore. I was talking with my mom and my therapist regularly, and both gave me advice I didn't want to hear. I had to consider my options. One of the options my mother and therapist suggested was unthinkable. If I was going to keep on living, then I would have to leave the boys with Eddie. They thought I should start a new life because Eddie was using the boys to control me, and that wasn't fair to anyone.

I thought about the whole situation long and hard. After all the crying and sobbing, I realized I only had three real choices. One option would be to change our identities and go into hiding, but what kind of life would that be without family or friends? The boys would never see their aunts or grandparents again, and we would be alone in the world. I didn't think I had the strength or the courage to make that choice.

A second option was to keep plugging away, maintaining the status quo. Maybe Eddie would someday accept the situation, or maybe life would become even more dire. Instead of you reading this book, you would have read a newspaper article about a murder-suicide and facts about domestic violence. I truly believed that if I stayed, he was at least going to kill himself and me, and then leave our boys orphaned with the shame of their parents' faults on their heads. At times, I thought he might even kill the entire family.

According to a 2007 report from Statistics Canada about family violence, there were 11,528 incidents reported to police by ex-spouses: 9,501 were female victims. Although these incidents take place after the majority of my abuse, the fact that 82 percent of female partners have suffered at the hands of their spouse or ex-spouse is alarming. According to the same report, the victims of attempted homicide by a spouse were also 82 percent female. That number is far too high for a civilized world. I thought I was alone so many times. I couldn't imagine so many people were suffering alongside me.

My last option, the only viable option, was to remove myself from the situation. This is the option that my mother and therapist were asking me to consider. I felt that we could be like other divorced families living apart. I thought if I could move to Calgary, where Eddie wouldn't know my address, I could visit Edmonton every other weekend and still be part of the boys' life. This seemed like the only solution. I would still be involved with the boys, see them regularly, and they wouldn't see any more violence and fighting.

It was life or death: I chose life. You may think you would not have made the same choice, but when you have lived intimately with violent abuse for a decade, you do what you have to do. The boys were never the recipient of Eddie's abuse, so I knew they were not in harm's way. If they had been, I would have chosen differently. My support team—the people that I put my trust in to guide me during this time—were telling me that this was the right choice. Even my lawyer supported my decision to leave. My lawyer told me that although Eddie was cruel and violent to me, he always thought Eddie loved the boys more than anything and would treat them well (unless they tried to leave him).

In the end I chose life: life for all of us. I wasn't sure what that life would be like, but our instinct to survive is amazingly strong. After a long deliberation, lots of tears, and heart-to-heart talks with people that loved me, I made the decision to leave.

I had reached my breaking point. To save myself mentally and physically something had to change. I felt that I had exhausted all my efforts in court so what was next. Even if I had a court order it didn't seem relevant or effective. Eddie would just do what he felt like. I didn't have anymore money to spend on a lawyer so I needed to explore other options.

At the time, I believed the situation was temporary. I thought we would only be apart until Eddie calmed down, or until I could get my life in order. I wrote to Eddie's lawyer begging him to explain to Eddie the consequences of continually ignoring the court orders. In that letter I wrote, "Once my life is in order and my ex-husband is no longer trying to harass or control me, I will get my boys back."

So many people say they would rather die than leave their children. I always questioned why I wasn't willing to die. It was my naturopath who told me. She told me that that within us all, there is a very strong instinct to survive. She told me that these women had never been faced with such a situation. My situation wasn't just about me—it was about preserving my children's lives as well. Leaving Edmonton felt like my only option, and I planned to see the boys every other weekend. We always had a joint-custody agreement—that never changed. We just agreed that Eddie would be the custodial parent.

Once I finally accepted that this was my only viable option, I took action. I decided that I would move to Calgary as it is only three hours away. So I started to look for a job in Calgary. My only requirements were that my new employer pay my moving expenses and a salary that would allow me to support myself.

Bryan was very disappointed with my decision to leave Edmonton. We had begun to talk about marriage. He had a good job in Edmonton, and although he was willing to move to Calgary, he was worried about getting a job and the stress that accompanies such a move.

I made the decision to leave in January, and by February 14, 1998 I was on the road to Calgary for a job interview. The company was an office furniture installation/moving company. This meant there would be no problem moving my belongings to Calgary! The next time they had a job in Edmonton, they would place my things on the truck and bring it to Calgary. The interview went very well, and we agreed that I would start my new job as controller on March 1. Bryan and I agreed that we would see each other every other weekend until he could find himself a job in Calgary.

I was very lucky to have some family friends who lived in Calgary. I was able to stay with them in March, until I could find myself an apartment. This was 1998, and there was a housing shortage in Calgary. Back then, everything was booming. I finally found a nice one-bedroom apartment in the Sunnyside neighborhood, and while I was on a business trip for work, some of the guys picked up my stuff and moved it into my apartment for me.

I loved that job. I traveled to Vancouver once a month, and there were plans for a trip to Dubai in October. That little hayseed that travelled from army base to base was now traveling the world. It was interesting for me to be so free and independent. I had never lived alone in my life. Living free of Eddie's control was incredible. It felt like I had just been freed from a one-room prison and was now free to feel the warmth of the sun and explore the world.

When I was with Eddie, I was certainly out and about, doing things like grocery shopping, going to McDonald's, and going to work, but I wasn't free. Back then, I was always aware of what I was doing and how it might affect Eddie. I was very careful not to do anything that would make him unhappy or, worse, angry. This type of emotional abuse, of being so monitored and controlled, was much more damaging to me than physical abuse.

With physical abuse, although so traumatic at the time, the bruises and cuts heal but emotional abuse gnaws away at you, first removing any self esteem you had at all and then slowly removing any hint of hope for the future. A life without hope is not a life worth living nor is it a life that meets your potential as a human being.

I met some nice people in Calgary. Soon after I arrived, my friend Danny and I drove to a restaurant. He pulled into the parking spot and got out of the car—a normal thing to do, wouldn't you agree? I didn't move; I was frozen in place. In the past, I didn't get out of the car unless Eddie directed me and allowed me to leave. Danny just looked at me and asked, "Are you coming or what?" I quickly got out of the car and tagged along side him into the restaurant. I was really like a deer in the headlights. It took some time and some guidance from some very dear friends for me to get past this point and to be comfortable thinking for myself and making my own decisions.

I was like a child experiencing everything for the first time and learning her limits. I had a lot to learn.

Parenting from Calgary

I moved to Calgary on March 1, 1998. In the beginning, I felt it was a good decision and a great move for me and, indirectly, for everyone else. It was my fresh start—a life with less stress and fear. To the best of my ability, I was doing everything I could to see Blake and Brett every other weekend. I would make the long drive to Edmonton and back just to see the boys' faces. I was eager for the opportunity to show them how much I loved and cared for them. I needed to reassure myself that they knew that I hadn't left them; I had left an unbearable situation.

I didn't like that I had to live so far from my children. I wasn't seeing them as much as I should have. When I lived in Edmonton I was seeing them four days a week. Now that I lived a three hour drive away I was seeing them four days a month. At the time I believed the situation was temporary. I thought we would only be apart, living in different cities until their dad calmed down, or until I could get my life in order.

Every time we had an arranged visit, I would get in my car and drive to Edmonton. Each time I made the drive, I felt the same wave of emotion. I would get up in the morning filled with anticipation and excitement. The excitement would continue until I was halfway there, and then fear and anxiety would set in. Every single time as I stopped for a rest break in Red

Deer (halfway point), the familiar feeling of anxiety grew and grew, until it felt like a medicine ball in the pit of my stomach.

Then my heart would race. My breathing would become shallow and rapid. I tried to calm myself by taking deep breaths, but it didn't seem to help. Then questions would spring into my mind. Would the boys actually be there when I arrived? Would Eddie bring them only to abuse me in front of them? The possible scenarios whipped through my brain like the scenes in a movie.

I thought if I could anticipate what would happen, I would be better prepared. But with Eddie, you really never knew. By the time I reached the city, I was trembling. I always tried to get to the exchange point first, so that I could let the police know that I had arrived to pick up my children for our visit and warn them about what could happen when Eddie arrived.

Eddie did everything in his power to maintain his control over me. The only way he could control me now that I had left Edmonton was through my visitation rights. This presented some challenges with him and some anxiety with me. Often, Eddie would tell me I couldn't come to see the boys because Blake or Brett had hockey. As far as Eddie was concerned, the boys' hockey took priority over everything else. If it was my time with the boys, I should have been the one taking them to their games. I would have loved to watch them, just like every other mother. I would have cheered them on when they got a goal, or commiserated with them if they lost. I would have been proud of them either way. Eddie took that from me, too.

Eddie and I exchanged an overwhelming number of e-mails about my visits. Most of them were Eddie's attempts to modify the court-ordered arrangements. Very rarely did our exchange go smoothly. If Eddie brought them, it was a struggle to get them in the car. They would kick and scream and tell me how much they hated me. To have my own children tell me they hated me after all I had been through was very depressing. Deep down, I understood that I was changing the situation and they wanted to be loyal to Eddie, but the sting of their words stayed with me for a long time. I remember during one exchange Blake yelled out that police were fascists. Where does a six-year-old boy hear such a thing? I was shocked. I couldn't believe Eddie would teach him these things.

When I did get the boys in the car they would eventually calm down once we drove off, but there were often outbursts and arguments during the weekend about how much they hated me and how they just wanted to go home with their dad. It was heartbreaking every time.

As the boys got older and bigger, the exchanges became more difficult. Blake was becoming even more loyal to his father and would often refuse to come. When I tried to put him in the car, he would yell and scream profanities and run away. Such episodes left me in hysterics. My little boy was running through the streets of Edmonton alone. What if something happened to him? My biggest fear was that he would be abducted or, worse, killed.

On one of these occasions, I ran into the police station. I was distraught, crying hysterically, and in a massive state of panic. I begged the police officer to go after my son. They just had to find him—there was no other option. I told the officer I was going in my car to look for him. The officer stared at me and said, "You are not going anywhere until you calm down." For a quick second I wanted to object, but her voice was so firm I realized I had to follow her request. She knew I would probably cause more trouble or an accident along the way.

If I was to find my son, I had to regain composure and think about the situation. I couldn't do that in the emotional state I was in. Finally, they sent out a car and found Blake a short distance away. He was safe and was trying to go home. I didn't force him to come with me after that. I realized that sharing our lives was becoming a potentially dangerous situation. I had to accept that I was losing Blake. For the time being, Brett was reluctant but still willing to come, and I appreciated every moment I was able to spend with him.

After months of difficult exchanges, I was at the end of my rope. I wrote a letter to my lawyer informing him of the details of the situation and asking for guidance. Both he and I knew I had little money due to my move and Eddie's lies and destruction. A broken driver's side window and an additional child support payment. Eddie had lied to the court and said that I had kept the monthly child tax benefit. This was not true at all. The money was deposited into my bank account but I transferred this money to him every month. Unfortunately I didn't have enough evidence to prove this and I was required to pay Eddie the money that he claimed he didn't receive. All of this just added to my depression about moving forward. I wanted to finalize the divorce, but I had no money, so I thought I should delay it a couple of months until I could get back on my feet.

I felt like Eddie was still controlling me financially as well as emotionally. I questioned whether the boys should be living with me. But deep down, I knew Eddie would never abide by such a court ruling, and the boys didn't seem to want that either. It seemed like a lose-lose situation. But I wanted and needed to spend time with the boys. Even to spend the summer camping with the boys would allow us to build a stronger relationship. I wanted them to be with me as much as possible.

As a result of my letter, my lawyer contacted Eddie's lawyer, and things were better for a while. During that summer of 1998, I saw the boys every other weekend and we had wonderful visits. The exchanges were still a nightmare but once I got them in the car and away from Eddie we had a great time. We had great weather that summer and were able to go to Kananaskis and Banff to explore the mountains. Our camping trips were unforgettable.

On one of our better trips, we went teepee camping. Just north of Red Deer there is a site that rents teepees. I picked up the boys and we set up camp at the teepee campsite. Strangely, but thankfully, we were the only ones there that night. We sat around the campfire and roasted hot dogs and marshmallows. When we went to bed, we heard strange noises like a woman crying. The silence of the night was very eerie and we were all nervous. We huddled together in our sleeping bags and soon fell asleep.

We did some exploring on our bikes after breakfast the next morning and were having a great time. We were crossing a bridge over a gully and Blake hit the side of the bridge and flipped over the handlebars and landed in the gully.   Thankfully Blake was okay, as it wasn't a hard fall, but my second thought was, *how would Eddie react if Blake had broken his arm and couldn't play hockey?* He would

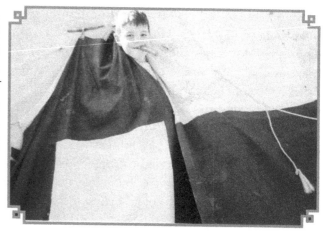

never forgive me, and he might punish me. I hated that I still had thoughts like that.

The camp was perfect and was only a five-minute drive to our favorite beach at Gull Lake. In the afternoon, we went to the beach and made sand castles and swam in the lake. We were having a terrific time together bonding as a family. There was no yelling or screaming—just playing and having fun. It was what we all needed. When we returned to camp in the evening, we sat by the fire roasting marshmallows. It was a wonderful day. We went to sleep that night more comfortable knowing the noises we had heard the night before were just the birds and not someone in distress. They certainly heard enough of that growing up.

We packed up the next day and started our drive back to Edmonton. It didn't matter that we had spent a wonderful weekend together—the closer we got to Edmonton, the worse things became. We had been driving about an hour when the comments started. Without any cause, the boys starting saying things like, "I hate your guts." I could tell they were turning their loyalty back to Eddie.

The remainder of the drive was very tense; I was hurt. How could such a wonderful weekend end so badly? They turned on me and I hadn't done anything. It was because of Eddie. Perhaps they thought that if they had a good time with me, they were being disloyal to Eddie. After I dropped them off, I returned to Calgary in a blur of tears.

Once September came, the boys were back in school and now both of them were playing hockey. So Eddie began interfering once again in our visitation schedule. I was doing what I could to avoid the additional costs of lawyers by trying to resolve it myself. I tried to appeal to Eddie in an informal manner, but he had his own agenda, which was to reduce or eliminate my presence in the boys' life. In order to find some resolution, I wrote Eddie a letter just after one of our visits was abridged because of hockey.

Eddie, what has happened to you? You used to stress the importance to me of knowing right from wrong. You seemed to have lost that knowledge.

As abusive and controlling as you were you were never the unfeeling person that you have become now. Why do you keep the boys from having two parents? You are hurting them so much. They need their mother. No matter how much you try and destroy my relationship with them I will continue to fight to see them.

You have to accept that I have a right to see my children and you have to stop keeping them from me and turning them against me.

Somehow we have to talk reasonably and figure out a visitation schedule that will be acceptable for both of us and that is best for the boys.

I do not agree with what is happening. I will be consulting a child psychologist regarding full custody but in the meantime we can't be putting our children though this.

Eddie, please realize that there is a court order in effect here and it must be abided by.

Move on Eddie, get help and let the children have two parents, hopefully two healthy parents. You may hate me and my leaving you but leave the boys alone. I will never give them up. I'd rather die than never see my children again. I love my children and I need to see them and they need to see me.

Please cooperate Stop doing this to yourself. Accept what has happened and move on. You are only hurting yourself and the boys. That isn't fair to the boys.

I really had no money at this time. The talk of consulting with a child psychologist was just that, talk, if only I had the resources to pursue that option. I just wanted all of the pain and suffering to end. I wanted us to both move on with our lives. I knew he had a serious relationship with his new girlfriend Corrine, and moving on would be better for all of us. If I could persuade him that it would benefit him, perhaps he might agree about the divorce. Dragging things on forever wasn't what I wanted or what I imagined his girlfriend would want. As for Eddie, I don't think formalizing anything, either custody or divorce, meant anything at all.

Eddie didn't acknowledge my letter, but then again, I didn't expect it. I had always hoped he would come around, but I never got my hopes up too high. Since the letter came from me not a legal representative, I don't think he gave it much credence. He continued to use my visitations with the boys as a means to control me. I did the best to fight for my rights, but the lawyer's fees and Eddie's reactions were more than I could manage.

As fall came and the weather became colder, camping with the boys, my only peace with them became more difficult. I had to find other ways to spend time with them during our visits. Sometimes, we would stay at my friend Darla's house. It was nice because she basically gave us free reign of the entire basement level. It was like our own little hideaway because it was finished like an apartment. On Friday nights, after what was usually a traumatic exchange, we would put our pajamas on, pull out the couch, and cuddle up to watch a movie.

Darla lived on several acres in the country, and the boys loved being there with the horses and the freedom to explore the nooks and crannies of the land. In the winter, Darla's husband Dave would occasionally take the boys out on snow-

mobiles. They had a lot of fun those weekends, and I could see them enjoying themselves. I had to hold on to those memories when the rough times began. And they always did—it was just a matter of time.

If they were feeling restless or bored, I would drive into the city and we'd go bowling or to one of the large indoor playgrounds with the climbing walls and the pit with the colored balls. It was a great day when I could sit and watch my boys laugh or smile while they played. When we felt safe and together, we had wonderful visits.

Eddie had refused to let me participate or even watch the boys' hockey, but I refused to let him exclude me from anything else. I wanted to be there for all the special moments in their lives. I had been able to attend the first two years of Blake's Christmas concerts, kindergarten and first grade. Living in Calgary wasn't going to stop me from attending Blake's second grade concert, or Brett's kindergarten concert.

It was December 10, just two weeks before Christmas. With the concerts that night, focusing on work was difficult that day. I planned to leave the office early and make the long, stressful drive to Edmonton to see their concerts and then drive back to Calgary late that night. The drive to Edmonton that day went as it usually did: it was a rollercoaster ride. I was really excited about the boys' concerts, but then the anxiety and stress of Eddie and his reactions filled me with dread.

This time, my anxiety was more extreme because I wanted to surprise the boys. I remember that when I was their age, knowing my parents were in the audience when I was performing in a school Christmas concert gave me a sense of confidence and love. I always tried to avoid occasions where

Eddie and I were together, but I knew Eddie would also be in the audience that night, too.

By the time I arrived at the school, I was trembling. The last person I wanted was to run into was Eddie. I thought I would go find the boys in the classroom first so they would know I was there and then go into the auditorium to watch the show. I thought they would be surprised, and happy to see me. As I walked down the corridor, I saw Blake. He was a smaller version of his father. The way he walked and looked reminded me so much of Eddie.

I beamed with pride when I saw him come my way. I was so happy to have found him, without his father being next to him. Unfortunately, Blake did not have the same reaction. When he realized it was me, he panicked. He marched up to me and demanded to know what I was doing there. He then told me he was going to tell his father and then ran off to get him.

I stood there in shock. Why would Blake have such a reaction? Had Eddie said something to him? It was like I was seeing Eddie question my every move. Before I knew it, Eddie was standing in front of me with both Blake and Brett hand in hand. He then began to call me names in front of the boys and some of the parents who happened to be in the hallway. He said if I didn't leave, he would remove the boys from the concert. It reminded me of a child's reaction: if I can't have it, no one can.

I was dumbfounded by his reaction. How could he do this? I had come as a parent to share in the joy of the season with my children. I know it was a surprise, but why did he have to react that way? I had driven three hours from Calgary just to see them perform, and he was taking it away, again.

I felt I had no choice but to leave. I didn't want the boys to miss their performances. They had been practicing so long, and I didn't want them to miss the opportunity to see them shine in the spotlight. I was in tears before the doors closed behind me. I could also feel a door closing on my relationship with the boys. Something had changed in them.

I trudged back through the wet snow to my car and sat there in the silence. The only sound coming was the sound of a mother crying for her lost children. The poet, Albert Smith said, "Tears are the safety valve of the heart when too much pressure is laid on it." My heart was truly broken. I had experienced so many situations with Eddie, but I had always thought the boys were my life. When they rejected me, it was more than I could bear. I could barely see the road through the tears on the drive back to Calgary.

That night when Eddie went home he sent me an e-mail about showing up unannounced at the school:

Sherri-Lee you cannot just show up whenever you want. I do not want anymore surprise visits it is very upsetting. Blake came and got me as soon as he saw you and he wanted to leave. Why can't you get it through your head the boys have a good life with me, and people that the boys are in contact with know it and support me one hundred percent.

I will always have very strong feelings for you. I miss you very much. I know that at this point the boys are happy with the way things are, you keep saying that the boys will adjust if you take them, my question to you is why should they have to? When you make those kinds of statements it shows that you are only thinking of yourself.

I am very sorry all I ever wanted was a family. A very big part of my family left, now Blake and Brett are my family. I wish I could undo all the mistakes, and I wish you were still part of my life.

I couldn't believe this was still happening. He was still trying to guilt me into coming back. We had a very liberal joint custody agreement and I had every right to go to Blake and Brett's Christmas concert. I had been threatening to obtain full custody of the boys because he was destroying my relationship with them. What he said really bothered me. He was so manipulative. There was no way I would ever go back to Eddie. I had endured too much for too long to walk back into that nightmare again. Whether he meant what he said about wishing to undo his mistakes, I don't know. I only know what I barely made it out of my marriage with my life. I couldn't do it anymore. I wrote back:

I had every right to be there last night. If I show up for a Christmas concert and the boys are upset you should be asking yourself why. Any child should be thrilled to have their mother come and see them. There is definitely something wrong there. Something has to be done to correct this.

About you and me, that will never be. I just wish for the boys' sake that we could get along. Our children can't even handle us being in the same school. Doesn't that make you wonder?

I told him I was looking forward to my next visit with the boys December 18th. We would be celebrating Christmas together and I needed some happiness and some quality time with the boys.

It was a long two week wait after the Christmas concert incident but finally December 18th arrived and I was able to see the boys. We celebrated Christmas and I splurged and reserved the truck room at the Fantasyland

Hotel in West Edmonton Mall. This was a real treat for all of us. The bed in the room is in the back of a pickup truck, and the boys thought it was fantastic. There was also a small round hot tub in the room. It had a tall statue of a policeman over it. We had so much fun just being in the room— it was an adventure.

We ordered a pizza when we first arrived, and then I filled the tub for the boys. I put in some bubble bath and turned the jets on. The bubbles went everywhere. They boys loved the tub and sprayed each other with their water guns. The laughed and squealed the way kids are supposed to.

Once the pizza arrived, I dried them off and put them in their pajamas. We all sat on the truck bed and ate our pizza. They were really having a great time jumping and going into the truck cab, pretending they were driving. After the pizza, we opened some presents and watched a movie so they could settle down before going to sleep.

The next day we woke up early and had a wonderful day in the mall. We spent some time at the water park and then played mini-golf. It was wonderful that we were able to spend so much time together it was like having a mini-vacation right there at the mall. And we needed it after the fiasco at the school Christmas concert. All in all, it was one of our better weekends together.

Life in Calgary
without the Boys

During the week, I lived my own life in Calgary. I was still trying to maintain my relationship with Bryan by seeing him on the weekends when I wasn't with the boys. During the week when I was on my own, I went to work every day and went to the gym in the evening with my friend Chantelle.

Chantelle is a beautiful, five-foot-ten woman who could be a model. She is elegant and charming and always knows what to say. She carries herself with poise and confidence. And her big brown eyes have men falling at her feet. Chantelle and I quickly became best friends. I've always had issues finding and keeping friends, but Chantelle is the real thing: the true friend that every girl needs.

We spent a lot of time together, and she showed me a completely different side of life. We were both twenty-eight years old, and she taught me how to love life. I had only started to enjoy life thanks to Bryan, but Chantelle expanded my horizons further. We would go to the gym two or three times a week, and sometimes we'd go dancing on the weekends when I stayed in Calgary. We enjoyed the nightlife.

Sometimes it was a bit awkward when Bryan came to Calgary. It was like my life was moving forward and he wasn't part of it. We still planned for him to move to Calgary so we could be together, but the longer I was in Calgary without him, the more I saw myself changing. We were slowing drifting apart.

Because I had met Eddie when I was fifteen and married him three years later, I never had the experience of going to clubs with my friends. This was a brand-new experience. Chantelle knew all the right people, and she was often invited to restaurant or club openings. We never stood in line or paid a cover charge; she simply went to a side door, batted her big brown eyes at the bouncer, and we were in. If there was a VIP section or room, we'd be escorted to the spot.

When I was with Eddie, I drank very little in order to look out for him, and for myself. When Chantelle and I started going out, enjoying a nice glass of wine or a cocktail at a nightclub became part of my new routine. I will forever be grateful to her. She helped me grow in a good way. I became more confident in myself as a professional and as a woman.

She would notice how I stood or walked or talked and would offer sound advice to help me improve myself. She told me to fake it until I made it. There is something in that old adage. If you smile more, you will want to smile more just try it. If I looked insecure, she would talk to me in a friendly way and help me to make the most of what I had. We were best friends for a great year.

I grew so much that year that I realized Bryan really wasn't the guy for me. Unfortunately, I discovered this just before he moved to Calgary. But he did move to Calgary, and we tried to make it for a while, but it was never the same. I was different, and I think he was different, too. He was a kind, caring person who helped me in more ways than I can count. But he was ready to settle down and I was just starting my life as a single person. It wasn't fair to him. I wasn't ready for the next stage in our relationship. So finally, we said our good-byes. The sadness settled over me when we broke up, but it didn't last as long as I thought it would. After all, we had been separated physically and emotionally for over a year.

Even though I was experiencing new things and was discovering a new world, there was still a very sad side to my life. The pain of not being with my boys and only seeing them sporadically was more than I could handle at times. Many nights I would sit alone in my meager basement apartment and think about what had become of my life. More importantly, I thought about who I was as a mother. My own mother had been a wonderful, loving, caring person and was always there for me. She was my rock.

Growing up and thinking about being a mother, I had envisioned picking the boys up after a fall or scrape, comforting them when their tears trickled down their faces, or being there when they woke up from a bad dream. I would kiss and hug them daily and ask them to tell me about their day at school or about playing with their friends. I so wanted to be that type of mother, their biggest cheerleader and fan in everything they did.

But life had a different plan and set of circumstances for me. Blake and Brett were just little boys who didn't have the daily, loving interactions only a mother could provide. They didn't have someone reading them fairy tales before bedtime or singing them songs in the car on the way to school. They wouldn't understand things like how a mom could just hear one word and then start singing a song out of nowhere. No one would be reciting the verse "bread, butter, pepper, and salt, fruit, sugar, and cream" to ensure everything was on the table for dinner. How would they learn all those little details?

Instead, what they learned during our brief time together as a family was a mother and father who yelled and screamed and swore at each other and who constantly fought about their children. They saw their father demean their mother in front of them, spit in her face, and try to choke her unconscious. Where were they to learn about loving relationships? In our family, all they learned was how to hurt someone.

They didn't get to see me the times I drove three hours in the rain or snow just to have a few hours with them, only to be turned away. All they knew was mommy wasn't coming to see them as much anymore. They probably thought, on their own or with a little help from Eddie that perhaps I didn't want to be with them.

They wouldn't know that their daddy restricted their time with me for his own selfish reasons. During one our visits Brett said to me, "I miss you, Mommy. I am going to build a house in Edmonton so you can live closer." Out of the mouths of babes. I had hoped that they missed me and hadn't forgotten about me, but when Brett said this, I wasn't sure if I could handle the separation any longer.

This just wasn't the way I ever imagined my life as a mother. The nights that I sat alone in my Calgary apartment, I wondered if continuing on was worth it. I would sit in my bedroom crying until there were no tears left. I would think about the unthinkable. I thought how easy it would be to simply overdose on some pills. I even thought about wearing my beautiful pink sateen outfit my parents had given me for Christmas years ago. That was the year I started dating Eddie.

I loved that ensemble, the three-quarter-length skirt, camisole, and long, flowing jacket that fell below my thighs. It's funny to say, but I felt beautiful and loved every time I wore it. Now it would be my funeral clothes. I imagined lying on the bed swallowing some pills and gently falling asleep into a dreamland of peace. My pain would be over forever.

I calculated the best time to do this for me and everyone else too. That's how thoughtful I was. I would do it on a Friday. I lived alone, so no one would expect to see me until Monday. Bryan would think I had stayed in Calgary and Chantelle would think I was in Edmonton with the boys. This would be the easiest thing for everyone. I was so crushed; life didn't feel worth living anymore. I had been beaten down so many times by life— hope was just a dying ember without any spark to keep it alive.

Here's an entry from my journal July 23, 1998:

The days are too long, the nights are too short. It is my dreams where I find peace, where reality doesn't exist. Reality hurts way too much. I need to see my children and they need to see me.

Would it really make him happy if I was no longer here? Is this what he really wants? Would he feel guilty? I know he hurts and I'm sorry for that, but why does he have to make all of us hurt? Would they be happier if I was gone? I really would do anything for their happiness.

I thought of suicide often. The pain and hurt were so severe that I couldn't see a way out of the despair. One day, in my search for a meager spark of hope, I went to visit a psychic. She was welcoming and took her time. First, she placed my hand in hers and read my palm. She spoke quietly and said: "I feel like there is someone close to you who is considering suicide." At first I thought, *how could she know that?* I mumbled: "It's me." She quite calmly said: "Don't do it. You won't succeed and you will end up in a wheel chair for the rest of your life." I knew she would probably convince me not to do it, but telling me my fate was like a slap in the face, and it woke me up. Although I had been contemplating suicide for a long time, I am grateful that I chose to see her. She may have saved me from an even worse life.

That year was an abundant year in so many ways. I partied and socialized far too much. I still drove to Edmonton every other weekend to be with the boys, but when I was in Calgary, life was crazy.

Almost exactly a year after I first moved to Calgary, I realized I needed to make some changes. The first problem was the amount of alcohol I was drinking. Not only was it costing me money, it was also costing me my health. One day, I looked in the mirror and saw myself for the first time. I had gained a lot of weight that year, and that was just on the surface. What was the alcohol doing to my insides?

The first thing I did was to quit drinking. Going dancing or hanging out in bars wasn't as enticing sober, watching drunk people got old quickly. I needed to find another type of entertainment. But not doing something wasn't an option. I started to feel lonely again. I knew if that continued I might fall back into a depression and do something drastic.

Maybe it was time to be more responsible. Since Bryan and I had parted ways, I wanted to be single. But after that year of craziness, it was time to settle down. They say everything in life is timing. Sometimes it falls into place, and other times we miss opportunities. Perhaps it is our destiny that we miss those opportunities.

I thought being in a relationship would help me settle down. I thought hard about what I wanted in a partner. My first group of friends in Calgary were nature lovers and enjoyed hiking and being in the mountains. They certainly enjoyed life and had fun, but it wasn't the right fit for me.

Then came my year of celebrating being single, in which I partied too hard and too often. The club scene made me very aware that I wasn't looking for that type of person either. The one thing I did enjoy was running. It was a wholesome, energetic, stress-relieving activity. I liked the way I felt when I was running. I liked the open air, the wind on my face, the sounds of life around me, and the beating of my steps on the pavement. It was hypnotic. It helped to clear my mind of the daily worries. It was just me, alone with myself.

I had been in a couple of organized runs and I loved the energy. Usually there was a social function after a run when you could mingle and get to know other runners. I decided my next step was to become more involved with running. Perhaps I would meet someone nice; if not, I would certainly get healthier.

I had to change my life, and I hoped this change would be the beginning of a brand-new me.

Another Life Change

Iknew that to meet a runner I needed to be in places they frequented.
So the next step was to join a running group. I decided to join the
organizing committee of the Stampede Marathon. It was a great
opportunity to meet new people and do some volunteer work at the same
time. My part of the volunteer work involved organizing the relay.

I was so excited about my decision to turn my life around that I had this
boundless sense of energy. I showed up to the first meeting very enthusias-
tic to begin my transformation. There was a gentleman at the meeting who
looked at me quizzically. He just wasn't sure that I fit in with this group.
I wasn't a die-hard runner, nor did I look the part of the corporate political
group. He approached me and suggested I try a running club he belonged
to: the Calgary Hash House Harriers. I thought to myself, *What a name for
a running club.* What kind of people would they be?

He explained that it was really a fun group of people that met every
Monday night. They would meet at a different pub, and the run would start
and end there. It was a great nonjudgmental group of people who were out
for a good time. At the end of the run, there was a social gathering where, if
you were caught doing anything silly or bad on the run, you were punished
with beer. Then, after imbibing, we would all stand around singing rugby
songs and acting silly.

His comment to me was, "It's a drinking club with a running problem." Just the sound of it made me want to join. He said I'd fit right in. I wanted to find out for myself, so he gave me the information for the next meeting.

I did show up that next Monday; I was a bit shy, after all, this was my first run. It was somewhat overwhelming, too. Everyone else seemed to have a rhythm to the meeting. I felt a little out of place at first. This new path to the new me brought some trepidation for sure, but I was willing and eager to get started.

I arrived at the parking lot of the pub, and there were a number of other runners milling about, so I cautiously walked over to join them. A nice gentleman asked me if I was new and then proceeded to tell me how the run worked. There was nothing normal about the Hash House Harriers. The members all have nicknames and they speak in an entirely different language. I found out later that the man's name was Butthead. His wife was Beaver, and the gentleman I met at the meeting for the organization of the Stampede Marathon was Hopeless.

I will never forget the start of the run. All the runners formed a circle and went around stating their names. Some of the names were beyond imagination: Party Pumper, Rag Head, Shack Shock, Mucky Dip. The nicknames helped to provide some anonymity if anything was spoken outside the running group. It was quite an experience. Butthead was very kind and stayed with me for the run to teach me the ropes. What a joy it was to be outside running with these people. Returning to the pub brought another experience for me.

I went to the run by myself and was still feeling a bit shy and intimidated. At the pub, I tried to stay in the back against the wall so I wouldn't draw any attention to myself. I was shocked when the group's "religious leader," the one in charge of punishing other runners for their faux pas, commenced retribution. I witnessed people sitting on blocks of ice, bums exposed, pants being pulled down for spankings, not to mention the multitude of songs that mocked the runner for doing something silly.

I thought the antics were hilarious, when they were being done to someone else, but I was horrified by the idea of being the object of such ridicule. I even witnessed a runner (hasher) drink beer from his shoe because he wore new shoes to the run. It was a good night—unnerving, but good.

The following week, I called the hotline number to get the information for the next run. I was a bit confused listening to the message—it was like they were speaking Greek. The message said the run started at an arena, but said the "on in" was a different location. What the beep was an "on in"? I didn't attend because it was too intimidating. Eventually I learned the "on in" is where the group gathers for beer and punishment after the run is completed.

I spent a few months going to the "hash" on Mondays. I would socialize with Chantelle the rest of the week and go to bars with her on the weekend. I was starting to live two separate lives. Then I realized it wasn't just a Monday thing for the running group. They had a social world outside the runs, too. There were fundraising dinner parties, Wednesday runs for the serious runner, a cycling group, and, what I enjoyed most: the full moon run. Of course, most times, there was socializing after the run, but it was all fun and quite innocent.

Chantelle was curious about what I was doing on my Monday nights. Often I would go on my run, and when it ended I'd change into evening clothes and meet her at the bar for drinks. She did meet me at the pub one night after a run but decided it wasn't for her. Perhaps she saw the punishment being handed out and was scared away.

It didn't take long until I started spending more time with the running club and less time with Chantelle. We had been best friends and inseparable for more than a year, now it wasn't working anymore. I needed to feel more stable. Everything is timing. I felt I needed a change.

I was twenty-nine when I joined the running club. I think the average age was around forty. Needless to say, I was one of the younger members. There were two other young ladies around my age, Laura "Left Bun" and Sandra "Right Bun." Who knows how they got those nicknames. They knew each other from university and were good friends. When I joined, we became friends and have been ever since.

I joined the club in April and by June was fully immersed in this new life. I had not run in years and wasn't very fit, so I ran slower than the rest of the members. I decided to add an extra night and attended the Wednesday night runs to get in better shape. Another member of the club, "Stranger," had been a runner for a long time but was injured and was slowly regaining his stamina by doing shorter, slower runs. Coincidentally, we usually ran together on Wednesday evenings.

We couldn't talk during the runs because I was out of shape and it took all my breath just to complete the route. But with a few words here and there, we managed to share a little information. He had been named "Stranger" because he travelled so much. He was a petroleum geologist for an oil company and grew up in London, England. Throughout his entire career he had worked internationally and had lived in many places including United Arab Emirates, Indonesia, Pakistan, and Texas. He was a nice guy. He was very interesting and had stories from everywhere. I really enjoyed our Wednesday evenings.

One evening I was attending a dinner at a Thai restaurant with some members of a new branch of the running club, the Rocky Mountain Hash. It was necessary for the founders or flounders as we referred to them, to organize a run. To organize a hash run, two people had to set or "hare" the run. It was all about the hounds and the hares. The hare set the run and the hounds followed. The duties of the hares involved finding a location within ninety minutes of the city limits in some rugged terrain like the foothills of the Rocky Mountains. Once the location was determined a trail had to be laid out (marked) with flagging similar to that used in construction sites or by forestry people. The trail should take about an hour and a half to two hours to run through dense bush and ponds, and rivers. It was always a challenge to make it a bit of a tough run.

During this dinner I was approached by Andy (Stranger) to help him set the run. I said sure. It was my first chance to set a run and I loved being in the mountains. We agreed to go out after work on Wednesday, June 17, 1999, which happened to be my twenty-ninth birthday.

Andy picked me up at my house and we drove to the mountains. Generally speaking, Andy doesn't have the radio on when he drives. I was uncomfortable with all the silence, so I talked the entire drive there. He must have thought, *When will this girl be quiet?* We had even more conversation setting the run near Sibbald Flats and again on the drive home. We enjoyed each other's company and learned a lot about each other that trip.

Although I had mentioned to Andy it was my birthday, he must have already known because when he dropped me off he asked if he could take me for champagne at one of the nicest restaurants in Calgary. As much as I really wanted to go to the restaurant and with Andy, I told him it wasn't fair. I was covered in mud and sweat from the run and felt dirty. He understood and we set a date for Friday instead.

I really thought Andy and I were just running friends. He was quite a bit older than me, and I didn't think he was interested in me that way. He was a wonderful man and an extremely romantic one at that. He absolutely believes in chivalry and treating a woman the way she should be treated. When he showed up at the house on Friday, he brought a beautiful bouquet of brightly colored flowers. No one had ever shown up with flowers for me before. I was thrilled.

We went to the restaurant and I felt like a deer in the headlights. This was fine dining to the extreme. The white linens, the gloved servers—it was like a scene from an old movie and I was actually in it. I will never forget the server coming to the table, after our meal was finished, with a cart of cheese and port and other libations. I didn't even know this was a course of dining: three courses were all I had ever seen. I had no idea that dinner could be so luxurious. I had often heard that you must enjoy your food, but this was amazing.

During the past year, I had dated a fair bit and had eaten at many restaurants, but I had never seen anything like this. Andy had to teach me a few things about fine dining, but it all worked out and we had a lovely evening. What a wonderful dinner, both in terms of food and company.

I was sorry to see the evening end, as I was having such a wonderful time. He drove me home and came to my side of the car and opened the car door for me. He took my arm and slowly walked me to the door. I thought to myself, *I think this is going to be more than just a friend.* I had a peculiar feeling he might kiss me. The anticipation was intense. I hadn't felt like this in a long time. Then we arrived at the door and he gently leaned closer and took my face in his hands and brushed my lips with his. Up to that point, I really thought we were just friends. I had to rethink where this was going and how I felt about it.

I was still traveling to Edmonton every other weekend to see my boys. Some weekends were better than others. More often than not, I would drive three hours to meet the boys at the police station and they would freak out by yelling and screaming that they didn't want to come with me. Heartbreaking as it was, I knew I was losing them. Sometimes I was successful and I would manage to get them in the car. Once we started driving away from the police station and they realized that their protests were futile, they would calm down and we would spend the weekend together in Calgary or Edmonton, depending on my finances at the time. I had stopped staying at Darla's house and tried to get hotel rooms when we stayed in Edmonton. It was more expensive, but I felt we had more family time that way.

On the weekends I didn't have the boys, I socialized with the running club. There were some really good, wholesome people in this group—they were good people to surround myself with. They looked out for me. Life was getting better. It felt calmer, productive, and normal. It was a better time than going to the bars every weekend. The group knew where I came from and some of them knew my family situation with the boys. I never felt judged by any of them. They accepted me for who I was, and I felt truly supported.

After my grand dining experience with Andy, we continued to run together on Wednesdays. The others probably noticed we were closer at other social events, too. In July, the club had a silent auction to raise money for Camp Horizon. Camp Horizon was a charity that provided programs to special needs children in Alberta. They might be suffering from cancer, diabetes, or other afflictions. Because they were the club's charity of choice, they would often use their facilities in the Kananaskis area for fundraisers.

The silent auction always included a multitude of items, some of which were far from normal. I wondered how they got away with some of those items. One year, a group of guys got together and auctioned themselves off as a "full monty" car wash. That's right—the highest bidder is treated to a carwash from a bunch of guys in the buff. The cost of the car wash: a few dollars. The gift to charity: worthy. Seeing those men in their morning glory: priceless.

The ladies felt challenged by their offer, so we decided to generate our own buzz of the night. We offered our services as French maids. The bidding for our services was very competitive. Andy knew I was one of the maids, so he made sure he had the highest bid. He already had a cleaning service, so I guess he figured it was for charity, or maybe he had ulterior motives...

The night we showed up at Andy's to deliver his prize, happened to be his birthday. We had some creative ideas about how to give him his money's worth. Some of the girls picked up the chemistry between Andy and me. So they made sure I was the maid beside him the entire evening.

It was all very innocent, though. We performed a can-can dance, cooked dinner for him, and prepared a bubble bath. Just so you know, Andy was in his shorts, and was the only one in the tub. Later we all sat on the deck and drank wine and chatted. The night couldn't have been better.

Our relationship progressed quickly after that. It was clear to our running group that we were more than friends from then on. By September we agreed I would move in with him. You might think we were rushing because I had only known him a few months, but when you're in a relationship with a loving, caring person, you know when the time is right. I heard in the movie *A Walk in the Clouds* that, "The heart wants what the heart wants." I couldn't agree more. A woman knows deep in her heart when it's right. There are no nagging thoughts, no whispers or doubts: only the calm of certainty. Time is just an illusion.

I was still driving to Edmonton every other weekend, but the number of times I succeeded in seeing the boys was plummeting, and fast. I never introduced the boys to Andy because I had enough to deal with just trying to be with them myself. The boys were now back in school and playing hockey. As in the past, Eddie wouldn't let me take them to hockey. I couldn't share in the one thing that made the boys happy. He continued to use hockey as a way of preventing me from seeing them.

Too often I would drive to Edmonton and be back in Calgary six hours later, sometimes without even a glimpse of the boys. I felt cheated in so many ways. But when they were there, a scene always followed—one that was dramatic, traumatic, and devastating for all of us. The kicking, screaming, and name calling that came from the boys as I tried to force them into the car was more than I could bear. Too often Blake was able to break free from me and run off. I was always so concerned for his safety. He was so angry and hurt I'm sure he wasn't thinking about looking both ways for cars.

During my marriage to Eddie and up until this point, I had always been seeing a therapist. I had changed therapists many times throughout the years but now that I was settled in Calgary I had found a therapist that I had really connected with, Sandy. Sandy and I would always discuss what was happening with the boys and how it was affecting us. She understood my daily torment about the boys. She understood and supported my attempts to see them, but she also knew it was hard on everybody. Many times she just listened through my sobbing. She helped me understand I had to do what was best for everybody, not just me. Sometimes it was difficult to hear her words. Many times I cried in the car and on the way home from her office.

After many sessions, we finally agreed that the best thing for everyone would be to continue driving to Edmonton, to show how much I wanted to see the boys. But I wouldn't force them to come with me anymore. I had to understand that the trauma of forcing them to be with me was not ingratiating them toward me, in fact it, might have had the opposite effect.

The boys were five and six years old, so little. It's hard to believe that they wouldn't want to be with their mother. Why were they always so dramatic at each encounter? Even though they were young, they still needed to respect me. This tug of war between mom and dad had to end; it was spoiling any bit of love between us. It was doing nothing but hurting everyone.

For the next year, I would drive to Edmonton at my negotiated times just so the boys would see I was making an effort. On one of my last attempts, I was already waiting at the police station when Eddie and the boys pulled into the parking lot. I walked over to the car and both boys were trying to hide from me. Brett was on the floor and Blake was off to the other side of the car. Blake yelled, "We're not going with you!" I said, "You don't have to, but I'm here if you'd like to."

Then Blake said, "I hate your guts!" Although my heart was breaking, I could only reply, "Well I'm still going to love you." Brett was very quiet, so I asked him if he'd like to go for lunch or ice cream. I offered to bring him back in an hour. He wouldn't come. I told him maybe next time he could come with me. He didn't shout or yell, but he had dismissed me. I saw it in his eyes.

Although I didn't get to spend any quality time with my children that day, I still felt I had made progress. Nobody was in hysterics, and I was able to tell them both I loved them dearly. They were able to see me there even if they didn't want to join me. At that time, I looked for any positive feedback at all. I continued those attempts over the next year.

After a year without any successful visits, things had to change again. With the support of my mother, my therapist, and Andy I made another heart-wrenching decision. I would no longer make the three-hour drive to Edmonton to see them. It wasn't an easy decision, I was heartbroken, but I felt like I was doing the right thing for my boys. Once again, my support team was there for me, supporting and encouraging me every step of the way. I still called the boys on the phone, but most of the time they refused to even come to the phone. They just hollered in the background that they hated my guts.

My mother had told me the story from Kings 3:5–14, in the Old Testament, about two women who approached Solomon declaring they were the mother of the infant child. They both had shared the same house, but one of the women had smothered her child during the night. She regretted doing this and took the other woman's living child. The other mother held a dead baby in her arms whom she knew was not her own, but she could not convince the other mother the living baby was hers. So they went to Solomon for judgment.

Solomon's judgment was unique. He listened to both women and then decided that the best answer was to cut the baby in half so that both mothers could share him. However, cutting the child would kill him. The mother who had already smothered her child was happy with the solution, but the other mother cried out and begged Solomon to let the other woman raise her child. Her love was so great for the child that she was willing to give up all contact with him so that he might live.

A mother's love is so profound. She knows she has to do everything for the child, not herself. She cannot be selfish. She would rather have the child not know her, be with her, or love her than to forsake him. That is a true measure of a mother's love: giving everything of herself so that her child can live and succeed.

You might think that a parent has authority over a child and not the other way around. They were very young, but through Eddie's interference, what chance did they have? Things were bound to develop as they did. I tried and tried and tried until I could no longer stand it. I was desperate for them to know I loved them. I sent presents for Christmas and their birthdays every year without even a thank-you or response from them. Sometimes I sent the cards to school to ensure they received them. For a few years, I even called the school photographer to get their school photos. I was desperate to know them and did anything that would bring me closer to them, even if it was only a picture. I wanted to be able to recognize them as they grew up. This was an awful time for me.

As stated on the Parent Alienation Canada Website[4]:

Parental alienation involves the systematic brainwashing, poisoning, and manipulation of children with the sole purpose of destroying a loving and warm relationship they once shared with a parent.

---

4   http://parentalalienationcanada.blogspot.com

This is what Eddie had done. Perhaps he had succeeded.

Andy was my rock during this time. He never judged me, he only supported me. He was always there to wipe away my tears and to hold me after my heartbreaking trips to Edmonton. He gave me so much, but he was never able to take my pain away.

Looking back, it's funny how Andy and I got together. We had been talking about marriage, but both of us had no desire to remarry. I'd had a bad experience and Andy wasn't sure it was for him either. But one night at a local restaurant, Teatro's, Andy and I were chatting about something silly when out of the blue he said, "*IF* I was to ask you to marry me, what would you say?" I said, "*IF* you were to ask me, I imagine I would say yes." A hypothetical question with a hypothetical answer. And that was that. No other talk or innuendos.

February of 2000, Andy took me on a vacation to Australia. He had been planning the trip before we started dating, but when we became serious he asked me to join him. I was thrilled to say the least. It was really an international gathering of the Hash House Harriers, our running club, so many of our friends were going to be there, too.

We had a wonderful vacation. I had never been to such a beautiful place. The scenery was breathtaking. Watching the sunset one night, I felt so connected to God and a peace swelled within me. It had been a long time since I felt such peace.

On February 29, Sadie Hawkins Day, we were visiting Honey Moon Bay in Tasmania. It was a beautiful day. The bay was amazing with water so clear that you could see right to the bottom. We were sitting on the rocks enjoying the sun when I gave Andy a card that stated, "*IF* you asked the question, the answer is yes." We both brushed it off without any further comments. Spending twenty-four hours with someone for twenty-one days is a true test of compatibility. We got along fantastically!

We arrived back in Canada in March. One cold Calgary day soon after we got home, Andy came home from work and had a small package in his hand. He placed it on the kitchen counter and said, "Here you go." To my surprise, I opened it to find a beautiful solitaire engagement ring. I said yes without any pause or second-guesses. I was thrilled.

We were married September 3, 2000 in a small but beautiful ceremony. I wanted to be married in our garden, but the weather didn't agree. Although it was a bright, sunny day, the winds were just too high. Thankfully we had a backup plan: the Fairmont Palliser Hotel. I spent the morning with my mom, my sister, and my best friends from the running group, Right Bun and Left Bun. We did the usual pampering and took time to rest, relax, and enjoy the day. From past experience, I knew I had to be prepared when it came to Eddie. So Andy and I decided to have some security guards that would be by my side until the ceremony and then outside of the room, just in case. I didn't want anything to deter from my day.

They say happiness comes to those who wait. Well, I had never been so happy. I certainly waited long enough through many trials to get to that momentous day. As Dad walked me down the aisle and told me he loved me, he could feel the happiness exude from my smile. He knew what I had suffered those years with Eddie, but now he could see the love between Andy and me, and he knew his daughter had met her soul mate.

I knew it too. I knew it was going to be a perfect day even with the weather. It would be perfect because I was marrying Andy, my true love. To paraphrase Elizabeth Barrett Browning, I loved him from the breadth and depth my soul could reach. And when he said "I do," my heart swelled with joy. I smiled at him, placed his hand in mine, and silently mouthed the words, "I love you." He winked and smiled. We were now one.

I knew from that day onward that Andy would stand by my side, no matter what. He was my rock. To this very day, he has been there for me: loving me, accepting me, and encouraging me to be the woman I can be.

Who could ask for more? No one.

The Years without Contact

I did stop driving to Edmonton on a regular basis, but I never stopped thinking about the boys. How could I? They were my flesh and blood and would always be part me of whether I could physically be with them or not. Even though I had decided not to physically attempt a reunion, I always wanted to know how they were and what was happening in their lives. I called often and tried to speak with them, sometimes to no avail. But I kept trying. Sometimes the boys would know I was on the phone; other times, I don't think Eddie told them.

I did my best to keep in touch and monitor their school progress too. For a few years, getting school photos kept me up-to-date, but one year was very sad. When I received them Brett wasn't smiling at all. The look on his face spoke volumes, and I began to worry, so I called Eddie. He told me Brett wouldn't smile because he had crooked teeth and felt self-conscious. To me it was more than just the teeth, but I wasn't involved that much in the boys' daily life. I had to let go. This was becoming torture for me.

Eddie was getting on with his life. He met a woman named Corrine. She had three children who were younger than Blake and Brett. In the early days of their relationship, they tried living together for a while. The time they were together during Christmas I sent the boys their gifts: Nintendo

Game Boys. I thought they would love the electronic games. They were the rage that year, and I felt it was important to give the boys something they might not get otherwise.

Anyway, because Corrine had a little boy close in age to Brett and Blake, I decided to buy him a Game Boy as well. I didn't want Christmas morning to be awkward by excluding one of the boys. When the Game Boys arrived at the house Eddie phoned me and was furious. I was stunned. He told me I had no right to buy Corrine's son a Christmas present.

Here I thought I was being especially kind and sensitive to the children at the house, but he had derailed me. He asked me where I purchased them so he could return all of them. I was devastated. Maybe Eddie thought I would upstage his gifts. Perhaps he just wanted the money. I don't know why he felt the boys couldn't receive the gifts from their own mother.

I don't know if the boys ever received my gifts or cards after that. I continued to send the gifts, but I started sending the cards to their school. I even copied some of the cards before I sent them in case the boys ever questioned me in the future about why I never sent them anything growing up. I thought about them daily and tried to do my best. I was so concerned that they would think I didn't love them or that I didn't care about them.

During this year, Eddie's dad became very ill and could no longer live alone, so he moved in with Eddie. It was pretty crowded with Eddie, the boys, Corrine and her children, and now Eddie's dad. It was only an eight hundred square feet house with one bathroom. It was too small for three adults and five small kids. Corrine thought it was too small as well, so she moved out and purchased a house nearby.

When Eddie's relationship with Corrine was going well, I never heard from him. I paid the child support every month on time without much contact. Three years went by without a word from him.

During this time I was hard at work on someone else: me. I continued with my therapy and started to accept the situation for what it was. I began to heal and not persecute myself for not being in the boys' life. It had been out of my control from the very beginning.

One day in late 2004, while I was working as a volunteer for the United Way, I received a call on my cell phone from Eddie. I couldn't believe he was calling me after such a long time. I knew he was receiving my support money, but there had been no other contact. The purpose of his call was... you guessed it. He wanted more money. He said he needed money for the boys' extracurricular activities. *What?* I replied, "You have the child support money. Isn't that enough?" He didn't respond. Knowing Eddie, he had probably spent some of it on other things.

A few weeks later, I learned why he was calling me. It was November and Andy and I were driving down the road. We were going to visit family friends in Airdrie, just north of Calgary. My cell phone buzzed, and, lo and behold, it was Eddie again. This time he wasn't asking for money.

He called and said I had to take the boys. They had to live with me now. Shocked wasn't the word. It had been three years without much contact and now he wanted the boys to live with me? After everything I had been through, I had finally accepted the boys would not be part of my life. I had started a new life. My boys didn't know me anymore. I doubted they would even want to live with me. I was a stranger to them now.

Eddie explained that he and Corrine had split up and he was going through a rough time. He just couldn't raise the boys anymore, and it was my turn to take them. The first thing I blurted out after the shock wore off was that I would need to get to know the boys again and they would need to know me before we could uproot them. I explained they were older now and they should have a say in the decision. He replied, "Yeah, whatever" in his apathetic way and hung up the phone.

I didn't know what to think when the call ended. It was so unlike him to want me to have the boys. After everything we had been through, that had been the one thing I knew about Eddie. He would never give up the kids. He probably wasn't serious. He was probably just venting because of the way things ended with Corrine. Although I did want to be part of the boys' life and said so to Eddie, I wanted it to be because they wanted to be with me and not because Eddie was fed up.

It was important that my relationship with the boys start on good terms. So, I just let things go. Through my therapy and just getting a little older and a little wiser, I had grown so much. I didn't hear from Eddie again for some time. I learned that he and Corrine got back together again for a while. When she was in Eddie's life, it was better for the boys and for me too.

It was only a few weeks after this call that Eddie's father passed away. This was a traumatic time for Eddie. Although he'd had some bad times with his father, after his mother left, his father was Eddie's only family. They were very close. He had been there for him through all his troubles.

He was the only reason Eddie could function, to the degree he could, in society. His father held him accountable on many fronts. Eddie never wanted to disappoint his father. It upset his father a great deal when Eddie drank or if he was unemployed. Eddie did his best to manage his drinking and to keep a job. Eddie tried hard to succeed in life because he wanted his dad to be proud of him. He was still drinking and still struggling with life but at least he was making an effort to keep his life together. His father was his reason to make this effort. Unfortunately when we were together, Eddie's dad never questioned my bruises or the way he treated me. But all in all, I liked him, and I was very sad to hear the news about his passing. It also put me on high alert as to what Eddie might do next. Eddie had trouble dealing with things emotionally, and sometimes he became erratic or violent as a result.

Generally speaking, Eddie never called me. He was quite happy with the arrangement: I paid child support every month and he didn't have to deal with me. However, one morning I did get a panicky call from him. He asked me if the boys were with me. I said: "Are you kidding me! They don't know my address, and they don't want to see me. Eddie, what the hell is going on?"

He told me that when he got home, after a night of drinking, the boys weren't there. This was very upsetting to me. The boys were only eleven and twelve years old. I called my mother and my therapist to talk about the situation. They both told me to let it go. There was nothing I could do. It was my father that told me that Blake and Brett must have created an island in the stream—a safe place to go when they needed to be away from Eddie.

His experience told him that when people feel threatened, they find a place and stay there until they feel safe again. Perhaps they had a close friend or neighbor that knew about Eddie's issues who was now watching out for them. I felt I had no choice to but to accept that. I hadn't been in their lives and didn't know their neighbors or friends. What could I do?

The death of Eddie's father was a life-changing event. I heard from his sister in Calgary that even with Corrine in his life, the downward spiral began. He started drinking more and more, both in volume and frequency. He drank to escape. Eventually, drinking just wasn't enough. He could still feel the pain, and reality wasn't looking so good. So, he needed to try something that would eliminate or reduce his pain.

He started calling me more often during this time. He continuously asked for more money and always used the boys as an excuse. The boys were growing and eating a lot of food, they needed to go to boxing tournaments, they had extracurricular activities. The excuses never ended. I didn't know what was really going on. I thought it was just another ploy to get money. I knew he was struggling with work, but it wasn't my responsibility to support him. I later learned that Eddie started asking his sisters for more money and gave them similar excuses.

He told me he didn't have a job and couldn't get one in Edmonton. But I discovered he had been driving and doing truck deliveries for a food company until the company started noticing shortages of goods, especially cigarettes. Eddie said it wasn't his fault, but eventually he was fired for stealing. Unfortunately that was the most significant job he held since college.

After getting fired, he bounced around from job to job. One of his jobs was driving a recycling truck. But that didn't last long. He said he couldn't be a garbage man and quit. You know, I learned that it takes all kinds to make the world turn around—all kinds of people to do all kids of jobs. Even a garbage man can take pride in his work. I remember watching a *Frasier* episode about Roz dating a garbage man, Roger. She felt ashamed about his job, but he enjoyed it and thought he was providing a worthwhile service. Why can't we all be like that? Eddie couldn't. He didn't like the status surrounding that job, so he walked away. What about the status of not being able to support your family?

By this time his drinking was so out of control that he was barely functioning. He would get an odd job here and there for part-time hours or temporary work. It was really the child support and the money his friends and family gave him that kept him afloat, when he actually paid the bills. Many times he didn't. Eventually Corrine couldn't take it anymore and left for the last time. Then Eddie really changed. Corrine had been a safety valve, and after she left Eddie became even more unstable.

Reuniting

Years had passed since I'd last heard from the boys. I tried phoning at least once a year, but every time I called Eddie would answer and call the boys and shout I was on the phone. It was always loud enough for me to hear on the other end; Eddie had no phone etiquette. But when they were home, I could hear them in the background shouting that they didn't want to talk with me. They would yell, "We hate her guts!"

Although I came to expect these outbursts, it was still very heartbreaking and sad. I tried not to let it bother me, but, to this day, those statements still hurt. I still called to reach out to them and let them know I tried to stay in contact. They were children, but they still decided not to take my calls. I continued to send Christmas presents and gifts for other occasions, and one year I even sent them home-cooked dinners.

In November 2007, I received a message on my cell phone from Eddie. He was asking for money, again. I mean, I wanted to pay my fair share, but I was getting fed up with the monthly calls asking for additional money. It was not only excessive, but it was also causing me to go more in debt. He would always use the boys for the reason he needed the money. I was torn. I knew I was paying sufficient child support but how could I deprive my children of any need that they had. Each time I reluctantly gave him the money. I believed it was going to my children.

I called Eddie back, and when someone picked up the phone I started spouting off why I thought it was just too much. Needless to say, the tone of my voice left nothing to the imagination. I yelled into the phone, "Why should I keep giving money to some asshole who took my kids away from me?" Suddenly the phone was disconnected.

I did feel satisfied for being able to finally vent my frustration and tell Eddie how I felt. I was somewhat surprised that he just hung up on me without even enduring a screaming match. Later that day I received another call. It was Eddie, he was out but Blake had called him on his cell phone upset. Blake told Eddie that he answered the phone and heard me yelling and didn't know what was happening. I was crushed. I hadn't talked to Blake for almost six years and the first time he heard my voice again was when I finally exploded at who I thought was Eddie. I hung up the phone and tried calling their house. It took two tries before Blake would pick up. I told him how sorry I was and apologized profusely. I told him I was angry with his father and I thought it had been his father who answered the phone. He listened without any response. I told him I loved him and that I would like to be in touch. Then I hung up the phone.

At least I was able to explain myself to Blake and the incident did have a silver lining. After that, whenever I called the house, both Blake and Brett would at least pick up the phone. It was mostly a one-sided conversation, but at least they were listening. It was a first step toward getting to know them again. I was able to share some of myself with them and tell them I loved them. That was so important to me.

Originally when Facebook came out I was reluctant to join. I had been in hiding for a number of years, and I wasn't sure I was comfortable with people knowing anything about me. Then things changed. I began hearing stories about how people who had given up their children for adoption were connecting again after a lifetime apart. I thought perhaps the boys and I could be those people too. After some thinking and talking with friends, I decided to join. It would be an easy way for the boys to start a relationship with me and get to know me without feeling pressured.

I am not a very patient person, so when I joined Facebook I quickly started looking for Blake and Brett. I found Blake first and sent him a friend request. It was ignored. I accepted that. Then one of my friends told me that kids didn't want their parents knowing what they were posting on

Facebook; that made me feel better about it. At least they knew I tried, and they could reach out to me in a noncommittal way when they felt ready.

It took a few more attempts to find Brett. But in his first response to me, he wasn't truthful about his identity. The responder said he was from B.C., but I could see where he went to school and his friends from Edmonton. I accepted that he didn't want to communicate with me for now, so I let it go. Brett ignored me for some time on Facebook, but after a while he did start e-mailing me.

He didn't contact me to get to know me. His first e-mail was about money:

This is Brett. My dad needed me to contact you. Blake has some hockey tryouts coming up with St. Albert and Grand Prairie and I owe money for my soccer program at school. Dad thought you were going to help out.

It was a start. Brett had a reason to open up communication, and I embraced it. Unfortunately, he did not know I had been sending money for all their extracurricular activities. It had been Eddie who wasn't using the funds to pay off the expenses. But I didn't want Brett caught in the middle, so I just asked him to get his father to call me and we'd make arrangements about the fees.

In my message, I also asked him how things had been going. I mentioned college when I got the chance. I told him if he ever thought about going, he didn't need to worry about those costs. I would take care of it. What I have learned from my years is that education can help you out of a bad situation, if you want. Having the inclination to learn is important. For a time, Eddie wanted to learn, and I thought his own experiences might have helped him in the field of social work. But Eddie's inner demons were too strong to overcome.

Brett would be graduating from ninth grade that year. I remember my ninth-grade graduation and the fun we had: the cherry-red dress and the Corvette. I didn't want him to miss out, so I offered to pay for graduation as well. I'm sorry to say that Brett didn't respond to my messages.

I didn't hear anything more from them for another few months. I had been so annoyed with Eddie that he no longer had my phone number. When the harassment became too much for me to handle, I changed my number. It meant separation, but at least the boys knew how to get in touch by e-mail. Eddie didn't appreciate knowing the boys could and sometimes did get in touch with me, so he actually called the information line for the government department, where I worked, and told them a horrific story about me not being involved with my children. He told them there was a desperate situation and he needed to get in touch with me.

That was a very vindictive thing to do. Not that I knew the person who eventually gave me the message, but this was my place of work and I had kept my personal life private. And now Eddie had created a lie about me. He had taken so much from me. He had done so much damage to my personal life; I did not want him to damage my professional life too. I decided not to call Eddie back. I would not give him the credit of letting him know he was affecting my work. I did contact Brett and Blake through e-mail and Facebook to see if they needed anything. I asked them when I could call and talk with them. I actually got a response from Blake. He hadn't been communicating with me up until then, and really he just inserted an e-mail that Brett had written (that I hadn't received) into his e-mail. It didn't matter. Blake had made a step toward communicating with me. I would take whatever I could get.

The e-mail consisted of Brett asking for some money. He had a boxing tournament in Montréal and needed spending money. I was okay with this request because I thought that traveling was important and rewarding. He was traveling with his boxing club, so it should have been a great experience for him. I deposited $200 in his account. I didn't get a thank you. I didn't mind giving money for these experiences, but I expected him to thank me. Instead, I received a rather ungrateful e-mail: *"Ya! What about school fees! They cost a lot!"* I was a leaky faucet that spilled money without even turning on a tap.

I was discouraged and upset by Brett's attitude toward me. I spoke to my therapist and other friends about this. I really didn't want to find myself being taken advantage of and used because I was so desperate for my children's love. They reminded me that teenagers tend to take and take. Their boundaries are nonexistent. They push you until you reach the brink. I was only involved infrequently; I could only imagine what it must have been like for other parents who had to deal with this day in and day out. No wonder there is so much trouble at that age.

Even though others warned me about teenagers' attitudes, I thought the responses were unacceptable, so I sent Brett an e-mail telling him how I felt. I told him: *"For your information I pay your school fees every year. If your* *father chooses to spend that money on something other than school fees then that is not my fault. You should realize that in addition to all of the extra money I give throughout the year I also give your father $850 a month to support you two. That is a lot of money. I wasn't able to see you growing up. You wouldn't even talk to me and I still give. Maybe your father should get a job."* I know it was inappropriate, but sometimes emotions spill out. Unfortunately the damage was done and I couldn't take my comment back.

Brett's response: *"Ya well my dad actually helps us out."*

It was much later and by accident that I discovered that there hadn't been a trip to Montréal. I assumed the money was spent on something entirely different, but I didn't bring it up again. I didn't want the relationship to be only about money; I wanted more than that.

I was relieved that our exchange didn't stop Brett from contacting me later. Both Blake and Brett were messaging me regularly through Facebook. It was great speaking with them again, but many of our conversations began or ended with more requests for money. They had been living only with Eddie for years now, so what they knew of me was mostly what they'd heard from their father.

Our own visits had been few and far between, and so they didn't really know me as their mother. And what they knew now was that I sent them money quite willingly. Believe it or not, although at times I felt used, it was still a relationship—a relationship that I hadn't had in so many years. I was willing to take any crumb I could. I wasn't trying to buy the boys by giving them anything they wanted, but I was trying to be involved in any manner available to me. I desperately wanted to be part of their life.

I used the e-mails from Blake (Brett's initial e-mail), to start a dialogue with him. Even though he had only forwarded Brett's previous e-mail without any personal comments, I thought I would take the chance and see if he was open to talking. In response to his message, I asked how things were going. He was starting twelfth grade that year, so he must have been excited about his final year of high school. I was so proud that my son was going to graduate.

Blake told me a little about himself. He was working part-time, but he too needed some money. Hockey fees were quite high, and he tried to contribute to them by working. Then he told me why he needed the extra money. He had taken his father's car, even though he didn't have a driver's license, and had been in an accident. Now his father was refusing to pay for hockey.

Of course I talked to him about taking his father's car without permission or a license, but I thought it was important to stay in hockey. I had heard so many stories about kids staying in sports and how it helped them stay out of trouble and gave them a purpose. I wanted Blake to be committed to that, too. I didn't think removing hockey was the best way to punish him for what he had done. I asked him for some details about hockey. I told him that I could possibly help him out, but I also wanted him to contribute from his earnings. He needed to understand both the repercussions of his actions and take responsibility for the financial ramifications. It was important to me to instill the value of a work ethic in him.

I started asking details about the money required and payments and said I would pay his hockey fees directly to the association. I couldn't understand why he got upset that I wanted to pay directly. Then the dates for payment and the amount required kept changing. By this point, I was getting suspicious about his reactions and the constant changes to what he needed. Because I had learned the hard way about things falling through, I wanted to make sure where the money was going this time. Blake got defensive and finally had enough of my questions and told me to talk to his dad.

I knew from that moment that I was missing something, or that some part of the story had been fabricated. There were too many signs. Our budding relationship was marred by finances. I was heartbroken. I couldn't even buy their love. What was I to do?

Since the boys and I started e-mailing and talking online, Eddie felt that he was justified with his continued requests for money. First he asked through the boys, and then he started contacting me directly. His e-mails requesting money were constant, and he always made a remark about the boys needing something or other. He had learned my weak spot, the boys, and was twisting me to accommodate him.

At the time, I didn't know that his life had deteriorated so much, which was the real reason he wanted money so often. He was drinking too much and getting into financial trouble. He was not able to pay the rent or his other bills. I sent monthly maintenance amounts that should have covered the basics, like rent, but he wasn't using the money for that. He was using it for alcohol and other things.

On August 5, 2008, I received a very desperate email from Eddie: *"This is very serious. There is no way out this time. I love them so much. We need $1,200 tomorrow or we will be on the street. I am going to tell the boys tonight."*

I was devastated. How could I let my boys get evicted? They had grown up without their mother—I couldn't let them be homeless too. Then I got angry. How could Eddie let this happen? Why wouldn't he get a job to help pay the bills? The economy was still booming in Alberta, so there was no reason not to have a job, unless you didn't want one. Even the local donut shop was paying above minimum wage.

It was time for Eddie to suck it up and take care of his responsibilities. He needed to take pride in himself and stop living off me. He had to make some changes in his life because he was primarily responsible for the boys. So I vented my frustration and let him know how I felt about him not contributing. But I gave him the money. I had no choice, and it was something I could do for my boys.

I know I was enabling him by giving him money every time he asked, but I thought of it as giving him money for the boys. I was financially able to help out, so even though I felt used, I had easier access to money than Eddie; I had credit. I had hoped from that point on things would change. Perhaps with this injection of cash he could get caught up. I paid the rent, the outstanding school fees, and Blake's hockey fees. In the end it cost me $2,400. In hindsight I see this was a big mistake but I did give him the money directly. I thought it might be humiliating for him if I was actually paying his bills and I really did want him to take pride in himself. I told him: "There better not be a next time. If there is you'd better be prepared for me to pay your landlord directly." And for a while there was peace.

As the months passed the boys and I were communicating more often. They would even talk with me by phone now and then. It was so nice to hear their voices. They had grown up so much; I could hear it in their voices. In October, Brett asked if we could meet. It was a very casual request through a message on Facebook. He suggested that it might be nice if we could just hang out some time. I was shocked and really couldn't believe it at first. I was excited that he wanted to interact with me and perhaps get to know me. I had been dreaming of this reunion for years. But it was just Brett and not Blake. I had hoped they would both want to meet, but I thought that if the meeting with Brett went well, he would talk to Blake.

I was counting the days until we would meet at the West Edmonton Mall. We arranged to meet on Saturday, October 25, 2008. We would spend the day together at the mall. The mall is so big and has so many attractions that you could spend days there. They have a water park, an amusement park, movie theater, hotel, and, of course, retail shops. It was going to be a fun-filled day. There would be just enough distraction for us to slowly get to know each other again, without any pressure. The last time we had been there together was the year we splurged at Christmas and stayed in the truck room. Maybe they would remember that wonderful time we had shared so long ago.

As the time drew closer for our meeting, Blake became curious and eventually asked it he could come, too. I was so happy. It was an opportunity that I had dreamed about and had built up in my mind. You know how it is when you look forward to something for so long; you have this image in your head how it will turn out. Sometimes the reality is even better, but other times you've built it up so much that the experience can only be a let down.

I was talking to Eddie a bit during this time. He was telling me that both boys were very nervous about the meeting. He said that he and Brett had a few heart-to-heart conversations about this. Brett was terrified that he might not like me; that we might not get along. What if he didn't remember me at all? His dad reassured him that everything would be fine. He convinced Brett that the meeting would be a good thing.

After I heard that both Brett and Blake wanted to meet, I was on cloud nine. You couldn't bring me down. Because I had been wishing for this day for so many years, I didn't want to blow it, so I called my therapist. I wanted to make sure that I didn't scare them off by overwhelming them with hugs and kisses. My therapist reminded me of the safety issue once again.

We went through some scenarios of how the day might unfold so I would be prepared for possible outcomes, even the outcome I didn't want. I wanted this to work so much that I didn't want to think about the possibility my heart would be broken again. My therapist provided some great advice about the reality of the situation to help prepare me. But how prepared can you be when you are meeting your own children after many years?

I did think that Eddie could use this meeting to ask for even more money. He had recently started working at a glass company, and I was happy he was working. Now he might be able to handle the financial responsibility of taking care of the boys. He might also build up some confidence and change his attitude. Having a job can do more for a person than just pay the bills. I was hoping it would do more for Eddie.

While Eddie had been unemployed for so long, he received many speeding tickets that went unpaid. Consequently, one day he was pulled over and his car was impounded. In October, Eddie sent me an e-mail telling me his car was in for repair, a lie. The repair was going to cost $1,700, and they wouldn't release the car until it was paid in full. He also said they were charging him $22 for every day the car stayed at the lot.

This didn't make sense to me, and after some inquiries Eddie finally confessed that the car was impounded. He proceeded to tell me that his car was the only good thing he had, and it would destroy him if he lost it. Then he pulled the boys into it. He said he needed the car for the boys. Winter was approaching, and it can get pretty cold in Edmonton. This I knew from living there, so I didn't want the boys to be outside in minus thirty-degree weather.

He promised it would be a loan and he would pay me back. He had a job, so now he would have some money. Everything he said sounded good—he had an excuse, but he also had a plan. I was only days away from meeting the boys for the first time in too many years. How could I disappoint them? I gave Eddie the money. Deep down I knew I probably wouldn't be repaid. I knew he could barely pay the rent, but he did seem genuine.

I lived in Calgary and the car wasn't registered in my name, which made it very difficult for me to pay the impound directly. Reluctantly, I had to give Eddie the money so that he could get his car out. In my mind, I thought I was just paying the support money a few days early. However, I should have known better based on past experiences.

Eddie didn't get his car out of the impound. Instead, he went to the casino and spent everything I gave him. Of course it wasn't his intention to lose all the money. He said it was his first time there, and perhaps it was. Maybe he thought he could turn the money into more and pay off his bills, I don't know. But it was a disaster. As they saying goes: "the house always wins." I asked him what happened, why he went there, and why he spent all the money. He told me he kept going to the bank machine, and he withdrew money until there was none left. How could that happen? Aren't there daily withdrawal limits? Was this another excuse?

Why did I keep doing this to myself? Why couldn't I learn from past mistakes? When it came to Eddie, whether I lived with him or not, I always seemed to fall into the same pattern. If he said something or did something and had an excuse, I always believed him or forgave him. Would I ever be able to break free of him?

This was the last straw, or so I hoped. I realized I could no longer give the money to Eddie. I didn't stop giving; I just paid the bills directly. I needed to know that my boys would be safe and that they had a place to live. I had to take charge. Maybe Eddie knew that too.

The car was still in the impound lot after I found out about the casino. The money was gone and the problem wasn't going away. Blake sent me a text me in desperation. He knew the situation. He told me his dad had to ask me for help. Now, he too was asking for help.

He said his dad made a mistake and that he wasn't normally a gambler. He didn't know why it happened, but now they needed my help again. Then he said, "Please, Mom, it's too cold to catch the bus." That plea did me in. I was just days away from meeting them. I was vulnerable and didn't want anything to mess up our reunion. I knew it was cold, so I gave in. I got a bank draft and managed to pay the impound fees directly. I paid the minimal amount I could to get the car out. This meant paying some of the outstanding fines, but there were still some more current ones remaining. Eddie would have to take care of them himself.

Five days later, I drove to Edmonton for our planned meeting. I was going to meet them at the 7-11 convenience store close to their house. On the three-hour drive to Edmonton, I was both excited and nervous to meet them. The moment I had dreamed of for so long was only a couple of hours away. My mind was abuzz with so many things. Would I even recognize them? What would we talk about? What would they think of me?

I arrived at the store a little early. I positioned my car so I could see people coming in and out of the door. I tried to call them on their cell phones, but it went straight to voice mail. Either they weren't charged or they were turned off. I watched the people come in and out and wondered, *Could that be them?*

Finally, a tall young man walked in the parking lot. He went into the store. While he was there I kept asking myself, *Could that be Blake?* It seemed like it could be, but I hadn't seem him in so long that I wasn't sure. When he came out, I called out to him. It was Blake. I was overwhelmed.

Here was my little boy all grown up. As he walked toward me, I felt over-come. Tears welled up inside me. Here was my little boy. I kept thinking that over and over. I couldn't get over it. I tried to contain my feelings as he drew closer, as I didn't want to make him feel uncomfortable.

A couple of days before the meeting, we decided to go to the water park at West Ed, as the locals call it. Blake told me he had to go home to put the dog in the kennel. I asked if his dad was home and he told me that he was working. I had to be prepared in case he wasn't. I said I would give him a ride to the house and I would love to meet his dog. We drove the few blocks to his house. We chatted a bit and I realized how polite and well spoken he was. It was a casual conversation, just about what he was doing. It felt great to be talking with my son.

We stayed a few minutes to take care of the dog and then we went to his friend T.J.'s house, to pick up Brett. Brett's face was just as I remembered it. His features were older and more pronounced, but it was definitely him. Unfortunately, he was more uncomfortable meeting me than Blake was. He had a hard time looking at me. He stole a glance every now and then, but he had a hard time looking at me directly.

The drive to West Ed seemed to take forever. It had been years since we had seen each other, so there were some uncomfortable silences. There was a lot of history to overcome, and I knew it wouldn't change in the first meet-ing. I was glad that both boys decided to come. It was nice just looking at them. But it also reminded me that I had missed so much of their lives. As much as that hurt, I knew I couldn't dwell on it or we would never go forward. This was a new beginning.

When we got closer to the mall we decided to have lunch first at Boston Pizza. It was a little awkward sitting down with them, but Blake was able to make some small talk. Having lunch with them was lovely; I reveled in every moment. When your children ask to meet you after so many years, you can't take anything for granted. Would there even be a next time? Nothing is guaranteed, so I absorbed everything. Every little thing they did, the way they gestured and the way they walked. Everything was new again.

I kept looking at them so I wouldn't forget. I wanted to emblazon their faces in my memory. I even paid attention to what they ordered at the restaurant so I would know what they liked to eat. I brought a couple of photo albums with me, with pictures from when they were little boys, to help start things off. I also wanted them to realize I was with them when they were younger and to show them proof of some loving times together. It didn't go as well as I had hoped it would. They just flipped through the pages. There was no reminiscing or talking about particular pictures. They weren't comfortable. They were a bit shy, and it may have been too much. I was disappointed, but I was still with them and that was the first step in rebuilding our relationship.

After lunch we dove over to the mall and the water park. Brett chose to sit in the front seat. I guess he thought as it would only be a couple of minutes that this would be a safe opportunity for him to check me out a little bit closer. He did glance at me many times. It was obvious that he was quite curious to figure out who I was and what I was about.

I understood that going to the water park with your mom may not be so cool at fifteen and sixteen, so I only asked that they stay with me when we got inside. They thought I would be going down the slides, too. I thought that might be overdoing it for the first time, so I just found a comfortable place on the side and told them where I would be when they were done.

After a couple of hours, they found me. I could see Blake's tattoo down his ribs. It was his last name written in Old English, and he was quite proud of it. I took the opportunity to take some pictures. At first they protested, but they eventually gave in. I wanted to cherish this day with my boys and a few new pictures would help.

After we left the water park, it was clear that Brett was becoming more uncomfortable. It must have been too much time without any distractions. I didn't want him to feel anxious or uneasy, so I decided to limit the day. As the boys were hungry, we went for some smoothies at Jugo Juice. Teenagers can certainly eat a lot! On the way back, we picked up some pizza and I drove them home so that they could be on their own and just absorb everything that had happened that day. I didn't want to crowd them, so I drove back to Calgary.

It was a wonderful day—a good first meeting. I didn't know if there would be a second visit, but I felt elated that the first one was more than I had hoped for.

Finally Help

After meeting the boys in October, there was no mention of another meeting. We didn't talk about the first meeting either, not like you would normally do. There was no, "it was so good to finally meet you," or "I'm glad we had the chance to finally get together." Maybe I was expecting too much. Maybe teenage boys just didn't act that way. But I was their mother and I wanted more. Don't get me wrong—I was so glad to have that first meeting, but it just initiated my desire for more visits.

One day I was doing some Christmas shopping for the boys and I felt like getting in touch with them, so I texted Blake. As I went to the various stores, I would text him about certain items I was thinking about purchasing. He would then text me back if he liked it or not. Sometimes he would text back a note about another item or a similar item to look at. It was so nice to have instant responses; it was like he was right there shopping with me. Technology is great when you can share moments with someone without actually being there.

Blake did seem more comfortable with me in October, and I was glad he felt comfortable now. He seemed engaged enough in our long-distance relationship, even if we were only communicating about gifts. Unfortunately I didn't get the same response from Brett. He was much more reserved at the first meeting, and he still seemed distant. Although he was younger when I had to leave, we had always been closer. Now it seemed we were much further apart. I think he was still holding on to some anger toward me for leaving.

Another day, I received more intense texts from Blake. Things weren't good at home. Things were getting pretty bad in Eddie's life then. Blake wasn't sure he could be alone. He was feeling sad, lonely, and depressed. There seemed to be desperation in the tone of his texts and e-mails that led me to believe he was frightened. Frightened of what, I wasn't sure. He was feeling desperate and asked for some advice. We were texting back and forth and I tried phoning him, but he wouldn't answer.

Brett was over at T.J.'s house visiting. I tried to encourage Blake to go T.J.'s house so that he wouldn't be alone. He could talk with Brett and TJ. TJ was his friend too. He needed the support from his brother because only he would know what they were living through. I didn't want him to feel alone. I was touched that Blake felt close enough to reach out to me, but it broke my heart that I couldn't be there for him.

Later that night I started to think about all the texts Blake and I were sending each other. Something was nagging me about what was said and the way it was said. I had been communicating with Blake quite a bit through Facebook and email and the texts I was receiving didn't have the same style of writing that Blake would use. It was just a feeling I had. I really felt that the messages weren't coming from Blake. I needed to confirm my suspicion so I sent a text asking the sender to confirm his identity. I asked a pretty basic question about what we did during our visit after the water park. Blake should have had no problem remembering. I didn't get any response from my request; so much for my wonderful day of shopping with Blake. It was another memory robbed from me.

I had given the boys phones so that we could be in touch, but during our day in Edmonton, Blake said his phone wasn't charged. At the time, it seemed a reasonable response, although I'd heard that teenagers usually charged their phones in order to be in constant touch with their friends. I assumed that Eddie had Blake's phone and was using it himself. Once again, Eddie took something away from me—a means of having a personal connection with the boys, and I was paying for it, literally.

Life for Eddie was spiraling downhill at this point. He continued to call me in desperation. At times, Eddie had tried to be responsible and help support the family. Those times were few and far between, but he did try.

He went from being a business partner in a club to a dispatcher job at a local trucking company to taking orders for a glass company.

Unfortunately, each day didn't get any better, and he didn't last long at any of the jobs. Because of his drinking he missed too much work. He had good intentions, but, like most of us, he was flawed and his flaws got the better of him. His consumption of alcohol was out of control. And when he had money, he used that money to buy alcohol. His drinking affected his work and he was eventually fired from all his jobs that year. He had never really recovered from his original knee injury, and through the years he always had workers' compensation topping up his income. To add insult to injury, they were also fed up with him and were threatening to stop his claim.

A few weeks after my visit with the boys; Eddie realized that he was going downhill fast. He did have the insight to reach out for some help and contacted a pastor in his neighborhood. The pastor, Howard, and his wife, Carmen, were wonderful support for Eddie and the boys. They did their best to make sure the boys were safe, and they tried to get Eddie the help he needed.

It was clear to Eddie and everyone around him that if he didn't get help for his drinking, and soon, that he would either lead a long, miserable life or a very short miserable life. Over the years, Eddie would come to these realizations every now and then, but was never able to commit and stick with it. Even when he was hurting me, he would later realize that he needed help. But he never did change. I wondered if he could do it now. I hoped and prayed he could both for his sake and for the boys', but it was a decision only he could make.

All this turmoil was also affecting the boys, as you can imagine. I learned sometime after our visit in October, Blake had been kicked out of school. I always thought that education could bring a person out of their socioeconomic limitations—that's why I went back to school. I was so discouraged when I heard that my son didn't finish high school. He was so capable, and I knew how much he wanted it, but everything just got to be too much. And now Brett wasn't doing well either.

I didn't really know what was going on. I paid child support and I paid the bills directly, but I didn't know any details of their daily life. It wasn't until later that I heard about what was happening.

It didn't take Howard long to realize the seriousness of Eddie's situation. He knew Eddie needed help and he knew the fastest way to get this help would be to have Eddie committed to the psychiatric ward at the Royal Alexander hospital. Eddie must have been desperate because he agreed. The plan was that the doctor's at the hospital would assess Eddie and treat him for whatever mental illness that might ail him. Once he was considered to be stable he would be admitted to a rehabilitation facility for his alcoholism and drug use. I didn't find this out until some time after the fact. Even if I had known, I couldn't have done much. I couldn't be with the boys and they made it very clear that they didn't want me to know anything or to be involved.

I was glad that Eddie had reached out to Howard for guidance and support. I don't know what he told Howard about me. I'm sure it wasn't good, but I couldn't change that. Hopefully Howard understood that there were two sides to every story and that because of Eddie's issues, he might not be getting all the facts. I assume that in his position as a pastor he wouldn't judge me or my actions, but that he was only there to help Eddie and the boys. While Eddie was hospitalized, nobody ever contacted me to tell me the boys were on their own. I guess they knew it wouldn't make a difference. The boys weren't going to let me take care of them. Howard and Carmen made sure the boys were taken care of. There were always people checking up on them.

Ever since I left Eddie and the boys, Christmastime was emotionally painful. I usually tried to go away for Christmas, so I could think about something else. This year I tried to be more involved to make things a little better for Brett and Blake. I knew Eddie was not doing well and was trying to improve his life with the help of the pastor, so I sent the boys an e-mail to find out their plans. I didn't get an immediate response.

I told them I was sending their gifts by mail and some home-cooked meals by bus. I thought they could use the home-cooked meals because I didn't think Eddie cooked very often. I knew Brett loved chili, so I made some and froze it in containers. The meals would be delivered right to the house. With little effort, they could have a nice family supper. All Eddie had to do was put the meals in the freezer and hide the gifts away until Christmas morning. I had no idea that Eddie was in the hospital, or I would have made other arrangements or would have delivered them myself.

Every Christmas I sent the boys an e-mail wishing them a Merry Christmas and letting them both know I loved them. That year I sent them an e-mail, but I didn't get any replies. This wasn't out of the ordinary, but as we had started communicating a bit more, I thought I would hear something. I found out later that immediately after Eddie was discharged from the hospital he had been admitted to the rehab facility for alcohol addiction. It turned out that Christmas morning the boys were by themselves. They visited their father on Christmas day at rehab, but there had been no Christmas morning breakfast, or opening of gifts, or lying down on the couch after a big meal of turkey and dressing: nothing.

They were just fifteen and sixteen that year. They were really too young to take care of themselves, but they were doing the best they could. With only one parent, Blake had grown up quickly. When I did find out about Eddie's treatment, from the boys and the pastor, long after the fact, I also discovered something that in some ways made my heart break and in other ways really disappointed me. I found out that when the boys got my packages, they just ripped them open the same day. There was no fanfare or excitement—nothing. I was sad that they didn't have a wonderful Christmas morning, but I also knew it wasn't that important in the grand scheme of things. They had to have been worried about their father and how he was doing.

Eddie loved attention, and he wanted to be the star of the party whenever he could. That didn't change while he was in rehab. I don't know much about addiction therapy, but I thought that caffeine, since it's so addictive, would be prohibited. However, Eddie asked his visitors to bring coffee with them, as much as they could. He also asked them to bring cream and sugar on the side. That way, he could hand out coffee to his fellow patients and be the popular guy and the star of the show.

In January, I still had no idea the boys were alone, taking care of themselves. No one, including the boys, thought to inform me. I was still paying the bills for the cell phones, and I would occasionally do a quick scan of the bill to ensure they weren't going over their minutes. Sometimes, though, I would end up paying an enormous bill. As they no longer had a home phone, this was their only way to communicate with anyone, but the minutes allotted to them should have been sufficient to cover their needs.

In January their cell phone usage was quite high. I kept warning them that when they reached their limit that I was going to suspend their phones. They never explained that their usage was high because they were talking to their Dad who was in rehab. If I had known that I would have done things differently. I believed it was important to follow through with consequences when the boys were told repeatedly what would happen if they went over on their minutes and I did suspend their phones. Obviously they weren't happy and I received a message on Facebook from Brett telling me how nasty it was to cut off their phones when their dad was in hospital. I had heard too many fabrications over the years to really believe that Eddie was in the hospital. I had no idea it was true. I realized later that my actions must have confirmed what their father had told them about me, that I was uncaring. I understand their reactions now, and I guess I should have looked into their situation more before I cancelled their phones. I did the best I could at the time.

The boys survived until their dad was released from rehab a few weeks later. Things were looking up for a while, and he was doing reasonably well. Eddie was getting help for his depression and alcoholism and had a support group. Things were better, for a little while, anyway.

Christopher Reeve said, "Once you choose hope, anything's possible."

Hope was something within Eddie's reach but the walk there was filled with obstacles he had difficulty passing.

Falling to the Bottom

Two months later, in March, Andy and I were shopping for blinds at Home Depot when my cell phone rang. I usually don't answer calls from numbers I don't recognize, but I did that day. Then I heard a recorded message telling me it was call from the Calgary Remand Center. When I heard Eddie's voice on the phone, I was absolutely shocked.

I knew life for Eddie wasn't great. I knew he had been in hospital and rehab in the last few months, and I had hoped he was turning his life around. I was surprised to discover he was now in jail. Despite all the abuse I suffered, Eddie had never gone to jail. And why would he call me? I should have been at the bottom of his list.

I asked him what he was doing in jail and, of course, if the boys were all right. Although I didn't think he would have physically hurt the boys, I just couldn't rule it out entirely. He said he was charged with uttering threats. Apparently he had told Corrine, his love; that he was going to kill her. They had been together off an on over the last ten years. This time, I think she had made a firm decision to end their relationship. While Eddie had often threatened to kill me, and occasionally tried, I'd never had the courage to press charges. I was empathetic toward Corrine, and part of me was glad Eddie was behind bars.

Eddie never did well when the women in his life tried to leave him. Sometimes, the women succeeded in leaving him behind, but other times was known to the police, they would sometimes be harassed on the street. The police called the house the Mandersons because only men lived there and their last name was Anderson. I found it odd that the police would deliberately set someone up like that, but I believed Brett. It actually made sense.

The more I heard, the sicker I became. How could my children be growing up in a place like this? When I left, their father had been a somewhat reasonable man. I was quickly learning now that he had been living on the edge. He had been living in a world of drugs, gambling, prostitutes, and gangsters. It was such a sad state. Brett seemed to be very laid back and not focused on his life at all. How could he be living with this? He just took everything in stride. It was like he thought this was the way life was supposed to be. I dropped him home and told him I'd be back the next morning. I drove back to my hotel and cried. I cried for my children's lost opportunities and for what could have been.

When I drove to the house the next morning, I decided the first thing to do was to get the house in reasonable order again. It was a cold winter morning so I drove Brett to school first then went back to the house. Blake isn't much of a morning person, so it took him a while to get off the couch and help. Once he got up, he was focused and quite helpful.

We started in the kitchen. We gathered up all the pizza boxes, beer cans, and garbage. We cleared away the dishes and threw out the rotting food. I knew the pastor and his wife had tried to be involved with the boys and Eddie. I could see recipes for simple meals posted on the fridge. I also knew they would sometimes bring meals over and eat with the boys. They were really trying to be helpful. They were good for the boys; they provided an example of a responsible couple and they also added a spiritual aspect to the boys' life. I was very grateful the boys had them during that difficult time.

In between chores, Blake and I did some grocery shopping. I told him that I wanted to buy food for him and Brett. I told him it wasn't their responsibility to feed all of their friends; I wanted the groceries to last. I couldn't afford to feed the whole neighborhood. After the grocery shopping we went to the Laundromat down the road. The dirty clothes in the house were so dirty and disgusting that I didn't want to touch them. Some clothes were covered in vomit and had been sitting there for weeks. It was an awful smell. I shoved them all in the washing machine and hoped it would come clean. We did twelve loads of laundry that day, and there was still more to come. Once everything was washed and dried, we went home, and I thought the boys would help fold and put away the clean clothes.

When we got home, Brett was just coming home from school with a few friends. It was a normal thing—gathering at the house after school. I let it go and went back to get the other loads of laundry at the Laundromat. It had been a busy day, and I was pretty tired from all the work.

When I returned from the Laundromat, the house reeked of hashish. I was livid. I guess while Eddie was away, this place really was the party house. There was no adult supervision, so they could get away with anything. I went downstairs to the source of the aroma and saw Brett and his buddies sitting around. I didn't catch them in the act, but they had clearly just finished smoking it.

I am normally a very civilized, calm, and passive person—until you cross the line. While I might be passive-aggressive, I'm capable of going ballistic when others push my buttons. Doing drugs in their father's house was illegal and disrespectful, but to do so in their mother's presence was unfathomable. Eddie, Blake and Brett had no respect for themselves or me. I couldn't understand how things had gotten so far out of hand. But I hadn't been there to mold the boys into good, productive men. Apparently neither had Eddie.

I yelled at Brett's friends: "Get the hell out of this house!" I just looked at Brett and said: "Why are you smoking drugs in your father's house? You know he wouldn't approve." Brett just looked at me and said: "I wasn't." I could see by the look in his eyes that he knew I was right. He would never want to disappoint his father. Brett's two friends ran past me on the way out the door. Brett wasn't happy and curtly told me so. His words were: "Who the hell do you think you are?" We were both on the verge of a blowup, so I left him alone to cool down. I needed to compose myself, too. I needed to be the parent, but I had only recently begun to rebuild a tenuous relationship with them. I didn't want my emotions to get the better of me.

I went back to cleaning to keep my mind off everything. I needed to get the house in order first, and then deal with the boys' lifestyle. After cleaning for a few minutes I heard some noise downstairs and went to investigate. Brett's friends had returned. I was shocked. I yelled, "Do you not understand? You are not to be in this house." They mumbled something about not having a ride. I really didn't care.

The guy who was supposed to drive them was still in the house with Brett. I just wanted them to leave. Finally the friend who was driving realized I was completely serious and the two dope smokers and the friend that was driving them all left. Blake had been upstairs hanging out with his own friends. He hadn't said anything about my interaction with Brett. This time he piped in with Brett and told me what he thought of me. "Who do you think you are? You haven't been in our lives for the past 12 years. What makes you think you can walk in here now and tell us what to do?" They wanted to have fun and party, and I was hindering their social life. I wanted them to realize what needed to be done. They were certainly old enough to understand the difference between right and wrong, but they didn't seem to care.

I continued cleaning late into the evening. It was monotonous, draining, and never-ending. Although things had mellowed somewhat after our yelling match, I was still the only one cleaning. The boys were playing a board game with two of their friends and listening to some music.

The mess didn't dissipate at all. The hours I spent at the Laundromat seemed ages ago, and the clothes were still not folded or put away. I mean, I wasn't asking for much. If I made some attempts at straightening the house, I expected them to do their part. But they didn't.

When I went into the kitchen to clean, later that evening, it was clear that everyone had been fed, even the two friends who were smoking dope. Blake had completely disregarded my request that he not feed the neighborhood. They hadn't even bothered to clean up, and it was all I could do not to explode. You know when you come to a point when you could either explode with raw emotion or just give up and cry? Well, I had reached that point. I felt like I wasn't being appreciated or respected for what I was trying to do. I told the boys I had to leave. I had done everything I could to help them get back on their feet while their father was away, but they clearly didn't want my help. They had all but told me to leave. Looking back, maybe they had been living on their own without any repercussions for too long that they didn't understand or appreciate the generosity of others. At the time I felt used and taken for granted.

I didn't drive back to Calgary that night; it was too late, so I went back to the hotel. I needed to have some alone time to collect my thoughts. I didn't want to leave the boys on bad terms when we had only just begun to get to know each other again. Where would that bring us?

When I woke up the next morning, it was pretty cold and the temperature was in the minus twenties. I was worried about Brett getting to school on such a cold morning. So I got in the car and went to the A&W drive-through to pick up a quick breakfast for Brett and drive him to school. I wanted to make another effort and help where I could. They say a married couple should never go to bed angry, and you should never part with anyone on bad terms. You may agree or disagree, but I needed to show the boys I still loved them.

When I arrived, Blake was asleep on the couch, but he did open the door for me. When I went in, Brett was still asleep in his bed, and he wasn't happy to see me. I thought maybe a night's rest away from me might have helped, but it hadn't.

I told him that I wanted to drive him to school. I gave him a warm breakfast to eat on the way. It may not have been the most nutritious breakfast, but he wasn't going to eat that early otherwise, and he needed some food before school.

The drive was very quiet, almost somber. We both stared out the window, unable to make small talk. I knew I only had a few minutes to make a connection, so I asked Brett if he remembered what it was like when I had been in his life. Did he remember the fun he and I had together? How we were buddies when Eddie and Blake went off to do hockey things? He looked at me in a daze. I'm not sure if he did remember and was afraid to bring it up, or it was a recognition of lost times. The only words he spoke were the instructions for where to drop him off for school. No connection, no breakthrough.

Although my heart died a little, I told him I loved him. There were no hugs, no "have a good day": there was only silence. The cold chill fastened to my heart when he shut the door on me. I drove back to Calgary thinking about another lost moment with my boys.

The Eviction

When I got back to Calgary I realized how important it was that I contact Carmen and Howard. I needed to know what was really going on and what action I should be taking. Having seen what was going on in Edmonton was a real shock for me and I needed some guidance regarding how I should proceed with the boys, with Eddie, with the whole situation. We communicated almost on a daily basis through phone calls and email. A couple of weeks after my return to Calgary, Carmen called to let me know that she would be coming to Calgary for a soccer tournament that her daughter was in. She asked if we could meet. I was grateful for the opportunity to sit down and talk with her. To tell her my story and to talk about how we could move forward to help the boys and Eddie. Andy and I met her at a coffee shop close to her hotel. We sat for a couple of hours so that she could hear my story and I could get caught up on everything that had been going on with Eddie and the boys. I appreciated their involvement so much. They tried so hard to have a positive influence on the boys. She was very understanding, and I felt we connected during that meeting. It was quite a relief to know she was in my sons' life. I knew she was someone I could reach out to.

Things didn't get any better at Eddie's house. At least while I was there Blake was doing his best to keep everything under control. It wasn't difficult for the landlady to know what was happening in the house. Each time the police stopped by for a visit or to address a complaint, they made sure she knew about it. They chose not to keep anything from her, and Eddie was very aware of that.

Unfortunately, the boys didn't get along with their neighbors. One weekend Blake and the boy next door got into an argument. It didn't become physical, but Blake threatened the boy and his family. The next thing he knew, the police had blocked the roads around the house. It must have been a scary scene. I only heard about it from the boys.

Blake was charged with uttering threats, which was the same crime as his father. Trouble seemed to follow the Anderson men, and now it was living in the next generation: my boys. Apparently Blake had threatened to blow up the neighbor's house. The landlady learned of the incident almost immediately. I don't know if the neighbors had told her, as she was also their landlady, or if it was the police, but there was no doubt that she would evict them.

Mrs. Olsen, the landlady, was aware that Eddie was in jail and that the boys were alone in the house. She was so upset that she served eviction papers anyway. She didn't want to wait until something major happened. It was bad for her house and the neighborhood.

With all the action at the house and the police involvement, social services got involved. Because Brett was still under sixteen, he was not allowed to stay in the house with his brother, who was still a minor. He was supposed to be living with the family of one of his friends, T.J. Brett thought it was pointless to live with rules, curfews, and schedules when he could stay with Blake and have run of the house. What teenager would choose rules over freedom? Not many.

Shortly after my visit with the boys in Edmonton, I received a call from a social worker at Children's Services. Michelle, the social worker, told me she knew that Eddie was in jail and Blake and Brett were living on their own. She explained that because Brett was fifteen and Blake only seventeen, Brett couldn't stay with Blake. Brett couldn't stay on his own, legally, until he was sixteen.

I told the social worker Brett was supposed to be staying with a neighbor while Eddie was away, but because the neighbor was just across street, Brett was always going home. I told her I had no control over the boys and that since I lived in Calgary, I was removed from their daily activities. She asked if I could go and stay in Edmonton until Eddie got out of jail.

Of course that was not possible because I had responsibilities and a job in Calgary. I didn't want to tell her that my relationship with the boys was very tenuous and that we were just beginning to make contact again.

I mentioned that Brett was only a few months away from sixteen and that if they tried to take him into custody, he might run away and live on the streets. That was something neither of us wanted. It was a tricky situation and we didn't want to spook Brett. She agreed to take the information and review the situation with her supervisor and then call me back. I only prayed and hoped the boys wouldn't be evicted and they would settle down. Maybe this scare would make them realize that things could get much worse.

At this time, everyone, Carmen, Howard and me, were concerned about Blake's safety when his dad was released from jail. Howard had been talking with Eddie and was concerned that Eddie might blame Blake for the eviction. Being the oldest, Blake was left in charge and should have had control over the situation. The truth was Blake was only seventeen and was doing his best. He wasn't an adult and should not have been forced to look after himself and Brett. Yes, he shouldn't have mouthed off or threatened the neighbor, but perhaps he was just blowing off steam. I don't think he ever intended to act on his threat. The problem was that nobody knew how Eddie would react when he was released.

Something had happened between Eddie and Blake over the years, and I wasn't there to know exactly what it was. When he was younger, Blake and his dad had been so close. They were best buddies and always did things together. I couldn't understand why they weren't close now. Unfortunately, it often seemed like Eddie treated Brett like second best when he was younger. Over the years, as the boys got older, Eddie's attention shifted, and Brett became his favorite. I'm not sure why he just couldn't treat them both equally.

Between Brett's possible apprehension by Children's Services and wondering what would happen to Blake when Eddie was released from jail, I was a nervous wreck. The pastor and I had talked about Blake moving out and getting his own place, but neither of us was sure if Blake would agree, or if he could even do it, since he was technically a minor.

I really appreciated having Howard to talk to. He was there, on the front line. He knew what the boys were going through. I knew I could count on him for sound advice. One morning in March I talked with him about the eviction, the boys, and Eddie and what we were going to do. I valued Howard's opinion. He was level headed and a little bit removed from the situation. As much as he cared about Blake and Brett they weren't his children. This allowed him to guide me to make more reasonable decisions and to come up with solutions. It was hard for me to do this with so much emotion involved.

I wasn't sure of the timing of all this because we didn't know when Eddie would be released form jail, and that precipitated everything. It turned out that time was on our side. Eddie had a bail hearing that day and Howard was there to post bail. He would be released very quickly. I e-mailed the social worker to let her know so she wouldn't start proceedings for Brett.

Bail was granted on Tuesday. Eddie was supposed to be released on Wednesday. You know about Murphy's Law. Well, something went wrong with his paperwork. He had to stay in jail and wasn't released for another week. His court date was set for August 9, 2009. This meant we had about five months to figure things out.

Initially the eviction notice was only forty-eight hours. As Blake had threatened the neighbors and police were involved, he was considered dangerous. When that happens, eviction can be very quick. When the pastor found out about the sudden eviction notice, he intervened in the process and thankfully received an extension until the end of the March.

When Eddie was released from jail, he called me. It was early in the morning, when he got home and the boys were still sleeping. His mood surprised me. I thought he would be so happy to be out of jail and at home but he wasn't. He was very depressed and feeling quite overwhelmed. He told me he wasn't happy to be home at all. He told me he'd rather be back in jail. He said when he got home he walked into the house and it was a mess he felt it was a reflection of his life. I was concerned and puzzled. I'd never known anyone to be released from jail before; was this reaction normal? I tried to reassure him that things were going to get better. I reminded him that he had a support system with Howard, Carmen and Brent his AA sponsor. I reminded him that he wasn't alone. I told him that he needed to stay strong for Blake and Brett. He still seemed very depressed when he hung up but he did take some action. He made some phone calls and immediately went to court to have the eviction notice extended. It was a big relief for me and all involved when the landlady, Mrs. Olsen, agreed to let Eddie and the boys remain in the house until the end of April. She had a place in her heart for the boys. She thought it was awful that the boys were growing up without their mother and that they had to live with an alcoholic father. She didn't think very highly of me. Then again, she didn't know the whole story. How could she unless she had walked in my shoes?

I realized right away that Eddie wouldn't be able to afford the physical move, damage deposit, or any other extra costs that would be incurred as a result of the eviction. I knew if I didn't do something; the boys would be homeless for certain. Andy and I talked about the entire situation and agreed that we needed to keep the boys together under one roof. They needed a new place to live, and the boys couldn't stay with us in Calgary, not that they wanted to or they would come. It would be inviting Eddie to be part of my life again, and he was too dangerous for that. So we did what we could, and Andy offered to pay for the moving costs.

I also realized that with an upcoming move they wouldn't have phone or Internet services. It would be hard to search for work without it. I was still very involved and would be responsible for the rent, so I felt it was important to find a place that was affordable. Eddie still had his car, but he wasn't allowed to drive because his license was suspended due to unpaid tickets. So, I had to look for places online and then contact Carmen and Howard to help Eddie view the places.

They were a great resource for Eddie, the boys, and for me. They helped reassure me and calm my fears when it came to the boys' welfare. I don't know what I would have done without them. They were there in the trenches and acted for me when I couldn't be there.

With my assistance, Eddie was able to find a nice place to live. It was the main floor apartment in a house just a few blocks from where they were living. Different tenants lived in the basement apartment. I was just glad it was in a nice neighborhood and the boys liked it.

I accepted that the boys didn't want me in their lives. It was hard because I wanted to be part of theirs, but you can't force someone to love you or want to be with you. It usually has an opposite effect. When I tried to force them, the boys rebelled and wanted to get away. I still loved them and I was doing everything I could, from the sidelines, to ensure their lives could be as stable as possible, given their situation. The first part of that was safety and shelter. And if Eddie was employed that would help tremendously.

I admit now I have problems with codependency. For many years, I was unable to admit it. You've probably seen it, too, in the ways I allowed myself to become involved with Eddie after our separation. At some point, it stops being love and starts being unhealthy. I was drawn in by guilt, but I continued down the path of psychological dependency. And Eddie took advantage of my need to give.

Eddie knew how desperate I was for him to get a job. He was feeling that same desperation. He convinced me that if his fines were paid off, he would be able to drive, which would enable him to get a job and start contributing financially. It was a reasonable plan and I bought it. The problem with these plans is that they were one-sided. The day I paid his traffic fines, Eddie had his license reinstated. The joy of being able to drive made him want to celebrate, so Eddie went to a bar and started drinking.

One of Eddie's bail conditions was to stay away from alcohol. He had been to rehab and sought counseling about his addictions, but he couldn't help it. After all, he was still an addict. That night he got very intoxicated and lost both his keys and his license at the bar. He stumbled home and passed out on the couch.

The next day, his sponsor, Brent, from Alcohol Anonymous (AA) stopped by to see how Eddie and the boys were doing. When he walked into the house, he was absolutely disgusted. He saw Eddie passed out, again. I'm sure part of him felt used and deflated. After all he and his wife, as well as Carmen and Howard, had done for Eddie, it was all for not. Eddie just didn't care. They knew about dealing with addicts and knew that it was impossible to help someone who didn't want to help himself. It appeared that Eddie fell into that group of addicts.

Alcohol had too big a grasp on Eddie's life. It was like a tapeworm that had taken hold over his brain and his heart, moving and conquering each vital organ until it could no longer function. Eddie could barely function. He would show a glimmer of hope and talk a good story, but when it came down to it, the addiction won out.

Brent had been very supportive of Eddie and the boys while they were living according to the cycle of Eddie's addictions. He had seen them through many difficult days. So when he came that day, the first thing he did was to ensure that the boys were okay. Once he did that, he left and called me to let me know what was happening. He told me he couldn't stand by and watch the degeneration any further. It was the final straw.

He told me this wasn't the first time Eddie had been drunk and in violation of his bail conditions. He said he felt that it was truly necessary to call the police and have Eddie picked up. He reassured me that between himself and his wife and Carmen and Howard, they would take care of the boys. It was the best thing and only thing that they could do.

Reluctantly, I agreed. What else could I do? These wonderful people were actively involved in their daily lives and knew what happened and what could happen. I had to trust their insight and help. So I told Brent that I trusted him and that he needed to do what was necessary. They picked up Eddie and took him back to jail the following day.

Now I had a different set of worries. I was doing what I could financially for the boys, but that only went so far. I needed some reassurance that everything was okay, so I reached out and e-mailed Carmen. I mentioned that Eddie going back to jail was the worst-case scenario, and I had no idea what to do next.

Carmen called and helped me to realize that I had to let it all go. There was only so much I could do for them, and if the boys didn't want my help, I couldn't force it on them. I hesitantly agreed and hoped and prayed for the best. That was all I could do now: just pray and pray.

The Lord must have been listening to all our prayers. Eddie was released within a couple of days. His bail was reinstated so he would be able to find a job to take care of the boys. At least, that's what I hoped would happen.

Some say hope comes into play when our circumstances are dire. Psychologist Barbara L. Fredrickson states that hope literally opens us up and removes the blinders of fear and despair and allows us to see the big picture.

That's the problem with hope. Hope is a necessary part of life. If we don't have hope, how can we live, how can we see beyond what is in front of us? I had hoped that we could have a normal, stable life; If not normal, then at least stable. I needed that. The boys needed that. Eddie needed much more, but I couldn't help him. I prayed for him because of the boys and because I didn't want to see anyone suffer. Suffering had been part of Eddie's life since he was a child, and there seemed to be no end to it.

Blake's Hockey Camps

etween Eddie's stints in hospital and rehab facilities that year, he had time to think about Blake and one of the dreams he had for him. Since the day Blake was born, Eddie believed he was going to be a NHL hockey player. He wanted Blake to live out his own dreams, and he tried very hard to make it happen.

When he was young, Eddie and Blake were very involved with hockey. They had their special time together and excluded me—not that I minded. A father needs to bond with his son. They need to share things and have some interests together. I wanted that for him and the boys, yet I wanted to share in the experience too.

Now Blake was seventeen and although he hadn't played hockey that past year, because he wasn't in school, Eddie's dreams never died. Eddie thought that since I was picking up the bill for almost everything—perhaps I could pay for this too. I wanted to help my children any way I could, and it's important to have dreams. They allow a person to see beyond the present, whatever that might be, and have an interest in life itself. I wanted to be part of fulfilling or aiding both their dreams.

Eager to do anything, I contacted some Junior A hockey teams to see if tryouts were still an option. I hadn't seen Blake play hockey in many years, but Eddie told me he was good. Junior A teams are the breeding ground for some of the draft teams for the NHL. He had to be good. Luckily, we received invitations to tryouts for several teams, including the Okotoks Oilers, Drumheller Dragons, and the Bonneyville Pontiacs. The tryouts required Blake and me to be on the road for three consecutive weekends.

Our first road trip was to Drumheller. Blake arrived in Calgary by bus. When I picked him up at the station, it was obvious he wasn't happy. He was sullen and miserable. I would have thought that the excitement of hockey tryouts would have been overwhelming and contagious. It wasn't. Perhaps spending time with me detracted from the experience. He wouldn't talk to me. We went for something to eat and then proceeded quietly to Drumheller. Because it was late, we checked into the hotel as soon as we arrived and went straight to bed. I had booked two rooms to help decrease the awkwardness Blake might feel. Things didn't change that weekend. We didn't have heart-to-heart talks and very little conversation took place during mealtime.

It was Easter weekend and the town was festive with decorations of Easter bunnies and chocolate. I couldn't help but buy some Easter eggs and put them in a basket outside his hotel door the morning of Easter Sunday. There was only so much I could do. I had missed so much over the years, but I was trying.

When Blake wasn't at the arena, he just stayed in his hotel room with the curtains drawn. I offered to take him sight seeing to a great dinosaur museum. It has wonderful exhibits that anyone would enjoy. But he didn't want to do anything. It was quite depressing. I was with my son on a glorious weekend, and he didn't want to be with me. It was so sad. We finished the tryouts and left in uncomfortable silence.

The following weekend we travelled to Bonneyville. We stayed in a two-bedroom apartment—separate, yet together. I had hoped things would get better, but they didn't. He went to his bedroom and only came out for hockey practice and food.

During our road trips, Eddie had been working on getting a new place and arranging the move. Eddie told me he was hoping for a fresh start and wanted to buy some new furniture to help freshen things up. He was quite depressed and hoped the new place was the start of a new life. The boys hoped so, too.

On the way home from Bonneyville, I received a text from Eddie telling me he didn't get his WCB check, so he couldn't buy the furniture. He asked me for help. I knew I couldn't—I was tapped out. I had given him so much money lately that I'd been forced to take out loans. I couldn't extend myself any further.

I knew Blake was happy to have a new start, so I wanted to help ease the sting of not getting that furniture before he arrived home. It broke my heart knowing he was going to experience more disappointment. On our drive back, I told Blake what was happening. He did not understand at all. It was a big mistake to broach the subject because it opened up a wound that had been festering for years.

Blake exploded. He yelled at me for a long time. He proceeded to tell me exactly what he thought of me and my maternal abilities. He yelled at me for what seemed like ten or fifteen minutes. I was tempted to pull the car over and ask him to get out. I was quite afraid of what he was going to do next. I knew leaving him on the side of the road was absolutely not an option, but I was livid and fearful. I hadn't seen this much anger in anyone since I had been with Eddie. I was being berated yet again by a young Eddie.

Although it hurt like hell, I learned so much from his rant. I always wondered what the boys were told about me, and I found out. Their father told them that I had left them and had taken all their savings. The truth was there were no savings—we barely made ends meet. I left that day with my few personal possessions, which fit in my small car. That's it. I had no money, no furniture, and not even all my clothes.

Eddie had also told them that he had paid for my education, and that was why he was in debt and why he couldn't go to school. They didn't know I had taken a student loan for my tuition and books. Eddie paid for the food we ate and the other household bills, but I had paid for my own education in its entirety. And I was proud that I did it on my own, without anyone's help.

Eddie also told them that I had cheated on him. Of course he never mentioned his affair with Jodi. In summary, Eddie had told Blake and Brett, just young boys, that I was a thief, a no-good mother, and a whore who had taken everything I could from their father. Nothing could have been further from the truth. No wonder the boys didn't want me in their life. If I had been them, knowing what they thought they knew, I wouldn't have wanted me either. They believed what Eddie told them. They couldn't remember the abuse, the choking incident when I asked them to call 911, or any of the other incidents. Eddie was a pathological liar and he was good at it. He spewed his garbage and they soaked it up.

took a baseball bat and smashed the windshield. He was angry and hurt and needed to act out.

The incident ended after the police were called. Once the police arrived, they took Blake to jail. He spent a few days there, and as part of his release he was not permitted to be in contact with his father. He was no longer allowed to be at the house.

Blake had to leave quickly. He needed somewhere to go, so he started spending time sporadically at his friend's sister's house. One thing led to another, and soon my seventeen-year-old was involved with a twenty-six-year-old woman and was playing father to her two little girls. I didn't approve, nor did Eddie. But what could we do? At least he had a place to live. Blake did return to Eddie's house to ensure things were okay and to collect some of his things, but unfortunately he and Eddie started fighting again. The fights were bad and once again Eddie called the police and had Blake arrested. Blake spent the next few days in jail. I couldn't help but be disheartened. Blake was following in Eddie's footsteps. I didn't want that for my son.

I did my best to keep in touch with Blake after he moved out and to let him know I was there for him if he wanted to make some life choices like moving out on his own or getting a job. There was a lot of talk among Eddie, the pastor and myself, about where he was living and who with and it wasn't good.

During this time, I also managed to reconnect with the boys' cousin, Courtney, through Facebook. Courtney was Kim's daughter and Eddie's niece. And while I was married to Eddie, Courtney and Kim had been a big part of our lives. She brought me up to date with what was happening in her own life too. It was nice to know her once again. She also mentioned she had been in contact with Brett through Facebook.

These days you can find people from your past through online websites and reconnect. I was grateful for it. She also gave me more insight into what was happening at Eddie's house. She said things were not good; in fact, they were getting worse by the day.

She told me that Brett had been kicked out of school due to a physical incident. The police had to be called in to remove him. He was called into the principal's office one day because he was in the halls when he should have been in class. The principal told Brett that she was going to call his dad. When she picked up the phone to call him, that's when Brett lost it.

He went into a rage. He stood up and in once clean sweep; he cleared everything off the principal's desk. He stormed out of her office and came face to face with the school police officer. The officer tried to calm him down, but Brett was too enraged to be reasoned with. Brett pushed the officer so that he could go by, and that's when the officer grabbed him and hauled him out to the police car. He was expelled and not welcomed back. He was also not allowed in the immediate vicinity of the school. My poor boy was traveling similar paths with his father and older brother. Things were spirally down rapidly.

This time, I contacted the school. I had started to get more involved since the boys and I had reconnected. I knew Brett was devastated about not being allowed to go to school. I sent him e-mails trying to encourage him, but his responses were both angry and sad. He didn't think his life had anything good in it. He wasn't yet sixteen, so legally he still had to live with an adult. Living at home wasn't working. I prayed and asked him to try and hold out for a couple of more months until he turned sixteen. Once he was 16 he could access various programs for supported independents. I hoped he could make it another couple of months.

I knew the situation was becoming more and more desperate when Courtney forwarded an e-mail Blake had sent her. He wrote that his father desperately needed help. He was doing heavy drugs and was suicidal. He also mentioned they had been evicted again. He was terrified that his dad and his brother were going to be homeless and end up living in his car. He was terrified that his dad was going to take his own life. I knew that for Blake to reach out to Courtney, it must have been bad. He had been estranged for many years from his aunts and cousins. He was grasping at straws to help his dad.

When I read the e-mail I was shocked. No one told me they had been evicted again. How could this happen? I was devastated. I couldn't bail him out again. Things were out of control. I had known drugs were part of Eddie's life, but his usage must have increased dramatically for Blake to reach out like that.

Eviction was another hurdle. I found out that the tenants in the basement apartment, an older couple, quiet and reserved, felt uneasy living there and feared for their safety. They sent a letter to the landlord. They never expected anything like this.

July 13, 2009
To: Landlord and Friend
From: The tenants of the basement suite in a home occupied by Ed Anderson

For your records, I wanted to summarize our experience in your basement suite for the short time we occupied it, from the end of May to the first week of July, 2009.

From the second day of our arrival onward, we heard the sounds of someone who was very angry upstairs. There was a good deal of yelling and loud swearing. Sometimes we heard the sound of things being thrown or smashed. The police attended the home on several occasions beginning the second or third day of our arrival.

We did not call the police, but we were becoming increasingly fearful as time passed. We were worried for our safety and that of some of the family members upstairs. At no time, however, did the renter upstairs, Edward, speak to us. Courtesy was maintained.

In the first week of July this changed after we communicated our worry about the situation upstairs. We know you talked to Eddie about the fighting. A few days following that, when we were driving away from the house, we saw Eddie returning home on his bike. He made motions that made us think he wanted us to stop the car. He appeared to want to tell us something. When we rolled the window down we heard him yell something about our big f***king mouths. He advanced toward the car with his fists clenched, and we had no doubt that he wanted to hit one of us—my husband is 67 and I am 59. We believe, because his voice was slurred, that he was drunk.

On that same night, we came to the conclusion once we quickly drove away, that we were no longer safe in our apartment. We paid for a motel that night and called the police so that we could safely remove our belongings. At that time, we learned that the police thought Eddie to be dangerous. They would not go to the house to see him with any less than three officers.

We have returned to the house two times now, and there are still things we need in the apartment.

At considerable inconvenience to you, we have now stayed in your home for four to five nights. Today we return to B.C. The generosity and kindness of you and your wife has taken some—a good deal—of the edge off this experience, but it has not been able to erase a good deal of the unpleasant memories, and all of the inconvenience that followed it.

With the best of intentions, you rented the suite to us on a short-term basis so that we could house hunt here. The problems Eddie has with his children and his own drinking have had far-reaching effects, negative ones.

The landlord was horrified. He obtained the complaints from the Edmonton Police Service and noted in the eviction that the police had been called to the house nine times between June 7 and July 9, 2009. Often they were called because of fighting inside.

It wasn't going to end. Moving Eddie from house to house only changed his surroundings. What didn't change were Eddie and his violent nature. I understood why the other tenants had spoken to the landlord. I lived through his violent moods. The other tenants just wanted to feel safe in their home. I had no idea things were so bad. I did not acquire this documentation until much later.

Once again, I reached out to Carmen for guidance. I updated her on what I had learned from my niece. I told her about the eviction and the substance abuse and where Brett and Blake were. I told her I was thinking about contacting youth services so that Brett could live on his own, away from Eddie. Based on what I heard from Blake and Courtney, there was reason to fear for his safety.

I knew Blake was living with his girlfriend, so he was safe from Eddie's behavior. But now Brett was alone with Eddie. I e-mailed Blake to ask what he thought of youth services. He didn't want me to contact them. He was fearful that they would simply take Brett away and place him in a group home. I explained that there were programs to help youth to live on their own that provided help and counseling. He wouldn't accept it. He begged me not to contact them.

I e-mailed Blake daily, trying to reassure him that everything was going to be okay. Finally, I told him that his Aunt Jolene, from Calgary, was in touch with Eddie. She was going to help him through this transition and urge him to seek professional help. The plan was that Eddie and Brett would move to Calgary and live with Jolene and her family until they could get back on their feet.

Financially that would help everyone, and it would also help Eddie and Brett in other ways. Everyone thought that having his sister close by would encourage Eddie to take positive steps in his life. She would also be a buffer between Eddie and Brett.

This would also mean that I would also be closer to Brett, if he wanted to be in touch with me. The downside to the arrangement was that Eddie might find out where I was. Since I left Edmonton, I had been in hiding. He never knew where I lived; he only had a cell phone number, and he knew I worked for the government. With his move to Calgary, there was the risk that he might find out where I live and start harassing me or Andy.

But right now, I couldn't think about that. I would deal with that if it happened. Most importantly, I had to ensure Brett would be okay. Their plan sounded solid, and I knew Eddie needed someone to keep him on track. His sister could do that.

I felt hope once again, though only for a short while. Then I received another e-mail, from my niece, Courtney, on July 19, 2009. She said Eddie had beaten Brett up pretty badly. There must have been a fistfight or something worse because Brett had two large lumps on his head. Brett left the house and went to his friend Kyle's house. She said Kyle told him to call me, and that I should expect a call or e-mail from Brett soon. But she also said there were other things she wanted to discuss over the phone the following day.

I was glad Brett got out and was now safe, but I couldn't imagine how he felt. All the abuse I suffered was at the hand of my ex-husband. Growing up, I lived in a warm, loving household and never had to fear for my safety. Most people take a loving home for granted, and I did, too. That changed with Eddie.

My children didn't have an environment that encouraged or inspired them to be better men. It was the opposite. If they remembered what Eddie did to me, they saw, at a very young age, how cruel people could be. And in the following years, they grew up believing I had abandoned them.

I could not change the past, I could only live in the present and try to do better. I had to remind myself of that over and over.

July 20, 2009

Monday July 20, 2009 was a wonderfully warm summer day in Calgary. I worked from home and I thought I would eat outside on the patio. I was sitting outside enjoying a nice fresh salad. I was enjoying the warmth of the sun as I stared into the clear blue sky. It was a glorious day. I felt hope from the sun. Sunshine always lifts me up and gives me hope. Unfortunately hope is beyond the reach of some people.

The phone rang so I ran inside to get it. It was Courtney. She blurted out in staccato, "Uncle Eddie is dead." And there it was. Just like that, he was gone. I was in shock and speechless. I didn't know what to say or do. I had to sit down and was silent for what seemed to be minutes before I could say anything to Courtney.

She told me what happened, the entire story. Eddie must have been feeling pretty bad after his fight with Brett. To try and cope with his emotions and stress, Eddie tried to self-medicate with drugs and alcohol. I was told that the next morning he was still stoned and drunk sitting at the kitchen table talking with Brett's friend, Frisco, who was staying at the house. I heard that there may have been some girls there too, but it hasn't been confirmed.

Frisco was going to be leaving on the bus later that day for Fort McMurray to look for work. This was going to be his last day in Edmonton. He had to get going with his day so he went to the bathroom to take a shower. When he came out of the shower, everyone was gone. He didn't think anything of it. He thought that Eddie had probably gone to bed. It had been a long night. Then he ran down to the laundry room to get his clothes out of the dryer to start packing.

He walked into the laundry room and was shocked by what he saw—shocked and quite distraught. There was Eddie's lifeless body hanging from an extension cord tied to one of the ceiling beams. On top of the white washer were pictures of Blake and Brett staring at the gruesome sight. The pictures were of the boys as children, young and innocent.

Frisco freaked out, understandably, and called the police. He must have called Blake and Brett next as they were at the house very quickly. Brett called his ex-girlfriend and she called Courtney. Courtney was living with her mother Kim in Whitecourt, a few hours away, so she was with her when they got the call about Eddie. Courtney then called me in Calgary. I called Eddie's other sisters in Calgary—Penni, Jolene, and Gerry—to let them know Eddie was gone. It only took minutes to inform everyone of the news.

I didn't know what to do next. I called the house and talked to Blake and Brett to make sure that they were as all right as they could be in such terrible circumstances. They were clearly upset but perhaps not surprised. In Blake's last few e-mails to Courtney and some of his aunts, he asked everyone for help with his dad. Eddie had threatened suicide earlier in the week, and Blake had actually gone to the house and found an extension cord hanging from the rafters in the laundry room. Blake was quite distraught and he felt helpless. He removed the extension cord. He wanted to do more but he didn't know what to do. Eddie had been threatening suicide since we were dating but he never acted on it. I guess this time he really couldn't take it anymore. His life was falling apart, and he didn't know how to get it back together.

Brett was more shaken. He was still living with his dad, and although he and Eddie had their share of fights, he still couldn't believe what had happened. What was going to happen next? Where would he go? Who would look after him? He wasn't quite sixteen. I told him I wasn't sure what would happen, but that we would do everything to keep him safe and happy.

Then I spoke to the police officer on site. He told me because Eddie and I were divorced there was nothing I could do. It would be the responsibility of his family to finalize all the details. His mother died of breast cancer and his father had died a few years later of heart disease. Eddie didn't keep in touch with much of his family and only recently started talking with Jolene in Calgary. His sisters had been fed up with Eddie's continuous calls for money and help.

Even though I knew I couldn't do anything for Eddie or the administration of the estate, I needed to be there for my children. Andy, my husband, was away at a conference in Banff. I tracked him down and told him what happened. He was as shocked as I was. We agreed I would travel to Edmonton that day to be with the boys.

Since I had known Eddie, he had threatened to end his life so many times. I didn't think he would go through with it. He loved the boys too much to do that to them. Not knowing what he was thinking, I can only guess that everything that was going on in his life—unemployment, eviction, the possibility of going back to jail—was just too much. He was to be back in court to face the charges of uttering threats on August 9, and he just couldn't take it any more. The stress took over.

I contacted Kim, and we arranged to meet at my hotel before going to the house. Gerri and Jolene were planning on staying at the house but I asked them to wait for us to get there. I was hoping we could meet at the hotel first. The boys had shared with me that they were unsure about all of this family showing up. They hadn't seen these aunts in years and they were skeptical about why they were showing up now. I wanted to reassure them that everything was going to be okay. Their family had come to support them. They were there to make sure they were okay, nothing else.

One of Brett's fears, which he brought up on our arrival, was that he would be forced to move to Calgary to live with one of his relatives. He really didn't know any of them well, including me, and he didn't want to lose his way of life along with losing his dad. To him, life had turned upside down in the last twenty-four hours. It was a difficult and stressful situation. He couldn't see that his family only had the best of intentions. All he saw were interlopers.

Both of the boys feared the influx of family would mean they would lose all their belongings. It would be like the scavengers after the dead, taking away all Eddie's possessions. I don't know what Eddie told the boys about his aunts, but that was the last thing they ever intended. They too were shocked about Eddie. They just wanted to offer their support—nothing more.

Unfortunately Gerry and Jolene did go directly to the house. Brett was there with a friend. Blake had been and gone. He had been coming by the house occasionally, but due to the court order he was cautious about being there. We actually called the police to see if, under the circumstances, the order could be lifted. They said it couldn't unless we went to court. Sometimes reason takes over the law. Since the complaint concerned Eddie, who was now gone, the issue was moot. Legalities!

A short while later, Kim, Courtney, two of Kim's other daughters, Janet, Tamara, and I arrived. The house was getting full. It was making Brett more uncomfortable. He wouldn't talk to me or look at me. I learned from past encounters to give him space. He knew I was there, if he wanted to talk to me. He did become more comfortable with Courtney. They were fairly close in age and he had been in contact with her over the last few months.

That first night, everyone sat around and talked and tried to get over the shock of what happened. We tried to relieve Brett's fears about moving and about any of us taking their things. We started going through some of the paperwork laying around, not snooping. All of us wanted to understand why Eddie would take such drastic measures.

Eventually someone found a suicide note in a box on a shelf in the kitchen. It actually looked like it had been written a long time ago. There was also someone else's writing on the note. It said, "Please help this guy."

We discussed the arrangements for Eddie and who would take care of them, Eddie's sisters decided that as the boys were closest to Eddie and I was their mother, that I should be responsible for dealing with the funeral and the estate. That way, the boys would be sure to have their needs and wants met. I guess I wasn't thinking clearly at the time because I agreed. At first, I assumed that I was in charge of planning the funeral, which I didn't mind. I wanted the boys to say their good-byes properly and celebrate their father's life. Then I realized there was a financial burden too. It was another of Eddie's bills that I was to pay.

During that night, we speculated a lot about Eddie's reasons for killing himself. We all knew Eddie was distressed and somewhat depressed, but we were all shocked he had committed suicide. Yeah, he talked a lot about doing it, but we all thought that it was simply talk. He often said a lot of things without following through. Why start with suicide?

There were so many questions. He had been planning to move to Calgary with Brett to live with his sister Jolene. He seemed ready, once again, for a fresh start. Eddie hadn't made these plans without some effort. We also wondered why there were two chairs in the laundry room where it occurred. He would only have needed one to do the job.

The next day the boys and I went to the funeral home to make arrangements. We agreed to cremate Eddie. The staff at the funeral home were very helpful: they helped with the paperwork, the obituary, and all the little details that you never expect when someone dies.

The boys told me that Eddie always said that: "the Pope went out in a box and I will, too." After some preliminary discussions, we were taken into a room filled with "boxes" and urns. First we needed to choose a coffin to use in the cremation. The coffins ranged from basic pine to other, finer woods lined with soft fabric and a pillow. Basic pine seemed too harsh for the occasion, so we chose a coffin lined with white satin and pillow.

Then we selected a light brown simple wooden box for the urn. It had a beautiful engraving that spoke about fathers. When we realized that the boys would not be living together, Penny and Jolene purchased another urn so that each boy could have one. We also chose some smaller, heart-shaped boxes so the boys could carry their father with them all the time if they wanted. Death is a part of life, and when it ends suddenly, dealing with the practicalities can become difficult for loved ones. While we were choosing items for Eddie, Brett grew upset. He thought it was sick that we were "shopping for his dead father."

I agreed to identify the body, and, at first, the boys didn't want to see him. I guess they wanted to remember Eddie as he was in life, not in death. It is a difficult task for anyone and would probably be very traumatic for teenagers. But they changed their minds and we arranged a small viewing for the boys, Eddie's best friend, Murray, and me. We planned to return a couple of days later for the viewing. We went home to find clothes Eddie would be cremated in. The boys chose some runners, jeans, a boxing jacket, and a baseball cap. It was how they thought their dad would be most comfortable. It was a task done without much emotion.

I also started making arrangements for a memorial service. I booked the hall and spoke with the pastor and Carmen and Eddie's AA sponsor, Brent, and his wife. They were truly supportive and helpful in making the arrangements. They helped me with food, flowers, programs, and all the little things that had to be done.

It was all so surreal. Eddie and I had been apart for over ten years, and there I was, arranging his memorial service. I was packing up his things and calling about storage facilities. I was paying for the service, cremation, and storage. The pastor and Eddie's AA sponsor and their wives did help with paying for flowers, projector, and the food. I only wanted to make things easier for the boys. At the time, it didn't matter what everything cost. It had to be done, so I did it. Emotionally I couldn't deal with an argument about paying, but I realized later there were other options and I definitely should have explored them. Eddie was my ex-husband, and I had no legal or moral responsibility to take on this task. I just wanted to make things as easy as possible for the boys.

We spent an entire week taking care of all the details. I packed up a few things in the house but most of the time I was arranging for the memorial service. The people that Brett had stayed with the night before Eddie died, Kyle's family, agreed that he could live with them. I met with them and they seemed to really care about Brett. It was a nice situation for Brett, as he could remain in the same neighborhood.

They were a nice family and did family activities on the weekends, like camping and riding quads. They had already taken Brett on a few of these trips and saw how much Brett enjoyed them. Based on what they knew was happening in Brett's house, they were happy to see him happy. In the winter, they said they planned to put Brett back into hockey. I was excited for Brett to experience a normal family atmosphere and good family fun. I knew moving to Calgary with me wasn't an option. He still couldn't even look at me for more than a few of seconds.

This was a really strange time for me. I really felt I had returned to the life I left behind so many years ago. All of a sudden, I was in my ex-husband's house packing his things. I noticed he still had clothes from the time we were married. I pulled out a blue Reebok sweatshirt and a flood of memories came rushing back. He wore that shirt a lot, often when we enjoyed our movie nights and ice cream on the couch. There was also his hypercolor shirt that Eddie was wearing when I gave birth to Blake. It was an unusual shirt because it changed color with heat. I remember clinging to it after many hours of labor. It was never the same color after that. I quickly placed the shirts and the rest of his clothes in the box and sealed it.

In some ways, Eddie had not moved forward in life. He stuck to the same old things. He stayed within his comfort zone to try and maintain control.

It was all kind of peculiar. All the time I had been with Eddie and the ten years since, Eddie's family had held no hard feelings toward me. In fact, they welcomed me with open arms. I felt at once at ease, but yet a little uncomfortable. What did they know of our past? I'm sure they questioned him about why I left the boys with Eddie. But they never spoke about it with me.

Unfortunately, the welcome by the boys wasn't as friendly. It was almost an uneasiness with the boys and this family that they weren't too sure about. Nobody really knew what Eddie had told the boys about their aunts and now wasn't the time or place to bring it up. Everyone was there to help the boys in any way they could.

Some of the people at the house were friends of Eddie's. Apparently they didn't know about me, which I thought was strange. They only saw me as some woman who had parachuted in and had taken over all the planning including packing Eddie's things. They probably wondered what right I had to do this. Needless to say, I had a few stares from them, but I just went on doing what needed to be done. So now they had something to talk about, but I didn't care. They only knew Eddie's side of the story, not mine.

I prepared a PowerPoint presentation for the memorial service. I searched through the house and found a few pictures of Eddie and the boys. It was weird that I actually had more pictures of Eddie than the boys or his sisters. I had kept a few pictures from when we were married and the boys were young. At least I had some memories to share with the boys. It's hard when you lose someone so quickly and during difficult, unpleasant times. It's hard to remember the good times.

Death is an equal opportunity event. Everyone will experience it eventually. Those of us who are left behind for the time being must deal with the repercussions, however dreadful they may be. Death is an opportunity to move on from any ugliness or disagreements in the past. The ugliness will always be there in the back, but the bad memories become less important. You have to move on.

The viewing happened later that week and was harder than the boys thought it would be. At first, the three of us went into the viewing room together. I was surprised to see Eddie like that. He looked so small. I didn't stay long so that each of the boys could have time with him. Brett left first and then Blake was there alone. Blake took quite a bit of time with his dad and I learned later that he had moved Eddie's head to see where the cord had been. He told me later he regretted doing it, but at the time he felt he needed to see it.

When Brett came out, he was quite distraught. I tried to hug him to comfort him, like anyone would do, but he pushed me away. I was crushed. How could my son not want comfort? Was it me? Was he so devastated no one could reach him right now? I did take it personally, but I knew Brett and I had a long way to go toward healing. When Blake returned, Brett went back inside to see his dad once again. This time he stayed a long time, and eventually we had to go inside and tell him we were leaving.

Eddie's friend Murray was there that day. He wasn't able to attend the memorial service, so this was his good-bye. It was good to have him there and he took the boys out for lunch after his visit. I was grateful they had someone to talk to. Murray had been Eddie's friend since they were kids, and he knew his bad side and his good side. Murray was a good person for the boys to talk to, whether it was about being mad that Eddie had done this or that they were sad to have been left behind.

I had been in Edmonton that week surrounded by Eddie's family. They are all wonderful people, but I started to feel like I was in quicksand and was being sucked back into my past. I went home that weekend just to connect with Andy and reassure myself that my present life was still intact and real. Andy had been wonderfully supportive and accepted there were things I had to do. He didn't question it; he just let me do what I had to. It was so wonderful to have a companion who thought of the other person first. Sometimes you take it for granted, but I will never do that. I lived a different life before Andy and I do not want to ever go back.

I went back to Edmonton on Monday to pack up the remainder of the house, put some things in storage, and ensure the memorial service went well. I was relieved to hand the keys back to the landlord and leave Edmonton at the end of the week. I really felt torn inside. I felt there was more I needed to do, and that I needed to stay longer. I could have stayed for the boys, but did they even want me there?

Andy helped me realize there was nothing more I could do. Brett was now living with his friend's family and Blake was living with his girlfriend.

They were on the road to their new lives. I hoped with all my heart their lives would be full of peace and love, even if I couldn't be part of it.

Henry Ellis said, "The art of living lies in the fine mingling of letting go and holding on."

It was time to let go.

Difficult Times

Brett's life was pretty tumultuous before his father died. He had been expelled from school, he was drinking heavily, and partying way too hard. I heard Dr. Phil say that the same-sex parent is the most influential parent. For Brett, Eddie was certainly influential, and not always for the better. Brett saw how his father behaved and lived, and now he was living a similar lifestyle.

Brett had had very little security in his life with Eddie, but at least he'd had some. Now this was gone, too. Life was more precarious for him. At the time he was living with Kyle and his family but nobody was sure this would be the answer. So much change was taking place. Would he fit in with the family? Would they get along? In the hierarchy of needs, the very first needs, food and shelter, are physiological. We can do strange things when these needs are not met.

It was also very hard to comprehend why his father had taken his own life. Everyone was shocked, even though he had been threatening to do it for years. There were so many questions that came to mind: the two chairs, the suicide note. The note itself wasn't out where it could be found easily. Eddie was telling the world he was sorry or why he thought he had run out of hope. Instead the note looked like it was written long ago and tucked into a box. Not that all suicides have a note. Dr. A. Leenaars, a Canadian researcher, indicated that the percentage of suicides who leave a note range only from 12 to 37 percent.[5] That's not a large percentage, but when I think of Eddie I thought he would detail his thoughts that morning.

So, I still had lots of questions, and after the shock wore off I remembered something Eddie had mentioned six months earlier. He said something to the effect of, if anything ever happened to me, so-and-so did it. The name didn't mean anything to me at the time, and I thought it was just Eddie being Eddie. I wondered who he had pissed off now. I thought nothing of it until that week. As far I was concerned, Eddie had taken his own life, and the police ruled his death a suicide. For those left behind, it is always hard to understand why someone would do that and to accept it. I remember watching a movie years ago, long before Eddie's death, about a young man who eventually committed suicide. I can't recall the title, but I remember how it struck the family afterward. I remember how depressed the person was beforehand, but when he finally decided to go through with it, calmness settled over him. Everyone thought he was cured, that he was on the mend. Instead he waited until his family members were out of the house and killed himself.

It was such a sad movie. I saw how the family tried to deal with the aftermath of what had happened, and it all came back to me: that sense of powerlessness. You can keep questioning why you did or didn't do a particular thing. But you can't always reach people who are in deep depression. They are too far down the rabbit hole and there's nothing that can be done. Eddie had been in treatment many times over many years. It didn't help. He had lost hope. When you lose hope, a part of you dies.

Brett was having a hard time accepting and dealing with Eddie's death. Thankfully Kyle's family was being very supportive. Brett was still so angry with me. Sometimes he was even aggressive—once he threatened me. We were at his dad's house packing up Eddie's things. Brett was there with a few of his friends. We were sitting at the table and he started to badmouth me. I told him that he needed to show a bit of respect. That is when he stood up and lunged over the table at me with his hand in a fist. He threatened to punch me. My heart was pounding, but I did my best to stay calm. Old memories came hurtling back at me. I got up, walked out the door, and drove away as fast as I could. I didn't know how this was going to unfold, but I knew I had to get out of there. Part of me understood he was angry

---

5   DistressCentreOakville.com

and probably felt isolated and abandoned after Eddie's death, but threatening me was not the answer. I could not and would not accept that behavior from anyone. There is only so much compensating a person can do.

Kyle's family was a nice, loving, stable family filled with activity and structure. At first Brett thought it would be great. Kyle and his family did all sorts of fun family things on the weekends, like camping and quadding, and Brett enjoyed spending time with them. They were fairly liberal with the rules, but there were some rules. Unfortunately, there were too many rules and too much structure for Brett to deal with. He had not had any real parenting in years, and it was all too much for him. He had trouble getting accustomed to rules and respect. An innocent family camping trip a few weeks after Eddie's death turned into an ugly incident. Brett decided he wanted to stay at home instead. He was dealing with a lot, and maybe he just needed some time alone. Kyle's parents weren't too happy that Brett didn't want to come. They were very aware of what he was dealing with, and they thought it would be best for him to have some adult supervision. They accepted that they couldn't force him to come, but they asked him not to stay at the house while they were away. He was a teenage boy, he'd just turned sixteen. They just wanted to make sure everything at their house stayed orderly while they were gone.

Not having a place to call home for the weekend seemed to really throw Brett for a loop. Through e-mail correspondence, he let me know how unhappy he was about this. Brett didn't understand that with every choice there is a consequence. He chose not to go on the camping trip, and, as a result, Kyle's parents chose not to leave Brett in the house alone. They were concerned that Brett might try and stay at the house anyway, so they arranged for Kyle's grandmother to stay for the weekend and make sure there was no trouble.

Maybe he was rebelling or lashing out, I don't know, but he and a friend made sure Kyle's grandmother knew he was unhappy. One afternoon that weekend Brett and his friend went to Kyle's house. They knocked on the door, but of course Kyle's grandmother wasn't going to let them in. This really upset them, so they started yelling profanities and sprayed the grandmother with a garden hose through the screen door. It was a very nasty thing to do. She called the police and Brett was charged.

After this incident, Kyle's parents asked Brett to leave the house. I'm sure it must have hurt them to take such drastic measures considering the circumstances, but the safety of their own family was paramount. I talked with Kyle's dad. He told me he felt that he had to take such a drastic measure because, in the end, he felt it would help Brett. He told me that he hadn't been an angel himself as a teenager. He had experienced his own troubles. In the end, he realized the error of his ways and was able to turn his life around. He was hoping that if Brett realized that there were serious consequences to his actions, then he might start to think about his actions and change his ways. This all happened before September 2009, it was less than two months after Eddie's death.

After leaving his friend's house, Brett lived on his own for a while. He would couch surf at friends' houses, occasionally sleep in the park, or spend the night with Blake and his girlfriend. I tried to keep in touch with him through Blake and some of his other friends on Facebook. I would hear from him every now and then if he needed something. His aunts also tried to keep tabs on him through friends and his cousins. We were a circle of caretakers who shared with each other what little knowledge we had about him. Sometimes, we only had a little bit of information, but we tried to make sure that at least one of us knew something about him.

I heard that Brett was drinking heavily during this time. I became very concerned for his well-being and his safety. There was never a consistency in the information I had about Brett, and I didn't know how much longer he could last. He had been burning the candle at both ends and with the emotional turmoil of Eddie's departure; I didn't know how much longer he could handle it. To this day, I have no idea how his body coped with all the alcohol he consumed, and I'm sure I didn't know it all, either.

I was aware of Brett's court dates for the incidents at the school and Kyle's house. I wanted to get him some help before those dates. I wanted to get him started on the right path, but he wasn't cooperating at all. His aunts and I tried on many occasions to help him. He emphatically said he wouldn't move to Calgary again and again. He had just lost his father, and all he had left were his friends. He wasn't going to lose them too. We tried to persuade him to think of his future. Friends grow up and move on. He needed to take care of himself.

In order to help him, I went to one of his court appearances. I didn't expect him to show up, but I was also afraid he might. He had been very unpredictable in my presence before, so I wasn't sure if just the sight of me there might ruin my chances with him. I knew he wasn't happy. I wasn't happy, but I wanted to help. The problem was that he didn't want my help or anyone else's.

I had a purpose for being there that day. I wanted him to see me there, in some ways, but I also wanted to talk to the prosecutor about possible detention after the hearing. I thought perhaps if he was detained for long enough, he could get some help. He needed to detox for sure, and he needed counseling. He had lost his father and was spiraling downhill in every way possible. I wanted him to have an epiphany that the life he was living wasn't what he really wanted. I wanted him to realize that he had goals and dreams and wanted more for himself. But I couldn't make him have it. That was one thing he needed to do himself.

I finally did get to speak with the prosecutor. He did warn me that anything I said to him could be used to strengthen the case against Brett. I told him that I understood that and it was my intention to get help for Brett. The prosecutor reviewed Brett's charges and his file. I was very disappointed when he told me that Brett would probably only have community service and no detention. He said they couldn't order counseling or rehab. Instead, he referred me to a social worker. You never want to see your loved ones incarcerated, but sometimes it might be the only thing that can help. I remember wishing that for Eddie, too. Brett was now following his father's path. I felt helpless. And yes, for a while, I felt hopeless.

So I contacted the social worker who told me about a PCHAD order. It is the Protection of Children against Alcohol and Drugs. This government program is delivered through Alberta Health and Wellness. It is a difficult process to have your child admitted into the program but it forces protection on the child. Unfortunately, I heard it didn't have a great success rate. Because it is forced confinement for five days, sometimes rebellion is the only thing they have left. The kids in the program can't leave the facility, but they don't have to participate in the counseling either. I was desperate. It was a very harsh step to take and I wanted to exhaust all other avenues first. When it came down to it, I just wanted Brett to be happy and healthy.

As the sadness of that summer passed and autumn leaves and cool fall mornings took their place, T.J.'s family once again came to Brett's rescue. T.J.'s parents, Linda and Jim, had been like second parents to both Blake and Brett. Geographically, they lived right around the corner, so the boys always knew there was a safe haven nearby. Linda was like an angel to the boys. She is very much a mom to both of them. She had a welcoming heart for Brett and wanted desperately to help him. She thought with the right environment and support, Brett might just turn around and get on the right track. She convinced her husband, Jim, to take that chance, too.

September was approaching and Brett was desperate to go back to school. He pleaded with me to contact the high school that had expelled him and negotiate a return. He seemed eager and passionate about return- ing to school, so I thought he had made a decision to change. I wanted to help, so I contacted the school and the Board of Education. They refused to allow him to return. I tried enrolling him in the Catholic system, but because he had been expelled for violence, he wasn't accepted in either school system.

The Board of Education said Brett would have to go to reform school. When he proved himself there, they would reconsider allowing him to return to mainstream high school. Brett still hadn't been to court regarding the issues of his expulsion, so until he could prove he had his anger under control for at least a semester, he wasn't welcomed back.

The bottom line was that if Brett wanted to go to school at all, he would have to go first to the "bad kids school," as he often referred to it. Linda worked close to this school. She thought if Brett just came to work with her each day, she could drop him off at school on her way to work. She knew the importance of Brett going back to school and she thought that he could do it with her support. She talked it over with Brett and he agreed to give it a try. One step at a time.

With Linda by his side, Brett enrolled in the school. He was very unsure of the whole environment, but I know he wanted to please Linda and would give it his all. He went for a couple of days and he realized that it really wasn't for him. He told me he wasn't happy there and it made him very uncomfortable. He said he felt some of the kids there were dangerous and he wasn't one of those kids. I felt that if Brett was that uncomfortable, he wouldn't give it a chance and the likelihood of success dropped dramati- cally. So I called the school and expressed our concerns over the situation.

The administration was very understanding and wanted Brett to suc- ceed. They were accommodating and mentioned a program about combin- ing traditional school and a trade apprenticeship. They indicated that he could spend two days a week doing regular schoolwork, which he could do from home, and he could spend the other three days at a job site learning carpentry skills. At first he seemed thrilled that there was an alternative.

All he had to do was meet with both teachers, one for the traditional school and the other for the apprenticeship, and get everything in motion. Linda was willing and eager to attend the meetings with Brett to get him started, but even after a few days of encouragement from me, Linda, and Jim, Brett never attended the meetings. In fact, he didn't continue with his education at all. Linda suggested other alternatives for his education, but Brett stalemated and wouldn't cooperate.

Everyone was devastated by Brett's refusal to further his education. He had been offered the opportunity of a lifetime, and he didn't realize it. He could get his high school diploma and be trained in a field that would allow him to support himself. But he couldn't see it, and so it was lost.

He had the best living situation he could have been offered. He was comfortable with Linda and Jim because he had known them since he was a child. He had his own big bedroom and regular meals with a family that loved and supported him. Unfortunately, he didn't know how to accept this and he began acting out once again. He continued his partying by sneaking out at night through a basement window. He wasn't picking up after himself. Sometimes he had people over to the house when Linda and Jim weren't there. He was disrespectful of Linda and Jim and the rules of their house. Needless to say, they were sad and upset that Brett didn't observe their rules. It was like he was doing everything to shut out everyone that loved him. I think it's a defense mechanism, but it doesn't change the hurt people feel when they give and give and there is no response.

Despite all that, Linda wasn't ready to give up yet. She had a never-ending heart and thought everyone could change with the right support. One beautiful fall day, Linda and Brett were in the backyard doing some fall cleanup. They picked some crabapples off the off the ground, raked some leaves, and cleaned up the garbage that always seemed to fly into the backyard. Linda told me that during afternoon, she saw a glimpse of the old Brett. Brett had said that Jim would be so pleased with all their hard work. He was pleased with himself too, and so was Linda. When Brett mentioned that Jim would be pleased, it broke her heart. Although Brett seemed to be the hard-nosed kid, always in trouble, here he was, like any child, just wanting recognition for a job well done. He wanted Jim to be proud of him.

We all go through life with our own baggage. I had so much baggage it was heavy to handle at times. But as a child, we always want our parents to love us and to be proud of us. I remember watching the movie *The Sixth Sense* with Bruce Willis as the psychologist and Toni Collette as the mother. This is the story of a little boy who has the ability to talk with dead people. I remember one of the last scenes, when Haley Joel Osment (Cole) talks to his mother about his dead grandmother. And the mother asks Cole the question she asked at the graveyard "Do I make her proud?" Cole responds, "Everyday." These are such powerful words. I remember being overcome with emotion when he said it. Even now, I can remember those feelings. There is so much weight on a child to have someone who is proud of him or her. He may not come out and say it, he may even brush it off, but everyone wants someone to be proud of him. When you make someone proud, it means that someone values you. We all want value and acceptance, even as adults.

For Linda, it must have been overwhelming, too, to watch a boy, who had experienced so much hardship and turmoil, become the young man he was becoming. She knew deep down inside the sweet young Brett was still there. He was lost and trying to find a way out. Unfortunately, he'd made too many wrong turns. She didn't know how long it would be until he was lost forever.

Brett was in trouble with the police on a regular basis. He never did show up for his court dates, so there seemed to be a never-ending outstanding warrant. It's odd how the justice system works. Every time Brett would get picked up for something, he would call Linda and she would go to the police station and he would be released to her custody. Eventually she realized she wasn't helping him by bailing him out. She stopped showing up, so they released Brett on his own recognizance.

Brett had been living at Jim and Linda's house for almost two months. There was definitely some tension at the house, as Brett wasn't following any rules. The last straw came when Brett, T.J., and some other friends stole a car and went for a joyride. I heard this wasn't the first time this had happened. But this time they were in an accident. The accident was so bad it knocked Brett unconscious, his friends managed to drag him out of the car, and when he woke up a few minutes later they all ran off. It wasn't long before the police managed to find out what happened. They showed up at the house with an ambulance to apprehend Brett. They took him to the hospital to be checked out first, and then they took him to jail. He stood before a judge and was released with a future court date. He hadn't shown up to the other court dates, so why would this one be any different?

The presence of a police car was starting to become embarrassing for Jim and Linda. It was happening far too often. Up until Brett came to live with them, they were a happy, normal family who lived a pretty routine life. They fit in well with their neighbors. Now they were starting to be concerned with what the neighbors might be thinking. With police there fairly frequently, they might be concerned that something would happen to their own homes, or that their personal safety was in jeopardy. The looks from other neighbors were too much. All the help in the world wasn't going to help Brett if he didn't want to change.

Jim was now at his breaking point. This last incident was the final straw. Linda tried to convince him to give Brett another chance, but he just couldn't do it. All this drama was too much for him. So he sat Brett down and discussed all the chances he had and the issues that were bothering him the most. Calmly, he said he had no choice. He loved Brett and he cared about him very much, but Brett would have to leave. Linda had discussed this with me, and I understood Jim and Linda's heartbreak. I felt it, too. My biggest challenge now was to find yet another place for Brett to live. For the time being, Brett was homeless once again.

Although Brett wasn't living there anymore, Linda and I kept in touch through e-mail. We were both in a mess wondering what was happening with Brett. It was now November and it was getting cold outside. How was Brett surviving, where was he sleeping? What else was he doing? There were too many questions and too many unknowns. And when you do not know, sometimes the mind goes to the worst place imaginable.

Over the next few days and weeks I would get sporadic messages from Brett through Facebook or text messages from his friend's phone. They were often cryptic and accusatory. Brett was lashing out at me for his circumstances. I tried my best to talk to him about getting help, but he didn't want to hear it. A few days later, he showed up late at night at Jim and Linda's house. He was with two of his friends and knocked at the door. He asked Jim if he could stay at the house. Jim refused.

Later that night I heard that Brett had shown up at one of his friend's houses, hoping to stay the night. It was a school night and the friend's mother just wasn't sure. She didn't feel comfortable with the situation, so she gave Brett a blanket and sent him on his way. Brett was going to sleep in the park that night. But the night was too cold and Brett showed up back at that house later and the friend's mom gave in and let him stay the night.

I guess Jim thought they had tried everything to get Brett to come to his senses and now it was time for tough love. I have heard stories and watched movies about tough love. For some kids, it really works. But they have to fall to the bottom first before they can slowly get themselves the help they need. The last few months, everyone thought Brett was pretty close to the bottom. He could only go up now, right?

It was a pretty emotional and sad time. At times, I just wanted to shake Brett and tell him to wake up and grow up, to be respectful and kind. But I knew that wasn't going to happen. I also wanted to hold him in my arms, to comfort him and reassure him that everything would be all right. I could want it all for him and pray and pray, but at some point he had to help himself. The situation with Brett was just tearing me apart. My heart was slowly being ripped to shreds. I couldn't even think about reconciliation with him. I could only worry about his safety.

I was so desperate I decided that, even if Brett never talked to me again, I had to get him some help. I seriously thought about the PCHAD order. At least with the protective order, he would be in custody for five days, detoxing, and forced to have some limited counseling. At a minimum, he would be off the streets and be safe for those five days. It would only buy a little time, though. But at that point, time was a luxury, and it would give me a chance to plan the next step.

The next morning I went to court and was successful in obtaining a PCHAD agreement. The difficulty is that the order is only in place for 125 hours. That meant I had to find Brett and have him picked up within that time. I had no idea where he was and the police didn't have the resources to track him down. We couldn't find Brett, so the protective order expired.

For many years I dealt with Eddie and the justice system to no avail. Now that a minor was involved, I actually thought the system would prevail and would work like it is supposed too. Brett was sixteen years old, a minor. He had multiple warrants for missed court appearances and various other charges, but the judicial system never found him. For the last few years, Brett had lived in the same area he had grown up, he never strayed very far, so why couldn't they find him there? Couldn't the police take action to locate him and bring him in so he could receive the treatment he so desperately needed?

By that point, I was truly exhausted and spent. I tried to help Brett in so many ways, but there were too many obstacles. And I was trying to do this living in Calgary when he was in Edmonton. I was beyond devastated. I couldn't understand why life had to be like this, again. I knew my relationship with Brett wasn't great, but I tried. He may not have wanted it, but both Linda and I tried to help him. We could see past his rebellion and lashing out. We saw the sweet young Brett hiding in the shadows of pain.

I didn't want to give up, so I tried another route. I wrote a letter to the Minister of Health in Alberta. I explained the situation, the past history, and begged for help. All I wanted was to get Brett off the streets into a program where he would have to listen to someone other than his family. He needed subjectivity and real help. One day I received a response in the mail from the minister's office. It was the typical political BS. I'm sorry we cannot assist you in your situation. And then they implied that I hadn't really tried myself. I felt like screaming at them. What did they know about us? Nothing.

I am a government employee, but I just couldn't take this crap. When someone asked for help in my office, I tried to help that person myself. If I couldn't, I put the person in contact with someone that might understand and know how best to help. I wanted to go right to their office or to the media and talk about the inefficiencies of our healthcare and justice systems in Alberta. But that wouldn't do anything for Brett and might actually make things worse between us. I had failed again.

I found out after a few days of couch surfing that one of Brett's friends, Donovan, felt sorry for him and let him stay at his house. Donovan was eighteen, he lived with his grandpa. He is a very enterprising and entrepreneurial young man. Donovan had a job as a plumber's helper but also worked as a DJ, a rapper, and an event promoter. It seemed like he had ambition, drive, and stability; the year before he had hosted a few booze-free hall parties in Edmonton. He made a lot of money, which he saved to buy a new car, a Dodge Charger. Donovan is a smart kid and knew hard work would pay off and help him to be successful.

Although Donovan was only a couple of years older than Brett, Brett was like a younger brother to him. Donovan wanted to help him and thought if Brett had the right environment and support he could make the right changes to be successful in life. He really wanted to give Brett the chance to make a change. Brett moved into their house and was living in the basement. At least now he was off the streets and safety wasn't an immediate concern. That was the first step.

After a short while, Brett talked to Donovan and told him if he could get an apartment without me cosigning for it, I would help pay an amount toward the rent each month. This was something Brett and I had discussed. So they talked that perhaps it was a good opportunity for Donovan and Brett to get a place together. I was going to cover a large chunk of the costs, so they should be able to afford to live together. Donovan, Brett, and I started negotiating the move and the costs.

Eventually we decided that Donovan would be the primary tenant and would buy the food and only pay rent in excess of our agreed-upon amount. This seemed like a good plan to me and a great deal for them both. Brett would have a place to live, with someone who was a responsible young man as a mentor. Donovan talked to Brett about finishing his education, too. He had goals and I thought that by living together some of his dreams and goals would rub off on Brett. Brett might get excited about life again. Everyone was happy with this arrangement.

Thank goodness for the Internet. I was able to do a lot of research from my place in Calgary, so I made a list of potential apartments and told Brett and Donovan I would be there on the weekend to view them. We met at the first house. Brett and Donovan were together. Brett still had a hard time being in physical proximity to me so we travelled in separate cars. It hurt, but that was the least of my worries.

After looking at a few apartments, the boys found a basement suite that they absolutely loved. They filled out an application for tenancy and the deal was done. While Brett was looking about, I discreetly talked to Donovan about the new place. I didn't want this to be a party pad with ongoing parties and drinking. He reassured me that they would be on the straight and narrow. I believed him; he had a good head on his shoulders.

They planned to move December 1. I would come back and help them move in and get their stuff out of storage. I now had hope. I hoped that this would be the change Brett needed to break away from the past and to finally move on. During the move I met Donovan's mom. She was a lovely lady. Her son was moving out for the first time and she was excited and proud of Donovan.

Christmas was approaching, and I knew it would be a tough one. This was going to be the first Christmas since Eddie died. Brett needed to be around people. I was glad he and Donovan were going to be living together. It was far too soon for Brett and I to be together—his anger and mistrust were evident when he was around me. I was going to be away for part of December, as it was Andy's mom's ninetieth birthday. We had made travel plans to go visit Andy's mom early December, and then I would be in Ontario to spend Christmas with my parents. Donovan's mom reassured me that Brett could spend Christmas with them. She was going to make it a special day for him. I was very grateful for her generosity.

Change is good for everyone but not everyone adapts well to it. It can bring stress and how you deal with the stress can make the change easier or more difficult. Brett didn't deal well with change. I had learned that while trying to initiate a relationship with him. And now he wasn't happy living with Donovan either. For an eighteen-year-old, Donovan had his life together and knew what he wanted. He had set rules and expected them to be followed. He and Donovan really had different expectations. The honeymoon of living on their own was soon over.

Donovan worked quite a bit and that left Brett alone. They say idleness is the devil's playground. Being idle and without purpose helped Brett start his old ways again. He wasn't going to school, he was smoking in the apartment, and he didn't seem to want to do anything. I was hoping that with time, Brett would settle down and things would get better. They didn't. He had only been living with Donovan a week or so when trouble started.

Although both Brett and Donovan really liked the apartment when we first viewed it, Brett now saw it as an encumbrance to his social life. The apartment was not in his old neighborhood, and I'm sure it was almost like moving to a new city. It was a long bus ride to get to his "hood" with his friends, and the distance started to create problems.

Just before I left in December, Brett called me. At first I was excited to hear from him. It didn't take long for his attitude and tone of voice to let me know that things weren't working, again. He started swearing at me and threatening me. I wasn't going to accept that from anyone anymore, so I hung up the phone. Then he texted me and told me he was going to kill himself on Christmas day. I didn't respond. I thought it was just another ploy to irritate me. He called again a short while later and as soon as I picked up the phone, he was swearing again. I hung up again. I was getting sick and tired of him manipulating and abusing me like that. He learned that from Eddie. I remember it all too well.

He called again. At first I wasn't going to answer, but I had to. I was worried about his frame of mind. He didn't swear this time. He asked me to call him a cab to go to Beverly, his old neighborhood on the north side of Edmonton. I said I would, so when we hung up, I decided to do something drastic. Instead of calling a cab, I called the police to take him to the hospital to have him assessed. At the time, I didn't care if I had destroyed any relationship I had with Brett. The situation wasn't about me: it was about Brett, and he needed help. It was tough love to the extreme. I cared so much I risked everything, any potential at a life together so he could get help. It was no-win situation for me.

Brett was very angry that I had him taken to the hospital for evaluation. What was I to do? I had to take his threats seriously. It might have been a ploy, but he may have been reaching out. A child psychologist evaluated him but released him to his brother, Blake. I had been in touch with the doctor by phone. I begged and pleaded with him to keep Brett, but he said Brett wasn't a threat to himself, nor was he intoxicated, so they had no choice but to release him. I couldn't believe they thought he wasn't at risk. What were they smoking? Had the doctor listened to anything I said? Or did he live in a fairy tale and believe everything he heard? They didn't verify a thing.

You know when you look at someone else's life or see it in a movie how so many troubles plague a person, people try to help but the help doesn't seem to be accepted. Brett was having so many troubles. I wanted so desperately to help but my help wasn't working. I didn't want him to end up like Eddie.

Donovan and I knew Brett needed help and we both wondered why the professionals couldn't see it too. I was leaving to visit my mother-in-law the next day and I felt helpless to deal with Brett and his troubles. I called the doctor again but he didn't give me any details. All he said was Brett was fine and there was nothing they could do for him. Surprise, surprise.

Brett had court dates on December 10 and 16 for various incidents. As I would be away, I arranged for a taxi to pick him up and take him to the court on the scheduled dates. I also spoke with Linda, and she promised she would be in court on those dates. Neither one of us expected Brett to show up. He hadn't shown up before, but we still planned for it anyway.

On December 9, Andy and I headed across the pond to England to help celebrate his mother's ninetieth birthday. I was at a loss with Brett. I had attempted so many times to get him help, but in the end, it fell through. I needed the break so I could recuperate and reenergize for the next hurdle. Sometimes I felt so drained that I'm sure I wasn't thinking straight. I really needed this break and I knew, for the time being, anyway, that both Blake and Brett were okay. Other people were looking out for them.

Andy and I had a wonderful time visiting with his mom and his cousins. We had a nice family celebration without any controversies. Because they lived so far away, and the last few months had been about me and my family, I wanted Andy to know that I cared about his family, too. I'm sure it must have been hard for him to be on the sidelines, dealing with all the issues we had this past year. I was grateful I had married such a warm, kind person to help me through it.

We spent Christmas in Ontario with my parents and family. It was nice to see them again, although the time was short. It seemed like we did a lot of traveling in December. First to England, then to Ontario, and finally we spent New Year's Eve in Golden, British Columbia with some friends. We had a beautiful, serene view of the snow-capped mountains from our cabin.

Nature has a calming affect on me, and I so welcomed the peace and tranquility and enjoyed its beauty. Unfortunately, it didn't last long.

A New Year

New Year's Day should be the start of a new beginning—a chance to wake up, refreshed and ready to make changes in your life for the better. I woke to phone messages from the Edmonton Police Services. Brett had been arrested the night before and was now detained at the Edmonton Youth Offender Center (EYOC). I heard that Brett had a party the night before at his apartment and someone had called the police.

Believe it or not, I was grateful the police had detained him. I had hoped that now perhaps he would be able to get some help. When you are detained in the youth center, you have to fill out a questionnaire. Brett's responses were symptomatic of a troubled person. I was told they put him on a suicide watch. As hard as it was to hear this from the police, I was grateful Brett was in a safe place. Perhaps finally being in police custody would prove to be the catalyst for change. I could only hope.

The next messages were text messages from Brett's roommate, Donovan. It was more bad news. He said that the party the night before was the last straw for him. He couldn't live with Brett any longer. He said he moved out during the night and moved back to his grandpa's house. I could feel his heartbreak. He had wanted it to work, but Brett was so far gone that Donovan couldn't help him. He said he tried his best, but it hadn't been good enough. He said I needed to do whatever I could. Brett was now losing his friends too and soon there would be nothing left for him.

I was on a roller coaster that never seemed to have any upsides. A heart can only take so much. It had been broken so many times. But as a mother, even though you are heartbroken over and over again, there is always a glimmer of hope that the next time will be better. I kept hoping for it.

I made the hard decision to get another PCHAD order. At least I knew where Brett was this time. I wanted this in place before he was released. As soon as the courts reopened after the holidays, I immediately went to the courthouse. I felt a minor victory in getting the order in place. I sent the order to EYOC right away and felt confident that once Brett was released he would be admitted for help. From what everyone was telling me, he needed the detox and counseling sessions without any further delays.

Brett had a scheduled court appearance on January 5. Given the way he was feeling about me at the time and the fact I just obtained a PCHAD order, I knew it wasn't going to be love fest. I was also not feeling that comfortable around Brett either. He had been saying some nasty things to me, and I didn't want to aggravate the situation any further. I got in touch with Blake who volunteered to go to the court appearance and to bring Brett directly to the detox facility.

I was keeping tabs on the situation from Calgary. Blake called and said that Brett was a mess in court. He was disheveled and looked like he was on the verge of a nervous breakdown. Blake said the judge decided to let him go. Because there was a protective order in effect and there was another court date in ten days, he thought it was best to release him so he could get the help through the detention in an AADAC facility, as opposed to Edmonton Young Offender Center (EYOC).

I spoke with the counselor at the jail. He said he felt it was good to have the order because Brett would be detained for five days and there was a possibility of extending the order another five days. That would bring him up to the next court date. At least he would be safe for the next ten days, and I was reassured that Brett would not be released unless he went to detox.

Blake went through the arranged plan. He went to pick up Brett, but Brett told him he didn't have to go to detox because he agreed to do one-on-one counseling. Blake believed this to be true, so he took Brett to his friend's house and went home to his family.

When I heard this, I was so upset. How could this have happened again? Once again, the PCHAD order would expire and Brett would not get the help he needed. I now had no idea where Brett was and no one was willing to tell me. I could only hope that the police would pick him up and deliver him to the facility. Brett was still a minor and it seemed he had free reign with no consequences at all. I couldn't believe how things were being handled. It wasn't right.

I called the jail, and because it was late, I had to leave a message for the person who told Brett he didn't have to go to detox. Blake didn't need this. He was only a couple of years older than Brett, and it was too heavy a burden to be responsible for Brett's situation. He was spending so much time dealing with his issues and it was making things difficult with his girlfriend. Blake had believed Brett; he was his brother. Brett's story also sounded plausible to Blake because Brett seemed to be clarifying all the things that had to be done. He said he didn't want to go back to jail and would do whatever was necessary to ensure that he didn't.

My plan for detention until the next court date wasn't met. I had hoped if Brett was detained he could get into the residential rehab at AADAC and start on the road to recovery. Unfortunately when the addictions counselor called me the next day, he told me that there was no requirement for Brett to go to detox. He had recommended it, but Brett wouldn't be arrested if he didn't go. This wasn't related to his criminal charges, so it wasn't deemed as important. It was a choice that Brett had to make. What teenager would choose to go to detox? Only one that wanted to change. I really felt betrayed, misled, and lied to, but there was nothing I could do.

Of course I still had the option of having Brett picked up for the PCHAD order. The counselor suggested I wait. He said when you deal with an addict you have to move at their pace. He told me that you can't rush them because that can make it take longer or, worse, backfire. He said he felt it would be a waste of time for Brett to be locked up at this stage of the game. Five days is a long time if you don't want to take part in the therapy and therapy is totally voluntary. If I enforced the order, it would be a waste of my efforts and might even force a bigger rift between us. Although his health was my main concern, I didn't want to damage whatever was left of the relationship either. I bowed to the counselor's expertise in this area.

Brett was released from jail on January 5, 2010. He returned to the basement apartment he had been living in. There was an eviction notice posted on the door. The landlord who lived upstairs wasn't happy at all to see Brett come down the driveway. The eviction notice had been served and Brett could legally stay there until the end of January, but he certainly wasn't welcome.

The landlord opened the apartment for Brett to get some of his things. Unfortunately, while they were there, Brett's anger got the better of him and he lashed out at the landlord. He was very upset about the situation and took it out on the walls in the apartment, leaving them pot-marked with his punches. While he was there he called me—angry and upset. He was not kind in his language or tone. In fact, he was so rude and belligerent I ended the conversation without waiting to hear any more spoken garbage. There was so much swearing the name-calling. It was like I was dealing with his father again. It was a lot of the same language his father used: F***ing Bitch! Whore! And the "c" word the word I hated the most: c**t! I just thought that was such a derogatory word to women and I told him often how much it offended me and that I didn't want him to use it. There were other things he called me, but it just isn't appropriate to publish them.

I was surprised when he called back a few minutes later. This time he asked for money for food. He had just spent a few days in jail and came home to an eviction notice, no roommate, and no food. I really did feel sorry for him. It was a lot to handle in a few minutes. He could have dealt with it better, but I wasn't there and his emotions got the better of him. I also knew he had been calling Blake many times and there was some stress associated with that too. It was like Eddie was reincarnated in Brett.

I sent him some money through a postal moneygram. I know I shouldn't have, especially because of the way he spoke to me. But when your children are hurting, you hurt too, and I really wanted to make that hurt go away. That didn't go well either. He went to a post office, but because he didn't have any identification, they wouldn't give him the money. It was like a trigger on a gun. He called me while he was there, so I heard everything. He verbally abused the women working at the post office by calling them vile names. I was sick to my stomach. How could my son act this way and speak to people this way? People he didn't even know. He was so disrespectful I hung up the phone.

When he called me back, we had an argument about being respectful of others. He had excuses of course, but I tried to make him understand that being polite and respectful goes a long way. The thing was, I don't even think he understood he was being rude or offensive. Maybe it was what he was familiar with. Sounds strange, I know, but I hadn't been there for too many years, so I don't know. I only knew I wasn't going to accept it.

At that point in time, I really had no desire to even be near Brett. Yes, he was my son and he was in trouble, again, but over the last few months, he had been verbally abusive, very disrespectful, and, a few times, had physically threatened me. Yes, he was angry with me for trying to send him away. I accepted that. He wasn't ready to make changes, but his over-reactions are a different story. His counselor said addicts had to go at their own pace. They needed to decide when they were ready to get help and what kind of help that would be. I wasn't sure I was ready for the wait. I told Brett I needed a breather. I couldn't deal with his situation, and until he was ready to make some serious life changes and start respecting others, I was walking away. I told him he needed help, help I couldn't give him. He needed to make that decision for himself. If he couldn't, he was going to lose more because people wouldn't want to be in his life.

I drove to Edmonton that weekend to remove Brett's things from the apartment. It wasn't my responsibility, but I felt bad for the landlord. It wasn't a good situation and I just didn't want it to get any worse. I opened the door to a disaster zone. Empty bottles of alcohol, pizza boxes, and garbage were strewn everywhere. Someone had actually made Kraft Dinner in the kettle and left it there to rot. With the help of Linda and Jim and their son T.J., we were able to get it all clean. I left Edmonton with a heavy heart and without knowing where Brett was.

A few weeks later, I heard from Brett. He called me in the middle of the night. His girlfriend was in hospital and there was something wrong with her heart. He had been drinking and, I guess, reflecting on life. He sounded so sad. His voice quivered as he spoke. He said he needed a parent. He knew I couldn't just pack up and move to Edmonton, but he said I could be his mom on the weekends. I felt like he really meant it. Maybe this was the shock that would change his life. He even said he would go back to school if I took him on Monday.

I wanted to believe him. I wanted to run to the car and drive to Edmonton and just hold him. I wanted him to want to change. It had been such a long time since he had shown any kindness to me, and I wanted to savor the moment. There was hope again.

I was really torn about what to do next. I needed to hear from Sandy, my therapist. I wanted to hear from someone that could see beyond my emotional ties and my eagerness to make things work. I e-mailed her and anxiously waited for the response.

I received a message the following day. She had some words of wisdom. She brought me back down to reality and made me realize it might have been Brett reaching out, but he might also have been trying a different tactic to get to me. Sandy said: "My guts say that you should be careful here. Brett is certainly targeting your soft spot. He may have reached bottom but perhaps not. He has tried numerous strategies to get to you. He has tried threat and force and attack." She mentioned that my giving in to Brett's request of working in Calgary and going to Edmonton every weekend would bring a complete collapse of my marriage and life as I know it. Brett expected me to sacrifice myself to save him. Sandy explained that this wouldn't work. She encouraged me to talk with him and recognize that he had so many issues he might feel overwhelmed right now. She said: "More would be served by challenging/supporting Brett to get involved in a rehabilitation/life skills program." It was her hunch that he wasn't ready to commit to such a thing. It was like the EYOC counselor had told me. Brett has to help himself when he is ready to help himself. Nobody can force him. She suggested I ask him to call the school, to get him to show that first initiative, and then take it slow.

Sandy told me a few things that were pretty hard to hear, but maybe deep down I had thought of them myself and she was just verbalizing my own thoughts. She wanted me to be strong and to help Brett realize he was the master of his life. I was there for support, but he had to choose the right path.

She ended with a word of encouragement. She said to listen to my inner divine wisdom. She had been encouraging me to listen to my heart and trust that the Lord would be there on Brett's path and on mine. He is there even when we doubt, when we have lost ourselves, and when our hope becomes entangled in mire. He is there. It took me a long time to believe that for myself, and I hoped that Brett would start to discover that for himself, too.

I listened to her advice and stayed at home in Calgary. I talked with Brett a few days later; he had indeed reverted back to his old ways. Unfortunately the verbal tripe and rudeness had returned. When I had the school call Brett to see if he wanted to return, I was told he was rude to the person there, too. There was only so much I could do. I couldn't rehabilitate him or to change for him. He had to take that step.

In February, I went to Edmonton again and saw both Brett and Blake. I hadn't quite given up, and Blake could keep Brett in line much better than I could. I had some good news. I was now a grandma. Blake and his girlfriend had a beautiful baby boy on February 11, 2010. It was a good visit with the boys and my new grandson.

I also met the friend Brett had been staying with on and off. Although I didn't know much about him, there was just something about him I didn't like. He seemed shady somehow. But he was Brett's friend, and I had to be content that he had a place to live. Brett seemed okay with the arrangements. There were three of them in the apartment, but his friend's brother spent most of his time working in Fort McMurray. Because he was away more than at home, it was like they had the apartment all to themselves.

I really didn't approve of Brett's living arrangements, so I wasn't financially supporting him. I wanted Brett to make changes, but my wallet wasn't the pot of gold either. I was willing to help, but I needed his commitment and he hadn't showed that to me yet. It wasn't long before the friend's brother also tired of the living arrangements and asked Brett to leave. He was wearing out his welcome everywhere he lived. So he went back to Blake's place to live with him and his girlfriend and the kids for a while.

Driving back and forth to Edmonton began to take its toll on me. I had been there in November, December, and January dealing with Brett's relocations. I had been there in February to meet my grandson, and I had to travel there again in March. I wanted Brett to actually attend his court date. In the past, I arranged transportation or had Linda attend with him, but it was never successful. He was so afraid of going back to jail, so he just wouldn't attend.

This time I thought if I was actually there to pick him up and drive him there he might go. I drove to Edmonton the night before the court date and got settled in a hotel. Brett and I talked on the phone, but he was with friends so we didn't see each other. He didn't seem all that enthused I was there to go court with him. Brett and I agreed that he would meet me in the morning and I would be there in court for support. Of course he didn't tell me where he was, but we were still in contact by phone. We didn't say much more, so I went and spent some time with Blake and his family.

Because Brett wasn't that keen on living with his brother and his new family, he did his best not to be there very much. So when I visited Blake, Brett was nowhere to be seen. He was with his friends. I really didn't approve of his friends. Blake and I chatted about Brett and where he was heading. Although Blake wasn't much older in years, it seemed his new responsibilities had matured him. He said that if Brett went to jail, he would have to go to school because he was still a minor. Blake liked that idea. I agreed it seemed like jail would be the best option for Brett right now. It might be hard on him, but it would be for the best.

The next morning I started calling Brett. After many attempts, he finally answered. It was obvious from the first sluggish word that I had wasted my time. I didn't think there was any way Brett was going to make it to court today. Of course I could only make assumptions based on the phone conversation, but I didn't think Brett had even gone to bed yet. It sounded like he was still in party mode from the night before.

As expected, he didn't show up for court. I did manage to speak to the prosecutor and the public defender for his case. I wanted them to know that I had made every effort to get Brett to court. The prosecutor told me if Brett had shown up they weren't looking for any more jail time. However, as he didn't come to court and the police would have to pick him up; this would definitely mean more time at the young offender center.

I left court feeling once again dismissed by Brett and misguided in thinking he wanted to change. It was a long, lonely journey back to Calgary that day. I began to wonder if there was any hope. I questioned so many things over the past year and how things could have been better. But even if he had lived with me, I would still be dealing with some rebellion with him. It was a no-win situation. Until he wanted to change, there was nothing I could bargain with to make him do it. I had invested so much emotionally each and every time there was an opportunity to make things right, but I was burned every time.

I started to distance myself from Brett. I know that you can only help a person who wants to be helped, and I had to stop pushing Brett. The addictions counselor had told me I had to effect change at Brett's own pace, not mine. But it was so difficult not to urge him in the right direction. It was hard as a mother to watch your child make the same mistakes over and not want to do better. It was hard to watch from the sidelines when the history of the past came back to haunt me. I found myself thinking about all the "what ifs" in life.

During this time, Brett was staying with Blake and his family, but I was paying Blake, Brett's rent. So it was helping Blake out, too, although I don't think anyone was happy with the arrangements. It was a strain for Brett to be living with Blake, his girlfriend, and three children.

In April, I did manage to spend a weekend with Brett. Unfortunately, it was under difficult circumstances. When I got home from work one day, Courtney, my niece who had been living with us in Calgary, told me she received a call about her mother, Kim; Kim, who had helped me in my greatest time of need, Kim, the boys' favorite aunt. She had suffered a massive heart attack while at work. Once we got over the shock, we packed a few things and headed straight to Edmonton. Kim had the heart attack in Whitecourt, but it was serious enough that they air lifted her to the hospital in Edmonton. We finally arrived at the hospital late that night. Once there, the doctors told us it was just a matter of time. When they turned off the machines, she died in less than ten minutes. She was only forty-eight years old. It was nine months and a day after Eddie's death; Eddie and his sister were both gone. Once Courtney and I got over the initial shock we carried on to Whitecourt to be with her family.

Brett was quite upset and wanted to be there, so he hopped on a bus to Whitecourt. I was already there with Courtney. There was a lot of family there, but Brett and I felt a little out of place, so we tended to stick together. This wasn't really our family. It was more Kim's boyfriend's side of the family. Brett and I actually spent some quality time together that weekend. He was very pleasant to me under the circumstances. I felt we were moving forward. I knew it was only baby steps, but it was in the right direction. After that weekend whenever I went to Edmonton to see Blake and the kids, I ended up taking Brett to breakfast or lunch and spending some time with him. It was nice.

Brett's failure to appear in court finally caught up with him. It was late May when the police picked him up after looking everywhere for him. He spent a few more days at the Edmonton young offender center (EYOC) before he was able to stand in front of a judge. Brett got off pretty well. He was given ninety hours of community service and one year of probation. This was the best thing Brett thought could happen. If he kept his nose clean and did the work, then he wouldn't have to dodge the police and could breathe a little easier. At least, that's what I thought.

I made the drive back to Edmonton for Brett's release from EYOC. I wanted to be there for him and to see if this time he was going to be different. When I picked him up at the center, he seemed to be acting strangely. If he hadn't just come from jail, I would have thought he was on something. Maybe it was all his adrenaline, but something was different. Maybe he realized he had his freedom back and it was a new day. I dropped him off at his girlfriend's house and headed back to Calgary. He was going back to Blake's later that day.

I'm not sure what happened at EYOC, but any steps that our relationship had taken forward were quickly reversed. He was rude and verbally abusive once again. No one would want to hear some of the things he called me. On my fortieth birthday in June, I didn't get a "Happy Birthday, Mom." Instead, I got a text from him that said, "Die, bitch." I just wanted to cry. You'd think I would have expected it, but I hadn't. You'd think I would have been beyond hurt, but I wasn't. I may have been a little shocked he would do it on my birthday, but I had heard so much garbage that it was just another day of Brett lashing out at me. I didn't curl up and crawl under my bedcovers, but this showed me how much Brett was like his father.

I refused to be treated like that, so I sent him a message. First, I told him I loved him. I explained that our relationship wasn't healthy. I gave and gave, and he took and took. I talked about the language he was using and the respect he didn't give me. I talked about trying to move on. He wasn't trying, and it had been almost a year since Eddie had passed away. I told him life isn't easy and we grow during life's most difficult times.

As hard as it was for me, I also told him I couldn't help him anymore. I told him if he wanted to work on the relationship through family counseling, I would be there. I gave him some information about finding help if he wanted it, but he had to make the decision and take the first step. I ended the message by telling him again that I loved him and how much I wanted him to succeed in life. As I hit the send button, a piece of my heart just crumbled away.

Brett's Move to Calgary

Maybe I was stronger this time. Maybe deep down I knew I couldn't do much more to help Brett, or maybe a piece of me had given up. For whatever reason, I didn't speak to Brett for a couple of months. I wasn't aware of what he was doing or where he was living. I thought of him often, but I knew there was nothing I could do. He contacted me first. He sent me a text on his birthday. I came to expect curt messages from him. He asked me what I was buying him for his birthday. I just shook my head in disbelief. I appreciated it was his way of reaching out, but with everything that had happened, it just didn't fly. I could only respond that our situation had to stay as it was until he was ready to get some professional help. I didn't want to get dragged into another pissing contest about parental duties or allow him to try and guilt me into something. I tried to appeal to him to make a change. Only time would tell.

The next time I heard from Brett was a few weeks later. He called asking me to buy a bus ticket for him to go to Calgary. He said he wanted to live with his Aunt Jolene. I hadn't heard anything about this. It was news to me. Although it might have meant a new leaf for Brett, I had to say no. I told him if he really wanted to move to Calgary, he would find a way to get there. You might think this was harsh, but if Brett was really changing, he had to be the conductor of his own life and take responsibility.

Apparently he wanted to come to Calgary bad enough because he did get his own ticket. I received an e-mail the end of August from Jolene stating Brett and his friend were coming to Calgary to live. At the time, I wasn't sure if I was happy or frightened. I knew how Brett had treated me in the past, and I wasn't sure I was ready to let him in my life again. Had he really changed?

I didn't see him the first few weeks he was in Calgary. He needed a few things like a bus pass, so I stopped by Jolene's house one day to drop it off. He knew I was coming, but he wasn't there. Eventually, after we exchanged a few texts, I agreed to take him and his friend out for lunch. We went to Applebee's and had a nice time. We chatted about nothing in particular, but the tone of the conversation was better than I expected.

Staying at Jolene's had a positive affect on Brett. Jolene was helping him look for a job, because Brett was only seventeen, it was a bit hard. Most times you had to be eighteen to be hired in jobs other than retail. At this point, though, any job would have been a good start. Jolene made sure the boys were not partying all night and were up before noon and out the door looking for a job. It was encouraging to see. Once again, he was being offered another amazing opportunity. Would he make this one work?

That fall, Brett and I were seeing each other on a fairly regular basis. We had some good days and some bad days. When we didn't get along, he would get quite verbally abusive. He was so much like his dad. He even asked me why I made him so angry. He recognized that he was overly emotional, but it usually didn't stop him from lashing out. He said he never wanted to treat me that way, but he didn't know how to deal with his anger. On those bad days, I began to wonder if we would ever have a warm, loving relationship. I didn't expect to have the type of relationship you see in the movies; I just wanted one where we could both be civil to each other, where we could be happy for the good times and be there for each other in times of need. I didn't think I was asking for much. Thankfully, Jolene was a great buffer.

By October of that year, Jolene had had enough of Brett and his buddy messing around. They had been living with her for almost two months and they still didn't have permanent work. She sent his friend back to

Edmonton. They may have been out of the house during the day, but Jolene didn't think they were taking the job hunt seriously. Freeloading wasn't going to be part of the equation. She was firm and wanted Brett to make the change.

When his friend moved back, Brett told us why he suddenly wanted to come to Calgary. Just before he moved to Calgary we weren't talking and I had no idea where he was living or what he was doing. He told us that he had been living in a house in Sherwood Park just east of Edmonton. It was a nice, big house and he shared it with his friend and his friend's father, along with a few other adults. His friend's dad's girlfriend owned the house. The two boys had all the freedom in the world there and were happy. Brett told us that one day, he got out of the shower and went into the cupboard to pull out a towel. Out fell $2,000 in cash. Brett thought it was a gift. He felt like he had just won the lottery. He scooped up the cash, got dressed, grabbed his friend, and they went on a shopping spree. I don't know exactly who was living in the house or why they would stash $2,000 in the towel cupboard, but needless to say, when the owner of the money discovered it was missing, he really wasn't happy. Brett realized he was in pretty big troubled and thought it would be wise to not only move out of the house, but to get out of town as well. Brett wasn't comfortable about going back to Edmonton and he was willing to do what it took to stay with Aunt Jolene in Calgary.

Shortly after his friend left for Edmonton, Brett found a pretty good job that paid fairly well. He worked in a warehouse and there was room to grow if he wanted. I remember this was the type of job Eddie had when I first met him. I was excited that he finally had a job, so I drove him on his first day. It was quite a bus ride from Jolene's house, and I wanted to ensure he was on time on his first day. I even picked him up at the end of the day. On the way home, we picked up some fast food and I dropped him back at Jolene's house. I had only driven a few blocks when I received a call from Jolene. Brett had been arrested.

How could that be? The police arrived shortly after I dropped him off. Jolene told me she was standing in the kitchen doing dishes when she saw someone run past her living room windows. She thought that was odd and she asked Brett to look out the window and see if he saw anyone. Brett's heart sank when he looked out the window and saw a police car. Before he knew what to do, they were ringing the doorbell and asking for him. Jolene was perplexed and Brett was devastated. Brett answered the door and they arrested him. They cuffed him and put him in the car.

I was shocked; it had only been a few minutes since we parted. She told me he was in custody outside her house right then. Jolene and I were both upset. We thought Brett was finally making a change. He had just landed a good job and seemed to be on the right path. We didn't want him to lose out on this job either; he had to be at work in the morning. She wasn't clear about the charges, but the police told her it was concerning a robbery. Until that moment, we actually thought his legal troubles were behind him. We were confused. When had this supposed robbery taken place? We knew nothing.

All I could do at that time was wait. I had to attend a meeting that night with some friends from the running club, but my mind was really somewhere else. Everyone knew it. My friends were very aware of what I was going through with Brett. I had my phone in my hand just waiting for a call; from Brett from anyone who could tell me what was happening.

I was desperate for Brett's call. I needed him to call me to tell me what needed to be done to get him released that night. After a few hours, he did call. He told me somebody would call and let me know the process for his release. He told me to tell them that I would take care of him and he would either be released to Jolene's or my custody. Eventually the prosecutor did call. I actually presented myself to court via phone. I thought this was odd but appreciated not having to stand in front of the judge. Apparently this is a normal procedure.

By this time, it was almost midnight. I was tired and exhausted and I had to work the next day. I went to court, filled out all the paperwork, and finally Brett was released. The court is open all night but at midnight the computers shut down and paper work has to be filled out manually. Unfortunately I got to the courthouse at five minutes past midnight. It was quite a wait before everything was completed. It was around three in the morning by the time I had Brett back to Jolene's house. At least we both made it to work that morning. I was very grateful they had released him. He would be able to keep his job. I never wanted to experience anything like that again.

The next day, Brett did tell us a few things about why he was picked up. It all stemmed back to when he was released from EYOC in Edmonton. When I picked him up at the center, I noted he seemed a bit strange. I chalked it up to him having his freedom back. I can't imagine what it must feel like to be released from jail. He said after he was released he was hanging out with of his buddies. They needed a cigarette and tried asking some guy walking by on the street if he would give them one. The guy said no, and Brett and his buddies didn't like the answer. I guess they harassed the guy and maybe went a little too far. I don't know what happened, but apparently that was the reason Brett was arrested. He said he knew the police were looking for all of them, but he didn't pay any attention to it. He didn't think that he was the one in trouble.

When Brett was in Edmonton he had a girlfriend whom he saw regularly. When he moved to Calgary, she would come down on the weekends for visits. Brett wasn't comfortable bringing his girlfriend to his aunt's house; he actually thought this would be disrespectful to his aunt. Brett and Jolene really connected. Brett really did have respect for her. I guess Brett respected people who were strong enough to stand up to him. When his girlfriend did come to town, they would stay with other friends for the weekend. I did meet her from time to time and when I saw how Brett treated her, I was upset. I didn't like the way he spoke to her either. But I had no influence over him. I had tried talking to him about being respectful in the past, but it went nowhere. When I saw Brett and his girlfriend together, I saw the possibility of my relationship with Eddie repeating itself. It scared me.

The problem was Brett really loved this girl, but he was terrified she would leave him too. So he became possessive of her. All his life, people had left him for some reason or other: me, his Auntie Kim, his dad, his grandfather, and on and on. He didn't want this with her. So he became an unpleasant version of himself. I remember Eddie being like this too. He would say he loved me and then treat me unkindly. I didn't want this for Brett or his girlfriend. They didn't need to be in that vicious cycle. I hoped they would figure it out themselves and soon. He needed a loving person in his life, and I didn't want him to drive her away because he was afraid she would leave. It would be a self-fulfilling prophecy.

Things started to look up. Brett now had a well-paying job and he didn't miss work. He had a friend in Calgary whose living conditions were a little crowded. This friend was eighteen, so he was able to get an apartment on his own. They both realized that it could be better if they were in their own place. It was a brutally cold winter in Calgary that year. Brett lived far away from work, so I drove him to and from work. With traffic, this added a couple of hours to each day. When I finally got home, I wasn't always a cordial person. This was starting to affect my relationship with Andy.

Brett had never been comfortable with Andy. He wouldn't have remembered my relationship with his father because he was too young when I left. He did ask a few questions every now and then about what Andy was like, but when he got in one of his moods, his questions and comments turned nasty. Unfortunately, I think he said some things to get back at me. His comments were not just derogatory but disgusting. Some of them made my stomach churn. I began to wonder if there was anything that could change our relationship. I had thought that when Brett moved to Calgary and got a job, we could rebuild our relationship. I had thought there would be less stress in my life when he and Andy could meet and get to know one another.

I was desperate for a healthy relationship with all of the men in my life: Andy, Blake and Brett. Sandy and I had been working toward this goal for quite some time. I wanted peace, love, and respect. I wanted to feel happy, or at least content that life was proceeding and we were moving forward. Often I felt like I was living two separate lives. Andy and Brett weren't sure of each other. They both had preconceived notions about the other. Andy heard my side of what was happening with the boys. I'm sure he must have felt insecure about having them in our lives. But he always supported me; no matter what. As for Brett, I don't think anyone would replace his dad. Everyone else was an interloper. We all knew his life growing up with Eddie had not been the best. We all knew about the run-ins with the law. But we were all trying to make a change. It was time for that change now that Brett was living in Calgary. I could not and did not want to keep Andy and Brett apart forever. They were a big part of my life and they needed to come to terms with each other. It might also mean a bit less stress for me. After some very intense discussions with my therapist, Andy, and Brett we decided to arrange a meeting.

As the day of the meeting approached, stress began to build. I hoped everything would go well. The actual day was a marathon therapy session. First, I discussed possible scenarios with Sandy. I needed to prepare for what might happen. Later Andy joined me at Sandy's office. We talked about how Brett might be feeling toward Andy and me and how he might react during the meeting. We also discussed the possibility that the meeting might fail. There were so many "ifs" that it was hard to plan. I just wanted to be prepared.

At the end of the workday I was going to pick Brett up as planned and take him to the Sandy's office, my third visit in one day. We planned to meet there since it was neutral ground and Sandy could act as mediator. Happily the meeting went relatively well. Brett was very polite and respectful. After the meeting, Andy was very open to meeting Brett again and getting to know him better. As for Brett, he still wasn't sure. But it was a start.

A few weeks later, Brett found a new place to live with his friend. It was closer to work, so that made life easier for everyone. He didn't have too many possessions, but Brett was able to purchase some furniture from Kijiji. Kijiji is a site where people list things to buy or to sell. It is a great resource to find used items or services that you may need for an affordable price. I rented a van, and on a cold Saturday morning we started to move everything into their new place. I kept thinking to myself that we had only done this a year ago in Edmonton. I hoped the outcome was going to be different. I think Brett was different. So much had changed since his move to Calgary five months before. He was making great strides toward becoming the man I wanted him to be.

Moving day was stressful. They usually are. It was so bitterly cold, I didn't even want to get out of bed that morning, let alone move furniture. But I got bundled up and went to help Brett with his move. His roommate and Aunt Jolene were going to meet us at the new place. Brett was not in a good mood that morning. I thought he would have been excited to be on his own again. His mood trickled over to his language, and soon my mood changed, too.

By the time we had the first load of into the new apartment, we had been arguing quite intensely. Words were flying. Brett became verbally abusive. He said things about Andy and me that I just couldn't repeat. By this time, the words I hated so much, the "c" word and bitch, were really quite passive compared to what he was saying to me now. He called me such vile names it made me ill. I actually took it for about an hour. Brett didn't know it but right in the middle of his verbal slaughter, his Aunt Jolene was standing within hearing distance. She was horrified. She couldn't believe that he would talk to me that way and that I would take it. I wanted to get the move over with. But I could only take so much. Once the load was delivered to the new place I returned the van to the rental location. I wasn't going to take that garbage anymore and I told him so. Aunt Jolene took over and finished the move.

Within a couple of days, Brett called me and wanted me to come over and see his new place all put together. He was like Jekyll and Hyde. One minute he was nice and kind, the next he was a completely different person. He sounded excited and eager for me to see his place. I was drawn in again. I kept doing anything to rebuild our relationship. That meant taking the good and the bad. Andy also wanted to be part of this side of my life and to build something with Brett. He suggested that he go as well. I didn't want to surprise Brett, so I called and asked how he felt about this. Brett wasn't sure about it for now. So I decided to take things slowly. Build it one brick at a time.

Now that Brett was living closer to work, I was seeing him a couple of times a week instead of daily. The time apart was good for both of us. He was thrilled to have his own place and was feeling independent. He was very proud of his accomplishments. His girlfriend was coming down on the weekends and that made Brett happy. When Brett wasn't happy, the people around him also felt the repercussions, so whenever he was in a good mood, everyone else was too.

He had been in his new apartment for a few weeks when he asked me to help him run a few errands one weekend. His girlfriend, his roommate, and his cousin were there and they were just relaxing that morning. Just before I left my place that Saturday morning, Brett sent a text to ask if I could pick up some breakfast at McDonald's. It was out of my way, but I didn't really mind doing it for him. He said he would pay me when I arrived at the apartment. As he sent his order to me by text, I was sure to order the right food. You know what it's like when you finally get home and the order is messed up. I didn't want that so I double-checked what he sent me.

When I arrived I said hello to everyone as Brett started unpacking the food. Within a moment or two, he said: "you got the order wrong". He was quite upset with me. "It can't be," I said and read his text back to him. I said: "you owe me $20." This was the cost of the meal, something he had previously said he would pay me. He yelled: "I'm not paying for it. It's all wrong!" I was still remaining calm at this time. I said: "Fine. I won't be bringing you McDonald's anymore."

It was like he flicked a switch. He started ranting and raving and spouting obscenities. More unmentionables (including the "c" word) that should never be put into print. Everyone else sat there shocked that Brett would behave like that over a breakfast order. Nobody was sure what really set him off. It couldn't really have been breakfast, could it? Was it Brett just messing around with me again? I was confused and terrified. I got the hell out of there and got in my car and drove home. At that moment I realized it was like a time warp. The cycle I had been in with Eddie was happening all over again. I was being verbally abused regularly. I was doing my best to keep my head above water financially, but I had such difficulty saying no to the boys. I was drowning in every sense. This incident really opened my eyes.

Brett's behavior was like his father's shouting profanities, exercising what he thought was control over me. He seemed to recognize all the tools that he could use to manipulate me. He probably recognized the fear and the disappointment that I felt because once again I was not able to please him no matter how hard I tried. Brett had learned a lot from his dad. He knew how to hurt me. Maybe it was a reflection of the pain that he felt. I don't know. What I did know was that I could never let myself be abused like this ever again.

When I arrived back home and calmed down, I sent Brett a message. It was very similar to the message I had sent him in June. I told him this latest incident would be the last time he would ever abuse me, I was done. I told him I could no longer carry on with our relationship because it just wasn't healthy anymore. I told him I wanted more than that and I deserved more than that. I told him if he ever wanted to have a relationship with me in the future then I would be happy to try again, but I wanted him to go to counseling before I could consider it. He needed to get his emotions in line.

He called me a few days later and tried to apologize. He even invited me over for dinner one evening. But I didn't want to get roped back into the cycle. It wasn't good for me, and it wasn't good for Brett. This would be the honeymoon phase in the cycle of abuse. I told him again I couldn't see him until he went to counseling. He seemed to accept what I said, but I could hear the disappointment in his voice. As disappointed as he was, I couldn't change it. He needed counseling, and we couldn't have a relationship until he was willing to make changes in himself.

This happened just before Christmas 2010. Andy and I were going to be in Ontario for Christmas with my parents. It was good timing because I needed the time away. While I was away, I didn't hear anything from Brett.

There was no drama, no one asking for money, no one calling me names or swearing at me. It was very peaceful. I decided I liked peace and quiet.

On December 26, 2010 I changed my phone number. I knew the boys could get in touch with me through Facebook if they really needed me. I needed to reduce the stress and anxiety that would overcome me every time my phone would ring or beep with a new text. I realize I didn't have to answer the phone or look at the text, but I never seemed to have enough strength to do that. I needed to be in control of my life again. My heart was quite tattered but I was much healthier after I made that decision. I will always be sorry that it didn't work out with Brett.

I don't know what happened with Brett that Christmas in Calgary. I heard from Courtney there were some incidents, but I never found out the details. A few months later I did receive an ambulance bill in the mail for Brett. He had been brought to the hospital that New Year's Eve. Since then, I heard from Linda, T.J.'s mom, that he moved back to Edmonton and has his own apartment. She tells me that he is doing really well for himself. He is working and has an opportunity to apprentice. It was really good to hear this. I hope Brett finds success. I tried very hard to make things work. It just wasn't meant to be. As hard as it is, it is something I have to accept.

The additional stress of my life with the boys was also affecting my health. As much as I wanted to be with my son, I realized I had to let go. My letting go was not part of a normal parent-child relationship, where the child moves out on his own. My situation was different. I may not know where he is or what he is doing, I may not know if he has found love or if he is happy, but I know I will always love him wherever I am.

Blake

As is common in families of alcoholics, one of the children often becomes the caretaker. This was true in Blake's case. Even though he and his dad didn't get along toward the end, and even though Blake wasn't able to go to the house because of the court order, Blake loved his dad more than anything. His dad was the world to him. I knew that from the very beginning. They were buddies and Blake loved him so much. He saw Eddie's flaws, but he loved him.

Blake's transition after his dad's death was not surprising. He was already living with his girlfriend and her two children, and he had recently found out he was going to be a father himself. Unfortunately, I don't know if Eddie ever knew he was going to be a grandpa. It may not have changed anything, but you never know.

His father's death caused Blake to become much more serious with his girlfriend. I thought the relationship was very volatile and a roller-coaster ride from the beginning, but what did I know? Now he had someone else to take care of. I didn't really approve of the relationship. I felt Blake was far too young to take on such responsibility with his new family. Blake was only seventeen and his girlfriend was twenty-six. The age difference alone was enough to make me unhappy about it. But he was going to be a father and now he was doing the right thing and trying to make it work. His was continuing his role in life as a caretaker.

When I see what he has gone through and how he interacts with his new family, I see a lot of myself in him. I too was the caretaker in the family. Blake had essentially been living with his girlfriend since May of 2009 the year his father died. She had been good to him regarding allowing him to live with her when he could no longer live at home. They were living in a very adult relationship with Blake acting as stepfather to her children. But since Eddie's death, they both felt I should be paying child support to Blake directly. Blake and I had many text messages back and forth about this. Even though he was seventeen, for a few more months, but living with an adult and not going to school, he felt it was his right to receive the money. It seemed a bit bizarre to me to pay it given the circumstances. I wasn't legally required and I refused. Money was continually an issue of contention among the three of us: Blake, me and his girlfriend.

Blake's girlfriend's youngest daughter was about to start kindergarten that fall and her mom thought it would be best to move to a better neighborhood. It was odd to think that my seventeen-year-old son had two stepdaughters and was going to be father himself. Of course, as a mother I will always have an opinion because Blake is my son and I only want the best for him, but based on my own history I have no right to judge. Relationships are hard enough, but if you become involved with someone with young children and you are not even eighteen, it can create a lot of stress. Couple that with your father dying a few months before and it might be more than one can bear.

The months following Eddie's death, I was seeing Blake regularly. I would make the drive to Edmonton at least once a month. I just wanted to make sure that both boys were doing okay and I was hoping that maybe we could create a relationship. Blake's girlfriend had only just begun to rekindle her relationship with her own mother after some trying times in her past. She understood the importance of having a good relationship with her mother and she did her best to bring Blake and me together. She and her children were a nice liaison between Blake and me.

Blake still wasn't that comfortable with being around me. He was very much the strong, silent type. Although he found it difficult to even talk to me, he was never rude or abusive toward me. Of course we had arguments, usually over money, but considering how Eddie raised him and the time in between, he remained respectful. I appreciated that. At least I could argue sensibly with him without it turning into a scene.

I did my best to encourage Blake to finish his education or to pursue a trade. He needed to be aware that in order to support oneself, the minimum requirement was a high school education. With a growing family, he would probably need more. He had come a long way in high school so it wouldn't take so much to complete his diploma. I told him if he wanted to continue his education, I would definitely help him out financially as a boost. I just wanted him to have a better life than he did growing up.

It was important for Blake to get a job to support himself and his new family. I tried to give him a helping hand whenever I could. Part of this was to be able to drive to a job interview and then hopefully a position with the company. Although Blake had been driving for some time now, he was doing so illegally. He had no driver's license. For this to be resolved, I paid for driving lessons so he could now drive legally. It was a first step. After he completed this, I then paid for Blake's forklift certification. Now he had a skilled trade that he could list on his résumé for potential employers.

After Eddie's death, Blake assumed ownership of his dad's car, a newer Buick. It had been Eddie's prized possession and Blake valued it greatly. It was a way to have his father there with him. Eddie had acquired the car in a business deal of some sort, but there seemed to be an issue surrounding the car, though I never found out the details.

One day while Blake was driving the car and stopped at a red traffic light, a group of men rushed the car, opened the door, and yanked Blake out of the car. He was stunned and had no idea what was going on. Then Eddie's former business partner appeared. He told Blake he was sorry, but he was taking the car. Eddie still owed him some money and the car would be used to pay off the debt. He threw some money on the ground and told Blake to take a cab home. Blake was devastated, but he had no recourse.

Shortly after this incident, Blake managed to find work. We had been talking to each other and I had been encouraging him every way I could. I was thrilled for him. But with a job came the issue of transportation. He started riding his bike to work. But the cold November mornings were becoming a problem. He wasn't wearing a helmet and it was dark when he left in the morning and dark when he came home at night. I became somewhat concerned with his safety.

As the mornings became colder, he started hinting that he needed a car. I understood and agreed with him, but I think he expected me to buy him one, and at the time, I couldn't really afford it. Owning a car is a big expense for anyone with gas, insurance, and maintenance. I was already helping out quite a bit financially with their regular monthly bills. After a lot of convincing and guilt trips, I caved. Blake assured me that things were different now. He now had a job to take care of some of those expenses, and soon he hoped to be more financially independent. He said I didn't have to buy a car for him but if I could get the loan, he would make the payments. It seemed reasonable, and I could see he was much more responsible, but something inside nagged at me. It reminded me of the same ploy his father had used.

Allowing others to take hold of my heart and ransom it was one of my flaws. My children and the guilt that I feel about not being able to be a part of their lives plays a big part in the decisions that I make where they are involved, where they have a need or a want that I could possibly help out with. So I bought the car for him. I wanted him to be successful and would do anything to help him along the way. I never did see a payment for the car, and as I write this book, I am still paying off that debt. In some ways I was okay with that. A parent tries to give her child a stepping-stone. I really believed the car was a huge break that would allow him to focus on other issues and perhaps make it work. I wanted him to succeed. I could see him growing into a responsible man taking care of his family. He was handling the situation better than I expected. Really, what is one car in the grand scheme of things?

Things always seemed to be rocky between Blake and his girlfriend. Often when I would visit, it appeared they were in the midst of an argument. Sometimes they wouldn't be talking to one another, or Blake would be home taking care of the kids while she was out cooling off. I could only imagine what they were dealing with. Blake had a lot on his mind. His father had killed himself and he was trying to find direction. Then came the news he was going to be a father himself, and his responsibilities as acting stepfather to two young children. It was a lot to handle for such a young person.

One thing that bothered me was that his girlfriend always took the car, the one I bought for Blake. She knew I had purchased it for Blake so he could find and maintain employment. I didn't want him riding his bike to and from work; it wasn't safe. Their fights appeared to be more significant each time. Sometimes I wondered if they would break up and she would ask Blake to leave. Blake would tell me things and sometimes would send messages on Facebook or through e-mail. He would message me telling me that they had a huge fight and she was telling him she was going to leave. He'd ask me what he could do to make her happy. How could he win her back? The fights were frequent. Sometimes when I'd go and visit and take the kids out Blake's step daughters would tell me that they were moving and Blake wasn't coming. I would often see his girlfriend's facebook postings indicating that she was spending weekends away from him at her friend's house. I wondered if she would then take the car from him. I did discuss this with Blake and he told me that he felt like he owed her. As he didn't have the resources to pay her in cash he felt obligated to give her the car. It was out of my control and really none of my business. He was my son, but he was an adult and he had chosen that relationship. Who was I to get in the middle? Yes, I bought the car for him, but it was his car, not mine.

Around this time, I decided I could no longer continue to pay to keep their dad's things in storage. I was spending a lot of money—between Blake's car payment, storage fees, taking care of Brett, and helping out Blake when I could. It was becoming too much. I couldn't keep up with all the extra expenses. Plus, I had my own expenses to pay. Blake lived in a place with a garage on the property. I thought he could store the items they wanted there.

One weekend, a few months after Eddie died; I drove to Edmonton to see the boys and to help Brett move in with Donovan. It was perfect timing to take the items out of storage and give some to Brett in his new place, and some to Blake. It was a cold November day. Why do our moves always seem to happen in winter? So we moved everything out of storage, and I was happy both boys got things to remind them of their father. I was also glad that the extra expense would be gone. That helped me too.

I did my best to help them out financially from time to time, and when I was, everything seemed to go relatively well. In the fall of 2009, I arranged for a cable package for Blake that also included home phone and the Internet, so Blake could be in touch and also to help with his job search. The cell phone I had purchased for him in the past never worked out. It was either not charged or lost. At least with the landline that wouldn't be an issue and I knew the cost upfront.

When I called the cable company, I had the package put in Blake's and my names. He was still seventeen for another month, so my name was required for the time being. I agreed to pay the bill when it came. One month I received the bill and was shocked when I opened it. The amount was almost $180. It should have been $10. This was far more than we had agreed upon. I reviewed the bill and noticed there were several charges for pay-per-view movies. I phoned the cable company that night and found out that someone from the residence had pretended to be me and authorized the changes to the package. I quickly advised them that I had never authorized it. I felt violated. After some serious phone conversations with Blake, we decided that since he was now of legal age, he could put the cable bill in his own name and take responsibility for paying it.

By the time Christmas came that year, I felt the boys were much more settled. Brett was living with Donovan and Blake was with his girlfriend. It would be their first Christmas without their dad. Although the last Christmas hadn't been a very good one with Eddie in rehab, I hoped and prayed this year would be better. The boys had somewhere to go and people to be with that Christmas. I knew it was far too soon to plan our first Christmas together, but we all had our own plans for the holidays and would not be alone. I think both boys preferred it that way, too. Trying to rebuild would take time, and I didn't want to rush it.

I did send each of them a message on Facebook over the holidays. Blake's response was cordial, but Brett's was less than kind. Messages played back and forth. Among the three of us, we could all see the conversation. My expectations weren't that high but when I read what Brett said it was another blow. I guess he knew being vulgar had an effect on me. Unfortunately when Blake read the messages, he asked Brett to stop being rude but then Brett was rude to Blake. It was a no-win situation for anyone. It was bittersweet. I could see that Blake was making an effort but Brett was still overcome with anger.

Shortly after Christmas 2009, I visited Edmonton again. Blake's baby was due in February, and it was important for me to continue to build our relationship. I was going to be a grandma soon, and I wanted to be involved in their lives. Regrettably, I was going to be away when the baby was due, but I wanted Blake and his girlfriend to know how much it meant to be part of their lives. I was very grateful for that. It was a nice visit, but I could see Blake was under a lot of stress. Still, he was doing fairly well considering what he was dealing with. I could see he was taking his responsibility seriously and was trying to do his best. I only hoped it would last, that he wouldn't buckle under the pressure. I had to remember he was still a teenager.

The problems continued. As Brett and Donovan's living arrangement had ended, I knew that Brett would occasionally stay at Blake's and sleep on the couch. I had been sending money to help Blake with the expenses, as I knew Brett was there more often than not. But in February 2010, just before the baby was born, I received an e-mail from Blake asking me not to send money that month because he didn't know where Brett might be staying. He thought he might actually move out and find a place of his own and would then need the money for deposits and rent. Blake's girlfriend learned of this and didn't agree. She was now becoming used to me sending money each month.

She sent me an e-mail talking about all the expenses they had. She said I had paid for Brett to be in a basement apartment, so I could pay to have him live with her and Blake. She basically said, if I didn't pay, then Brett would have to find another place to live. She wanted the money deposited into her account that week. When I read the e-mail I felt used. I knew there were going to be additional expenses because of the coming baby and Brett, but I felt she went about it the wrong way. I felt trapped between a rock and a hard place. My relationship with Blake was really improving. I was about to become a Grandma and I really wanted to be apart of my grandson's life. I couldn't risk upsetting Blake's girlfriend and losing all of this, so I paid the money to keep Brett in a place and Blake's girlfriend happy for another month.

A few days after days that visit to Edmonton, I received a knock at my door. It was a Tuesday evening just past six and I thought it strange because I wasn't expecting anyone. Normally, Andy and I are reluctant to open the door at night. You never know these days what might happen. But then Andy said it might be the neighbor returning the house key. She had looked after our cats over the Christmas holiday. So I went to the door and was surprised to see two rather rough looking men. At first I didn't know what to think. Was this going to be the home invasion I had always feared or some sales spiel to buy something I really didn't need?

Before I had a chance to prepare a rejection to their query they flashed their police badges. Okay, what's happened now? I asked if they were there about my son. They confirmed they were as they walked in the house. I was expecting to hear news about Brett. We had been through some tough times and there had been detention at the young offender center, so I just assumed it had progressed into something else.

It wasn't long before they mentioned Blake's name. Immediately I panicked. The first words that rushed out were "Is Blake dead?" They promptly said no and apologized for not clearing that up sooner. They said Blake had an outstanding warrant and they thought he might be at my house. I told them I was aware of the warrant as it resulted from the confrontation between Eddie and Blake. I told them as Eddie had died the year before, Blake and I assumed that there was no longer an issue and that the charges had been dismissed. Then they explained that Blake would have to turn himself in so that they could dismiss the charges. The officer said it wasn't a big deal, that it could be cleared up pretty quick. He gave me his card and left. I called Blake as soon as they left and explained what he needed to do. I thought he would take care of it the following day.

The next morning, I received a call from a detective at the police department. She mentioned two of her colleagues had been by, but she was hoping she could come by and have me identify some pictures. We arranged for a time the following day. I thought it strange she would ask me to identify anything because the other police officers just mentioned the warrant relating to the incident with Eddie. So when she arrived the following day I just assumed she would have me look at a picture, but I had no idea of what. As it turned out, there was a lot more to it.

We sat in the living room and she laid out a few pictures on the table. With the tape recorder running, she asked me if I recognized the person in the picture. The first one was a mug shot. It was Blake. They knew it too, as his name was at the bottom of the photo. Then she showed me a grainy picture of a person. It was like a still taken from surveillance photo like you see on crime shows. There was no way I, or anyone else, could identify that person. I told her as much, too. She pulled out another picture, clearer than the last one. Although it was clearer, I still couldn't say for certain it was Blake. There were some similarities, but something seemed off with it. I told the detective I didn't think it was Blake, but I couldn't say for certain.

The detective then explained why she was there. I waited for the bombshell. There were too many things that didn't sit right. Something was terribly wrong. She said there had been two bank robberies in Calgary and one in Edmonton and the suspect from the bank video looked like Blake; my heart just about fell to the floor. Could this be? I knew we weren't extremely close, but our relationship had come a long way. We had had some deep conversations and he'd shared some personal things with me. At one point, he even asked me for relationship advice. Did he just forget to say, "Oh, by the way, we're okay for money now because I just robbed a bank?" I couldn't believe it. No way. I started to think about it logically. Why would Blake drive three hours to Calgary, rob a bank, and then drive three hours back? It didn't make any sense at all.

She asked a few more questions about Blake and his girlfriend. She asked if Blake could be influenced to do something like that. She asked what was happening in his life—did he have a job? How was he living? There was so much speculation on their part, and in conjunction with the grainy picture, they were trying to cover all angles. I guess when you look at his history and the trouble and the pressures he was under, it's plausible he might have done such a thing, but I didn't want to think like that. I had faith in him. He knew the difference between right and wrong. He had set life goals to be a plumber or a police officer, and he was moving toward them. There was no way he could have done this. I repeated that over and over again. I don't know who I was trying to convince more: the detective or myself.

When the detective left, she asked that I not mention any of this to Blake. They planned to talk with Blake very shortly and they didn't want him on the run. When she said the words, they seemed so foreign. It was like I was watching a movie about a fugitive. But here it was. They were talking about my son. I agreed not to say anything to Blake, but I asked the detective if she could keep me informed and let me know when Blake had been cleared of this mess. And it was a mess. Hopefully it was just a case of mistaken identity.

After she left, I became a mother on a mission. Blake wouldn't rob a bank and I had to make them realize it. I searched my files for documentation that supported how Blake was able to live. I had been giving them money for a few months now and I wanted to provide the evidence that would support it. It would explain how they were covering some of their monthly bills. While I was doing this Blake had called and left a message. He needed some help with a speeding ticket. He felt this was why the police were trying to get hold of him. I wondered about that, too. If he had robbed a bank why would he worry about paying a speeding ticket? There wasn't enough evidence to prove he had done this.

I was completely distraught that night. I tossed and turned all night long and couldn't get the image of Blake at a bank robbery out of my head. I felt a little disloyal to Blake because I hadn't told him about the meeting with the detective, but I also didn't want him to worry. There was nothing he could do at the moment. And I was sure it would all get settled sooner or later. He had so much on his plate right now. His girlfriend was nine months pregnant and they were not getting along very well. I didn't know if they would continue living together and raise the baby together, or if Blake would be forced to leave. I called my mother in Ontario that night. It was late, but I couldn't bear it any longer. She had always given me good advice, and this was too much for me right now. I needed her stability and calm approach to the issue. She convinced me not to tell Blake and adhere to the police request. When it came right down to it, I didn't believe Blake could have robbed a bank. It would just take some time to clear his name. He couldn't handle any more stress right then, so I wasn't going to add to it if I didn't have to.

After a night of sleep, the little bit I was able to get, my head was a little bit clearer. I told Blake's aunt what was going on and she did some research on the Internet to learn more about the bank robberies. She found the article with the pictures of the suspects and the dates of the incidents. There were four robberies, three in Calgary and one in Edmonton. She reassured me that it definitely wasn't Blake in the picture. I felt immediately at ease when someone else confirmed my own intuition. She said the boy in the picture had a chubbier face than Blake. Blake had a longer and leaner face, like mine.

She also gave me all the dates of the robberies and I started to put the pieces of the puzzle together. At once, I realized Bake couldn't have been involved. I was actually with him on one of those days in Edmonton. It was the day we had moved furniture to Brett's new place. The furniture had been delivered to Blake's place the night before, so we just had to move everything to the new place the following day. We were all there, so there was no way he could be involved. Blake was also working during some of the robberies, and I thought that if the police checked with Blake's employer, they could clear him for the other robberies. I e-mailed the detective and gave her all the information I had. I knew they wouldn't believe my statement that he couldn't have been involved. I'm sure they heard that from other mothers all the time. But now I had proof. Brett and I were his alibi.

I was now confident that Blake had nothing to do with the robberies. I showed Andy the pictures and told him of the police interview. He was shocked at the similarities between Blake and the man in the photos, but because I was with Blake on one of the dates, he knew he was innocent. He told me that if the police didn't clear Blake's name, we would hire the best criminal lawyer in Edmonton. A bank robbery is a federal offense and is extremely serious. Andy said that although Blake had done some things in the past, this was outrageous and he wasn't going to be punished for something he didn't do. He was innocent.

Unfortunately, the police never did check out Blake's alibi and the investigation continued. Andy and I were about to head south for our winter vacation and Blake's baby was due any day. With us being out of the country and the stress of the new baby, we didn't want to take any chances, so we hired a criminal lawyer in Edmonton for Blake. All I told Blake was to call the lawyer if anything should happen. I told him the bill was taken care of, so he had nothing to worry about.

On February 11, 2010, my son became a father and I became a grandmother to a beautiful baby boy. Everyone was so happy. It was exactly what we needed to overcome the sadness and drama of the last seven months. With new life, there was hope—hope for the future and new beginnings. Blake had started a better job at a bigger construction company. Things were looking up. That is, they were until the detectives showed up at his door a few days later.

They took Blake to the police station that night and in typical interrogation style continued to ask questions relentlessly through the night. He was so grateful we had arranged for counsel for him before we left. He was so young. It was a lot to bear. He called his lawyer and did as he instructed. The police made it very clear to Blake if he was found guilty of robbing the bank, whether he had committed the crime or not, it was a minimum of five years in prison. I'm sure this must have frightened the heck out of him. Luckily the lawyer had talked him through some things and the next day he was released. It must have been a long, stressful night for Blake. Within a few weeks, Blake was cleared of all charges. But the experience changed him.

Blake finally went home to his newborn son. Finally, he could have joy in his life. The police incident was over and all that was left was the time he could be a father to his little boy. I arrived back in Calgary nine days later and headed straight for Edmonton to see the boys and my new grandson. He was absolutely beautiful. He had such small fingers and toes. He was the spitting image of Blake. And when he smiled, my heart melted away.

Over the next few months everything was going quite well. I was going to Edmonton almost every other weekend to spend time with the boys and my grandson and step-granddaughters. I loved hearing the girls call me Grandma. It wasn't perfect by any means, but perhaps we could let the past go and move forward. I wanted that relationship with my children and grandchildren. It was important and I tried my best to keep it going. In April I took all of my grandchildren for an overnight visit. We shopped for toys and crayons at Wal-Mart, ate pizza, and hung out and watched movies in our hotel room. I will always cherish that wonderful memory.

But the good times never lasted. And in May, they started to go downhill. Brett and I had made up once again and had been speaking to each other and he told me things were not good at Blake's house. He told me he wasn't comfortable living in the house any more. He didn't have a room to himself and it was sometimes awkward at mealtimes, as there was nothing for him to eat. He told me not to pay the rent there anymore. He told me the money I was sending wasn't going to pay the bills. I changed the arrangement I had with Blake's girlfriend. I started to pay only a portion of Brett's rent and gave a portion in grocery gift cards to Brett. This ensured that he was safe at night and could also get some food when he wanted. She seemed okay with this at the time.

In June 2010, almost a full year after Eddie's death, it got even worse and everything fell apart. Brett's rent was due, but I wasn't sure if he would continue to live with Blake and his girlfriend. Brett kept telling me things weren't good for him, Blake, or my grandson. I started to worry. I still only had his side of things and wasn't sure I had all the facts, but what he told me did not make me happy. I'm sure it must have been stressful for everyone. There were so many living in the house now: three kids, Brett, Blake, his girlfriend, and her brother. I heard that Blake and his girlfriend were continuously fighting. It was a possibility I would have to help Blake and Brett move out. I wondered if there would ever be a time when there would be peace in my life.

Shortly after this, I received an e-mail from Blake's girlfriend. It was the last straw. She made some pretty derogatory comments about Blake. She did tell me she was leaving. She sent me a text stating, "I'm taking the kids and we are out of here by the end of the week." In the end, it turned out to be a threat, but how was I to know? Blake was my son. He wasn't perfect, but he was still my son and my son's happiness was my priority. I refused to pay her any money that month. I felt that I needed that money to set up the boys once she had kicked them out. We had an exchange of words through text messages. I told her that I didn't like the way my boys were being treated. We had a pretty serious argument. Both of us said unpleasant things. It really wasn't nice. She texted me and told me that I knew nothing about her and Blake's relationship. In her words, "You know *nothing* about my and Blake's relationship. I gave it to you…I can take it all back! Take care. I don't think we will be seeing you any time soon." Then she posted a rather unnerving status on Facebook: "I love it when people's LOSER parents try to involve themselves in your business when CLEARLY they have NO CLUE wtf is REALLY going on! Nice try, though! What you DON"T know is that . . . I"VE GOT MAGICAL POWERS heheheeh. I can make people disappear! Try Me!!" I took her comment seriously. I considered this to be a threat to my life. I was just trying to stand up for my boys. They deserved better.

Blake sent me an e-mail coming to his girlfriend's defense. I respected his loyalty to her, but I also felt now was the time for me to remove myself from the situation. By this time, I felt manipulated and used. I refused to be bullied anymore. I was not going to be sucked into that same vortex of darkness I had been in with Eddie. It felt like my relationship with the boys was still only about money. I only wanted respect and eventually love from my boys. I knew it was going to be an uphill battle, but it just wasn't working. I felt like Blake did respect me, but there were too many other factors influencing our relationship. I believe that if Blake wasn't in the relationship that he is then there would be a possibility for us to have a relationship.

At this time the only phone in the house was Blake's girlfriend's Blackberry. The only way I could communicate with Blake was through her. I did try and she basically told me that this wasn't Blake's e-mail—why was I bothering? Since that day I have not tried to contact Blake, and he has not tried to contact me. It is very sad but it is what it is.

The last message I ever received from Blake's girlfriend was on Facebook in June 2010. It was only two weeks before my birthday. The cryptic message was very hurtful. She said, "Take down the pictures you have up of you and my kids. You don't deserve to be called Grandma!" That hurt. It really hurt. I had tried and tried and tried. It didn't work. All I wanted was to be part of my boys' lives and my grandchildren's lives. I felt very used. They pulled at my heart and asked for money. When I paid it, things were good when I didn't pay; my relationship with my son and grandson was severed. I always felt that both boys wanted a mother, but maybe they didn't know what a real mother was supposed to do.

And Now...

I have achieved many successes in life. I graduated college and became a certified management accountant. I managed to find love and happiness again. But with all those triumphs, I don't think I was successful at one of the things that matters most of all: parenting. Maybe if I'd had the opportunity to raise a child from birth to adulthood and be there every day, I could have been successful. But my situation was different. Eddie had taken that opportunity away from me, and I will have to live with that for the rest of my life.

You can't go around in life saying, if only I did this, or didn't do that. You will only make yourself crazy. I learned many lessons in my life. Some of them were good and some of them I wouldn't wish on anyone. But you know what? No matter what you experience in life—no matter how many times you've cried or were stressed to the breaking point, no matter if you wanted to give up a thousand times—all those experiences make you who you are. Some people can rise to the occasion, while some crumble under pressure. We all have our imperfections. I know I have many. I also know I did the best I could at the time. When I watched an Oprah show one day, she said a few things that resonated with me. "When you know better, you do better." I realized I had done the best I could at the time. Could I do things differently now? *Of course.* Everyone would. My experiences have changed who I am, so going back now would change everything. I would know what didn't work. I would know that being strong hurt. I would know that there are some things I just cannot change, no matter how much I want to. But I cannot go back. I cannot live in the past. Life does go on.

I did have another chance at parenting in someone else's life before I reunited with the boys. Andy and I became the caretaker and guardian of my niece Jessica from Ontario. She is my sister's daughter. Jessica lived with us while she was a teenager, and we tried to help her grow into the woman she was to become. We sat with her when she was ill, helped her with her homework, took her for driving lessons, and gave her love and support in her times of need. Both Andy and I wanted to give her everything possible to be successful in life. Of course, there were some struggles along the way, but there were also some wonderful, happy times. It took her a few years to find her way, but the point is that she did and now she is a compassionate, caring mother and one of the stronger members of our family. I would like to think I had a small part in her path to adulthood.

Over the years I had also been involved with Eddie's niece Courtney. She was my link to the boys at times. She helped me out during and after Eddie's death. A few months after Eddie's death, she went to Germany to work as a nanny. While she was gone we talked regularly via Skype and email. When she returned to Canada she wanted to go to school to become a travel agent. She asked Andy and me if she could stay with us and we agreed. When she came back, however, she was sick and couldn't continue her education until she was better. She lived with us while she got better and finished her education. Andy and I did our best to help her as well. She had many medical appointments and hospital visits. We were there for here every step of the way. When she was finally well enough, she continued with school and was able complete her education.

I know I am a nurturing person. I want and love to be involved in the lives of the people I love. I tried this with Brett and Blake, but unfortunately they were not receptive to my help. They say it is better to give than to receive. I gave so much to the people in my life; some would question why I continued to give after I had been shot down or mistreated so many times. Upon reflection, I think it is because of my love for others and my faith. My mother believes that I reach out to others when I perceive they need guidance. She thinks that no one can really fail as a parent. We can only teach as well as the circumstances and the environment permit. My mother used to sing me a song about parenting: "Now, my love I have

taught you all I know, and now you are set free to test your wings and fly."
We are not the result of our upbringing. There are so many factors that
decide your life's path. I had a great upbringing, but my experiences during
my first marriage changed me.

Growing up as a child in a warm, loving household, I saw the joy and
love within a family. That is not to say we didn't have issues. You may recall
that I rebelled as a teenager. But my parents were there for me. Every time
I did something stupid, every time I made the wrong choice, they were
there. It was their loving guidance and support that helped me get through
some of the things I had to endure. I will forever be grateful to them
both.

When you have these wonderful experiences growing up, you naturally
assume that your life will continue be like that. Well, as you know by now,
mine wasn't. You may have been thinking while you were reading, why
didn't she just leave? It took me a long time to finally realize that I was
worth something. I think Oprah said once, "Because you are here, you are
worthy." It is such a simple statement, but it's so profound that it takes my
breath away. I am worthy. For a long time, during the years with Eddie and
many years after, I did not believe I was worthy. I'm sure my therapist tried
to hammer that into my head many, many times. From time to time now, I
question it too. I am worthy. I matter. I could not leave until I finally realized that I was worthy and that I mattered. When I realized that, I chose
not to be a victim. I accepted that I was finally free of my captor.

Our journey through life is full of good times, happy times, sad times,
and hurtful times. I lived all of them, and for a long period of time, my life
was only sad and hurtful. But you can make anything out of your life. You
have to have the desire to make it better. There are stories around the world
of people who grew up in horrific surroundings only to become an inspiration to others and make good with their life. They saw past the hurt and
pain and realized they too had something to give. Many times, these people
were able to give back to others or inspire others. I hope that by reading
this book, I have given you an insight into the life of an abused person and
that we can all change our lives.

The cycle of abuse is strong and is very hard to break. Many women will
leave one abusive relationship only to find themselves in another. I was able
to break the chain. With the love and support of my family and my wonderful, caring husband, I am now free. I am free to be the person I always

wanted to be. I am free to think the way I want and to do what I want. I will not take that for granted ever again.

It is also my hope that reading this book will help you to understand the extensive damage caused by alienating children from their parents. Unfortunately, everyone suffered in this family. My parents never got to know their grandsons. My sister never got to be an aunt. My niece and nephew never go to know their cousins. And my sons lost most of all. Eddie took a loving mother away from her sons. He took a warm family unit and shattered it to pieces. He destroyed how the boys would see a family unit later in life and robbed them of the necessary skills to grow. Then he took his life. And now the boys are essentially orphans trying to find their way in a messy world.

I will not blame everything on Eddie. He was only one piece of the puzzle. It was the corner piece that was needed to solidify the family, but the remaining picture would still be beautiful if the boys had made different choices. I tried to help them each and every time to make better choices and to get them back on track when they veered off the path. I am not perfect. I know my kids are not perfect. I tried to help them, but they didn't want my help. I cannot live their lives for them. I can only help guide them on their way. We are all accountable for the decisions we make, the good and the bad. I made some good decisions and some that I would change. But my love for them was paramount.

I was diagnosed with Multiple Sclerosis in 2007, the stress was pretty unbearable. I had issues with Eddie. I was trying to have a motherly relationship with Blake and Brett, and then I had medical issues. MS is a serious disease and I knew I had to change some things in my life. I knew the prognosis of the disease and knew that I would eventually experience some serious side affects. I knew about the possibility of being wheelchair bound and potentially losing my sight. It was far off in the future, but the doctors told me that reducing my stress would help the disease to remain in remission, possibly for the rest of my life. At this point in time, I am generally symptom free, although while writing the last chapter of this book, I was also diagnosed with another treatable illness. I am learning a lot about my health and the need for balance, the need for minimal stress. So now, I try to be calm and have peace in my life and be thankful for the loving people that surround me daily.

I have had to be very strong with some of the actions and decisions I made over the years. Sometimes I wasn't strong enough. You may not agree with what I did, but my heart was pure and I made those decisions with the love I had for my family. The consequences are what they are.

I made a life-changing decision that I thought was for the best. I chose to be a survivor. I left a dangerous situation and felt the best way to protect my children was to leave. I knew Eddie could be volatile with me, and I wanted to neutralize any potential occurrences of violence. He loved the boys and tried to be a loving parent. I wanted my children to be safe, and if that meant I couldn't be with them every day, then I was willing to accept it. It wasn't about me; it was about my love for the boys. I loved them enough to set them free.

Eddie thought that by alienating the boys from me, I would come running back. I know that if I had returned, I may have become a horrible statistic. Murder-suicides within families of domestic violence are sadly a common occurrence. I chose not to be a statistic. Lives were definitely destroyed, but at least my boys have the opportunities to make their own lives. They have the opportunity to make good choices. They are now in charge of their own destinies.

I love my boys with everything I have. I still cry a lot for the loss of my time with them. It shouldn't have been that way. When I gave birth to the boys, I expected our love would be shared and we would be in each other's lives until the very end. That life was robbed from us. I still love them dearly, but it's not our time to be together. It feels like my heart has been ripped from my chest over and over. But each time that happened, I grew stronger and wiser. It doesn't make it easier, but I have the skills to cope. I have learned I am worthy of love and respect.

The pain that I experienced as a result of parental alienation is beyond what some people could ever imagine. I know many people have judged me and wondered how I could have left my children. It goes to show that you don't always know the life your neighbor, coworker, or friend is dealing with until you walk in their shoes. Maybe now you know a little more about me and why I did what I did. Maybe now you will ask that other person that looks distressed or in need if they need help or if they just need someone to listen. Maybe now you will understand that there are no correct decisions in life. We do our best and hope that everything will turn out for the best.

So now you know my story. Life with my children wasn't a fairy tale with a happy ending. It was full of trauma, setbacks, dragons, and heartbreak. But there was also love, strength, and courage. You saw how I dealt with a mountain of problems; was physically abused almost to the point of death, and came out on the other side. You saw how I beat the odds of domestic violence and became a productive, happy person who contributes to society. You also saw the tears and struggles I faced trying desperately to mend my family.

My intention in writing this book was to explain to my children why I wasn't part of their lives. I wanted them to know my side of the story. It is not my intention to judge or critique their lives, so there are some things I must leave unsaid. Their lives are very different from mine, and there are some things and people in their lives that I just can't have in my life. It's very sad that it is this way. It's heartbreaking.

Who knows what the future will bring, but for now, Blake and Brett, I must send you my love from afar. Please know that I always have and always will love you. From the depths of my heart, I will love you.

"Letting go doesn't mean giving up, but rather accepting that there are things that cannot be."—Anonymous

CPSIA information can be obtained
at www.ICGtesting.com
Printed in the USA
LVHW040843260420
654457LV00002B/393